THE SLOW FARM

TARN WILSON

Judith Kitchen Select

OVENBIRD

Ovenbird Books
Port Townsend, WA

Ovenbird Books Nonfiction Series
With a foreword by Judith Kitchen

This book is published under the Judith Kitchen Select imprint of Ovenbird Books, a new publishing venture designed to bring literary nonfiction titles to the attention of the reading public. In the interest of quality and individuality, Judith Kitchen acts as editor and introduces each book; the writer has complete autonomy over content and design.

Book Design: Mark Gleason

OVENBIRD

Ovenbird Nonfiction Series
Judith Kitchen Select

Ovenbird Books
Port Townsend, WA
www: ovenbirdbooks.org

Library of Congress Cataloging-in-Publication Data is on file.
ISBN-13: 978-1-940906-06-5
ISBN-10: 1940906067
Library of Congress Control Number: 2013920862
Ovenbird Books, Port Townsend, WA

For my sisters, Jack's daughters:

Tammy, Rima, and Tori

ARTIFACTS:
AN INTRODUCTION

In 1971, at the age of four, Tarn Wilson was taken by her parents, Jack and Janet, to live on an island off the coast of British Columbia. This was the beginning of their back-to-the-land experiment and what she remembers is indelible: the myopic and miraculous world of the child—the farm, the water, the freedom, her body wholly her own as she explores and discovers and forges her way. There's more, of course, and this evocative rendition chronicles fear and delight, enchantment and disillusionment, along with a growing hunger for knowledge. But the author's underlying impulse is to understand, not to disclose. How can she resurrect her unconventional childhood without being self-indulgent?

Artifacts, that's how. *The Slow Farm's* many small segments are stitched together with an amazing array of photographs, quotations, news stories, timelines, native lore, pop songs, recipes—you name it, Tarn Wilson has found it—and the commune finds its proper proportions within a larger canvas. The radical sixties form a base. Root cause asserts itself in these cultural relics: snippets of Jack Kerouac, Betty Freidan, Timothy Leary and A. S. Neill's *Summerhill: A Radical Theory of Child Rearing.* Real ghosts of Vietnam haunt these pages along with the requisite utopian dreams. But the artifacts also move forward as the seventies parade across the screen in all their freewheeling glory.

Wilson uses this device—an excavation of sorts—to get a fix on what she had no way of knowing at the time. There's more at stake than memory. Small moments are writ large as her world expands, first to her needs, then to ours. Language becomes essential. "To me, words were not human inventions, but a manifestation of the natural order," she says, and we watch her struggle to reconcile one world with another as the nation's history begins to inform her own.

So this is important . . . DO NOT skip these interstices.

They provide framework—and context. By stepping outside her personal version, Tarn Wilson deftly turns memoir into an interactive project. The reader is invited into the structural design and the book becomes a kind of chess board on which we make strategic moves, superimposing a recorded world on one that might seem limitless. In the end, we sense an inevitable collision with history—both personal and political.

The marvel of this book is that it feels so true to childhood and yet conveys an adult overview. Its double-edged perspective gives this memoir depth and richness; we trust this writer's intellectual instincts and her questioning mind provokes revisitation. First, she goes back linguistically, rediscovering her love of language and how it reveals herself to her self. Second, she fills in the gaps in her knowledge and probes past and present emotions. Third, she physically returns to the island as an adult. Time itself has slowed. There, she unearths a solid artifact and *The Slow Farm* blossoms again in the reader's mind as we—all of us—come to partial terms with an imperfect past.

—Judith Kitchen, October 2013

This book is published under the Judith Kitchen Select imprint of Ovenbird Books, a new publishing venture designed to bring literary nonfiction titles to the attention of the reading public. In the interest of quality and individuality, Judith Kitchen acts as editor and writes an introduction; the writer has complete autonomy over content and design.

www: ovenbirdbooks.org

IN THE BEGINNING

Late summer 1971, my father quit his job in Washington, D.C. as the Brookings Institution's first computer programmer, bought an old school bus with "Suck Nixon" painted on the side, and packed us off for British Columbia.

This is what I remember: my sister and I loved our bus, a house just the size for children. My father had gutted the interior, tucked a gas stove behind the driver's seat, used green bus seats as benches around our kitchen table, and built us bunk beds. I got the top bunk because I was almost four; my sister got the bottom because she was almost two. My parents' bed was a foam mattress on the floor in the back, which my mother covered in an Indian spread. She sewed bright curtains for the windows. We trundled along Canadian back roads, cozy and warm, as close to our parents as we would ever be, and watched the blur of trees out the window.

This is what I didn't know then: while living in Alexandria, a suburb of D.C., my father had been reading the Beats, stories of Ken Kesey's adventures in his psychedelic school bus and the essays of Timothy Leary urging him to "turn on, tune in, and drop out." Our parents trained us to call them by their first names as a statement against oppressive, traditional family structure. Our mother cried as she watched the news, when she heard the daily death count from Vietnam, when the National Guard opened fire on the students at Kent State, when police blasted civil rights demonstrators with fire-hoses and beat anti-war protesters with billy clubs. Our parents had marched too, often enough to have their names in the FBI's files. They'd been preparing for the Revolution. They argued about whether it was more ethical to fight the Establishment or abandon it. My mother wanted to fight.

My father won, and we were off to find our own Eden. Set loose in the primeval Canadian wilderness, my sister and I were to be educated by the land, released from shame, fear, insecurities, sexual hang ups, and shallow social conventions imposed by a corrupt and repressive culture. In our natural, unspoiled state, we'd be happy and free.

Only children and idealists believe paradise lasts forever. In the beginning, I lived fully in the present, blissfully unaware of any world other than the one my family had built on the edge of our lush island. My father believed he could maintain our Eden by the force of his vision and will. We were special enough, he thought, to escape the inevitable end of the story, the path from the world as we wish it were to the one that exists.

This is what I didn't know then: a year and a half after we nestled into our little coastal logging camp on Texada Island, my mother would leave my father. I wouldn't see it coming. Years later, when I'd ask my parents what happened, both would go mute. I'd have to rely on my own small and peculiar memories. I'd research around those memories to understand my parents' choices, the context a child can never see. I'd hold my little beads of memory, stare at them, try to understand why they were so vivid, why I held them so tightly. I'd dissect them for clues for how we lost our Eden.

This is what I didn't know then: no one escapes the slow walk out of Paradise into the flawed and lovely world.

POCAHONTAS BAY

SPRING 1972 – SUMMER 1973

FINDING EDEN

By early spring 1972, the bus was broken more often than it moved. When the carburetor blew in Gibson's Bay, British Columbia, Jack sold the bus for fifty dollars, bought a 1950s Volvo, and drove us north along the mainland coast, looking for home. Finding more suburbia than bush, we turned back. At Comox, by the ferries, Jack saw the sign for Texada Island and spontaneously decided to take a detour.

First we drove the length of Texada's two paved roads, Blubber Bay Road and Gillies Bay Road. Janet, next to Jack in the passenger seat, wrapped her arms around herself, as if to keep herself warm, and didn't speak. The sun lit the blond highlights in the hair piled on top of her head. I leaned against my window and drifted in and out of sleep, waking to roadsides overflowing with pink fireweed and sweet peas, and behind them, a wall of Douglas fir. My sister Rima slept soundly, stretched out the full length of the seat. Jack turned down rough, unnamed logging roads that shook me awake. The car rattled. Dust covered the windshield, puffed inside the car, left grit in our eyes and teeth. Rima began to cough and crawled between the seats and into Janet's lap.

"Can we close the windows?" Janet asked.

Jack rolled up his.

Janet tried to roll up hers, but the handle just spun. She'd forgotten. She sighed, turned away from Jack, and hung her arm out the window.

All Jack's roads faded away or ended abruptly at streams, gullies, or piles of logging scraps.

"The girls are hungry, Jack. We need to think about a place to sleep."

Jack hit a hole, gripped the steering wheel to keep it from shaking out of his hands, and bounced north. I knew he was having too much fun to stop. The thick canopy of evergreens gave way to an alder grove and then opened to the sky. Pocahontas Bay. A half-moon shaped cove, which looked out across Malaspina Strait to the faded outline of the mainland. A small logging camp with a cluster of buildings, abandoned piles of logs, yellow logging equipment, and three small matching houses, backed against a mesh of cedar trees and salal bushes.

A shirtless man with a long, blond ponytail leaned in the doorway of the middle, and only occupied, house.

We all crawled out of the Volvo, glad to stretch. The air smelled of seaweed and creosote.

The man held out his hand to Jack. "Ken.'"

"Jack." Jack shook his hand and waved toward us. "My wife and kids."

"Want some weed?"

"Sure."

Janet shook her head no, leaned against the house, and closed her eyes.

"I'm leaving tomorrow for India," the man said. He took a toke and held his breath.

"Ashram?" Jack said, as he took the joint.

The man, still holding his breath, nodded.

"Far out," Jack said, and put the joint to his lips.

Rima and I chased each other between the grown-ups' legs, then headed for the pile of logs, as if they already belonged to us.

"The house," Ken waved behind him. "You can have it. The rent's free if you keep an eye on the place for Old Mr. Hagman while his loggers are away. They're only here for a couple of months, just during the day. He'll hire you if you need any work."

A native people of British Columbia, the Tla'amin, tell a story about Texada. They say the island is the back of a whale. It has sunk and risen six times and will sink and rise once more. So, in the old days, they refused to make a home on Texada, Si'yi yen. They landed their canoes on the beaches to collect clams and oysters, to hunt for seal, otter, and black-tailed deer, to eat salal berries, salmon berries, thimble berries, to camp for a season, but they wouldn't stay. Only a fool makes his home on the back of a whale.

STILL LIFE: PARADISE WITH SHADOWS

On the bus, we were always together. But in Pocahontas Bay, Jack and Janet released us into the salty air.

Alone, usually naked, Rima and I tramped on old logging roads into the bush. Cedars and firs circled us and exhaled their cool, green breath. In the specked light under the branches, we transformed into fairies. We wore sword fern fronds for skirts. We turned giant leaves upside down on our heads as hats: the stems made a point like an elf's cap. When we were hungry, we munched on fiddleheads, not because they were tasty—they were dry and grassy—but because we were so proud we could feed ourselves and didn't have to go home for lunch. Thimbleberries were furry mice on our tongues. Red huckleberries were small and sour, but when we held them to the sky to let the light shine through, they were ruby-luminous.

On the curve of beach to the west of our house, we held hands and jumped over waves so cold we were numb to our necks. Salt and fishy-smells soaked our skin. We caught purple crabs and let their needle feet tickle our palms; they waved their boxer's glove pinchers at us. We piled seaweed onto a bark-plate, crumbled dead crabs on top, and pretended to eat crab salad. A giant tree root, which had washed ashore, made a house. We decorated with smooth pebbles, mussel and clamshells, and polished bits of glass—white, brown, green, and cobalt blue. I liked the rare blue best. I could disappear into that color, like looking down a long blue tunnel.

In the beginning, Jack spent hours next to the house, chopping wood on an old chopping block, the noise an echoing background rhythm. He split cedar shakes to sell as roofing and siding. He cut and bundled salal for Mrs. Hagman, who sold the greenery to florists all over North America. While he worked, his jeans slipped too far down on his narrow hips. He'd pause, hike up his pants, and watch a raven flapping over his head. His hands calloused; his biceps grew.

Janet spent most of her time in our two-roomed house, learning to cook on the elaborate cast-iron wood stove with three fancy black legs and one plain white one. On one side was a cooler, a plywood box built into the wall, which pushed out behind the house; on the other, a little window, a counter, and a deep sink where Janet gave us baths with water she hauled from the creek. A nine-paned window opened the front of the house to the bay; under it, Jack built a double bed—with a bookshelf as a headboard. The kitchen table leaned against the one interior wall, which separated the main room from Rima and my bedroom—a space large enough only for our toy box and the bunk bed Jack had made for us out of unpeeled alder logs. While bread dough rose, Janet scrubbed our disintegrating floor on hands and knees.

Our parents gave us no rules, no boundaries, so we made our own. We didn't peek under the house, even when Rabbit the cat slipped into the blackness. We didn't walk behind the house where there were spider webs and layers of wet leaves. Even though the outhouse was on a little cliff overlooking the bay, we didn't like to use it. It was too dim and damp, with a sweet, rotting smell. A faceless creature with long arms probably lived in the pit and might reach for us. The hole cut out of plywood was too big, and if we fell, the gooey blackness would muffle our screams for help.

We didn't like the Clubhouse next to the road at the top of the hill, a one-roomed dilapidated shack, which had been built for the Girl Guides and used, at one time, for their overnight trips. Inside, the air was heavy, the floors sagged, moss grew in the corners. A mysterious fungus might attach itself between our toes and to the backs of our ears. In a corner I found some orange and brown yarn wrapped around two crossed twigs: Janet said it was a God's eye. I kept it for a while but soon threw it into the woods—if there was a God, I didn't want His eye watching me.

We avoided dark places and floated through Pocahontas Bay in patches of light. We pressed down rooms and hallways in the marsh grasses, which grew at the mouth of Whiskey Still Creek. The edges of the grass slit our fingers. We lay on our backs in the scent of bitter green and watched the grass blades slice the sky like scissors cutting white paper.

Then Jack or Janet would call for us, and, although we were not by nature disobedient, their voices seemed as far away and impersonal as a raven's gargling cry.

STILL LIFE: PARADISE WITH SHADOWS

Sugarloaf
May 30, 1968

Dean W.E.
Dean of the College of Arts and Sciences
University of Colorado
Boulder, Colo.

Dear Dean Briggs,

I expect to receive my Bachelor of Arts degree from the University of Colorado on June 7. I am requesting that I officially be excused from the graduation ceremony for the following reasons:

1. that I am not proud of earning my degree in a world in which there is not equal educational opportunity for all men,

2. that I do not consider my education to be in any way completed,

3. that I feel the symbolism of the cap and gown to be an anachronism from an age in which scholars were considered to be the sacred elite of their society,

4. that I do not consider myself in need of a stamp of social approval,

5. that I wish to be judged by my actions and not my titles,

6. that I already feel sufficiently involved with the "outside" world to forgo any initiation rites or puberty ceremonies,

7. that I have no feeling of identity with the class of '68,

8. that I was not informed of the necessity of attendance when first enrolling in a degree program,

9. that the formal structure of the University has hindered and not helped my acquisition of knowledge,

10. that my parents, wife, children, friends, and associates have no interest in my participation in the graduation ceremony,

11. that I feel I can better occupy my time.

Thank you,
John A. Wilson Jr.

WHAT I BELIEVED: WORDS

I loved to say "Pocahontas Bay," hear the tumble and roll. The name went loud and soft, loud and soft, like ocean waves. Poc-a-hon-tas. Cut logs bounced, slipped, and splashed down the log slide into the water, making Pocahontas Bay say its own name. Poc-a-hon-tasss. It didn't occur to me someone had named Pocahontas Bay. I assumed its name was as old and naturally formed as rocks. When Jack told me we were related to Pocahontas, an Indian princess from the olden days, I wasn't in the least surprised.

Jack tried to teach me to say "disestablishmentarianism," but the word wouldn't stick. To me, words were not human inventions, but a manifestation of the natural order: the strongest logger on Texada was named "Stump"; a prominent logging family was named "Woodhead." Jack and Janet, who were married, had names that started with matching J's. My name, Tarn, meant a small mountain lake, and I had lived in the Colorado mountains when I was born. Rima was named after the beautiful woman who could talk to the birds in the book *Green Mansions*, and Rima was beautiful and liked the woods.

One afternoon, all four of us strolled along an abandoned logging trail, through leafy shadows, looking at ferns and lacy mosses. Sometimes Jack and Janet's hands touched as they walked. We stopped to look at a huckleberry bush, which grew out of an old fir stump. "The other day in Vananda," Jack said, "I met a man named Al, who lives in a hollowed out cedar stump." Rima and I didn't understand how the man could fit inside, but Jack explained the stump was gigantic and he had added a wooden room on the front.

Rima and I skipped and chanted, "Owl lives in a tree; Owl lives in a tree." Of course a man named Owl would live in a tree. The inside of his house probably looked like Owl's in *Winnie-the-Pooh*.

Jack and Janet laughed. "No," Janet smiled. "*Al* lives in a tree."

"That's what we said, Owl lives in a tree." We ran ahead. We refused to hear otherwise.

At first I was confused that the big yellow logging vehicles were called "cats," because they looked nothing like cats, but then Jack told me "cat" was short for caterpillar, and sure enough, the vehicles were bright as the black and yellow fuzzy caterpillars who dropped to the ground from the alder trees, and they moved the same way, with a smooth, rolling crawl. Rima called the moon "the moon agloon," and I believed her. She'd heard the moon's full and proper name.

I found a small piece of driftwood twisted like a piece of taffy and formed into a capital "I," with a bumpy cross bar on the top and bottom. When I showed Jack, he explained driftwood was formed by storms, waves, rocks, and sun. I liked Jack's story, but I also thought nature could spell and flung alphabet letters onto the beach where I could find them, letters as magnificent and ordinary as stones and deer droppings.

**Pronunciation
of Texada:** Tex - ay - da

Popularity: Even though many consider Texada the
largest of the Gulf Islands, the island is off
the main ferry routes and rarely appears
in guidebooks as a tourist destination.
Most people in Vancouver have never
heard of it. (In 1996 my research at the
University of British Columbia yielded
only a geological memoir from 1914 and a
dissertation on the shrew population.)

First charted: July 12, 1791 by Spanish explorer Don
Jose Navarez

Location: Approximately 50 miles/80 km northwest of Vancouver and 5 miles/ 8 km
southwest of Powell River; runs parallel to the Sunshine Coast and forms the
western boundary of Malaspina Strait.

Length: Approximately 31 miles / 51 km

Width: Approximately 6 miles / 9.5 km

Highest Point: Mt. Shepherd 2,924 ft

**Average annual
rainfall:** 39 inches/ 992 mm

**Average summer
temperatures:** 52-74 degrees Fahrenheit

**Average winter
temperatures:** 30-40 degrees Fahrenheit

Number of paved roads: 3

WHAT I BELIEVED: PERFECTION

I believed Jack and Janet were perfect: Janet's singing voice, the soft skin on the inside of her arms, the oblong turquoise stone on her silver ring, the way she could knead bread and then bake it until the top was perfectly crispy, the way she smelled like bread baking; the way Jack could split a perfect shake with just one tap of the ax, walk with perfect balance on the boom frames, and read the scratchy voice of Witch Wookie calling after Peter Pitkin: "Is that you Peter Pitkin? Did you steal my magic hen? Will you come back again? Then you'll catch it!"

One late afternoon, Jack and I walked along the beach. He picked up a pebble, flipped it in his hands, then flicked it toward the water. The rock skipped one, two, three, four, and almost five times before sinking. I threw a rock and it sank with a blurp. Jack laughed and showed me how to find smooth, flat rocks and flick my wrist.

All my rocks sank.

"Mine are too heavy," I said.

"It's not actually the weight of the rock that's important, but its shape." He showed me the rock in his hand. "Here, try this one."

I was frustrated and wouldn't take it.

So Jack skimmed the rock over the water—six skips—and then ambled down the beach. I followed just behind, worried I'd disappointed him.

I picked up a clamshell. It was smooth-pink in the center and grooved-white at its edges, each side a perfect match of the other. Then I thought about how people—and dogs and cats and deer—all have two sides too, two eyes and two ears and two nose holes, perfectly opposite of each other. Jack liked new and interesting ideas, so I'd impress him and make up for my rock-skipping failure. I handed him the shell and told him how clams and people are alike.

"There's a word for that," Jack said, "symmetrical."

He didn't seem surprised by my observation. He turned the shell in his hand. "It means one side of something is the mirror image of the other." Then he told me what he thought was merely an interesting fact, "You know, no one's face is perfectly symmetrical. One eye or ear is always bigger or higher or a slightly different shape." He handed my shell back to me. "A lot of people have one foot that's about a half size larger. And most women have one bigger breast." He added, thinking, as he did, like a mathematician, that although he and I could imagine a perfect shape, a perfect circle or square, none actually existed. All circles, if measured, would prove a little lumpy, all squares a little wavy.

On the walk home, the salal leaves, which before had seemed glowingly whole, were speckled with insect holes and unsightly bumps. That night at dinner, I noticed our plastic plates with the brown and olive trim were chipped on the edges.

After dinner, I sat on Janet's lap and stared at her face: high-round cheeks; full, peach-colored lips with a light colored mole on the right side. Her blue eyes were large, but her right eye seemed smaller and lower than her left. While Janet talked to Jack, who leaned against the counter drinking coffee, I stroked her cheek, to lull her to distraction. Then I eased my hand up her face to her eye. I pressed under it, pushed at the side of it, trying to force it into symmetry with the other. When it popped back, I pushed again, harder.

"Tarn!" Janet leaned as far back from me as she could. "Stop it."

I poked my finger into the soft side of her breast. "Is this one bigger?"

She laughed. "Yes." She grabbed my wrists. "But you're not supposed to notice."

I was disturbed I'd never seen this imperfection before, this secret chaos, a world slightly off kilter. I'd overlaid perfection on imperfection, seen perfect faces where there were none. I was anxious over this for days.

Janet and I have been thinking of moving to British Columbia in a year or so . . . we were very impressed with Canadian attitudes and ways of life while traveling through Ontario and have heard similar reports from people who have been in other areas, including British Columbia. People are generally friendlier and less anxiety ridden, and especially more tolerant. The schizophrenic middle class vs. hippie dichotomy disappears in a truly sympathetic exchange of ideas. Traveling through the U.S., people both rural and urban either categorized us as hippies or non-hippies according to their personal criteria, and treated us accordingly, while in Canada we met only friendly helpful people from a Lieutenant Commander in the Royal Canadian Navy and family to a garage attendant. They just don't conceive of the world as good guys and bad guys.

Letter from Jack to his parents,
October 26, 1967

STILL LIFE: JANET'S HANDS

With one of Jack's first paychecks from Mr. Hagman, Janet bought bright purple paint. She painted the front door and the trim of the house—and then finding she had extra—the inside door frames, the kitchen shelves, the cooler, our toy box, and, finally, even the kitchen table and chairs. The paint was shiny and the color of kings' capes in my illustrated fairy tale book. I knew we had little money, so I loved the extravagance—Janet's protest against so much gray sky.

She was intent on bringing color to our misty world. She lined the front of the house and the path to the outhouse with daffodil bulbs. Then she planted an acre garden on the top of the hill by the logging shed. She turned the soil. "I've never seen dirt like this," she said, "so rich, it's black. No wonder people grow so much marijuana here." She planted some. She planted vegetable seeds. She pulled weeds.

After the deer nibbled all the tender, new plants, Jack built a ten-foot fence from poles and fishnet. Around the perimeter, Janet planted marigolds, little yellow and orange suns, because she'd heard they repel slugs. But the banana slugs—yellow, bruised, and green around the gills—slimed by anyway, leaving a trail of silver behind them. Someone advised her to put a lid full of beer next to each plant—the slugs would fall in and shrivel—but she couldn't bring herself to kill them.

I pulled up fistfuls of electric orange carrots. Pea tendrils curled around my fingers. I could eat all the pea pods I wanted. At night Janet held the small, shiny pages of *Peter Rabbit*. As she read, I imagined Peter sneaking under our fence and eating our new lettuce and radishes. I hoped his blue coat with gold buttons would stick to our fence and he'd leave it behind for me to find.

I watched Janet's hands, her rough, red knuckles. They were large, "large as a man's," she said. But I knew they were a woman's hands because her fingers were long and gentle and she moved her wrists gracefully. On one wrist was a pale pink birthmark, with darker pink spots, the shape of an undiscovered continent.

As we squatted between the rows, sifting the dirt between our fingers and tossing out rocks, Janet told me that after her father died, her family moved from Louisiana to Boulder, Colorado. Her mother Wuh-Wa wanted to plant flowers in the front yard of her new house. When she couldn't find her box of gardening supplies, she pulled on her long yellow evening gloves and stabbed at the dirt with a kitchen spoon. Not long after, Janet's sister Travis, who was in high school, was asked out on a date. As had been custom in Louisiana, she wore a Jacqueline Kennedy style dress, pumps, and white gloves. Her date arrived in jeans and hiking boots. After a speechless moment, he blurted, "We're just going to the movies."

Janet laughed, a bitter laugh. "After that, I swore I'd never wear gloves."

Along one edge of the garden, Janet planted sunflowers, which grew taller than the fence. They were almost people, friendly people with skinny necks and heavy heads. They ignored me as I ran back and forth between their hairy stalks, but they seemed to watch over Janet, nod over her, like older sisters with big faces and messy hair. They were nicer than her real mother and sisters, who hadn't spoken to her since she married a hippy and moved to Canada.

Janet let me harvest potatoes. The ground was lumpy with them. I sifted through clumps of damp earth, separating tubers from clods. The dirt was thick with worms, and I was afraid of touching them: worms were someone else's skin, living fingers without bodies. But I kept searching. Like curled animals or Janet's stories, the potatoes waited for me to find them, to brush them off and settle them in a basket.

As she worked, Janet told me that once, at a party, a palm reader had grabbed her hand, looked at the deep, crisscrossed lines—her lifeline stretched full across her palm like a baseball seam—and told her she'd have a long and complicated life.

Another time, when she was newly married and sitting alone in a cafe in Boulder, a man approached her table. He was a poet, he said, and he'd written a poem about her. He handed her a napkin. It was about the weathered hands of a Colorado ranch woman. I imagined Janet smiling to herself and putting the napkin in her pocket. Janet was glad that poet didn't see her Southern softness; she'd have preferred to come from sturdy ranch stock.

The women didn't want to be '50s style wife and mothers, they didn't want to be <u>plastic</u>. So they gave up all the modern conveniences, prepared foods. They admired the Indians, so they wove, made their own bread. Everyone made their own bread. But after a while, it became its own form of entrapment.

Interview, 2006, with Fayette Hauser, member of the Cockettes, the 1960s psychedelic gender-bending San Francisco performance troupe.

WHAT I BELIEVED: PEARLS

Rima and I pulled up the sheets on the bottom bunk. On the side of the mattress were two metal circles with little holes punched in them, shiny in the afternoon light. We thought they were microphones. I pulled on the mattress handle to turn on the microphone, while Rima talked into the holes.

"Call Ishkin and Bishkin," I said.

Before bed, almost every night, Jack would curl up with us on Rima's bottom bunk and tell us stories about Ishkin and Bishkin, the elves who flew in a silver airplane and lived in the Colorado mountains, where we lived before I could remember, before there was Rima.

Rima talked, turned her ear to the microphone to listen, then reported Ishkin and Bishkin were coming to pick us up in their airplane. I yelled to Janet, "The elves are coming to pick us up. We might not be back in time for dinner."

She was in the kitchen, preparing to cook the oysters Jack had harvested. Jack sat on the front steps. He pried open the oysters with his pen knife, plopped them in a bucket, and tossed the shells in a pile. They made a sound like muffled broken glass. Soon, Janet would roll the oysters in cornmeal, fry them, and serve them with ketchup.

We dressed up for our trip, which meant wearing all our favorite clothes at once: T-shirts, corduroy pants, calico dresses, long skirts. Rima finished her outfit with a blue wool button-up sweater and red tennis shoes; I pulled on a crocheted poncho and my yellow rubber boots with Big Bird on the side.

At the log pile across the street from our house, we waited for the elves. We leaned against the stack. We threw wood chips at each other. Soon, the heat tightened around our necks.

When we returned, the first of the cornmeal-encrusted oysters lined the counter. Janet looked at us sideways, a little fear scrunching her mouth and the corner of her eyes, as if she were worried the elves hadn't come. But our faith was unshaken. "Ishkin and Bishkin went to the store," I yelled on the way to our room. "They'll pick us up tomorrow."

Rima and I stripped to our T-shirts and left our clothes in heaps on the floor, like big wilted flowers.

"Girls! Janet!" Jack called from the front step. "I found a pearl!"

A pearl!

In "The Little Pearl Heart," which Jack read to us, a princess has a hailstone for a heart and, in order to love, must always wear a magic pearl around her neck. In the picture, the pearl is incandescent, swirling with pink and turquoise, perfectly spherical and large as a marble.

We gathered around Jack. Rima pulled back his fingers to get a better look. In the center of his palm was something small, dull, oblong, and slightly lumpy, not a princess pearl at all.

"What's a pearl?" Rima asked.

"Sometimes an oyster gets a piece of sand in its shell. It's uncomfortable, like having a rock in your shoe. When the oyster can't get the sand out, it coats it with calcium carbonate—like what your teeth are made of—until it's smooth and doesn't hurt anymore."

Jack handed the pearl to Janet, who stood behind him on the step. For a moment, the pearl was held equally between them, and Janet smiled her quiet, internal smile.

"Let me see," Rima pulled down Janet's arm and poked it with her finger.

I didn't look again. I was too jarred by the gap between the vision in my mind and the lumpy imitation in Jack's hand, a crusted-over bit of annoying sand.

But the rest of them were pleased with the pearl just as it was—that dull tooth of a jewel, which Janet set on the windowsill above the kitchen sink.

How to Make a Boom Frame: Pocahontas Bay

Step 1

Step 2

Step 3

Step 4

WHAT I BELIEVED: SAFETY

Sometimes Jack disappeared into the bush with the loggers to fell trees. From the house, I could see the tips of the firs, hemlocks, and cedars tremble, and then disappear. A sound of ripping branches. Then the eerie silence afterward. I didn't like to see trees, which seemed so permanent, tumble. Jack told me a tree sometimes fell in an unexpected direction and could kill a logger. So each silence carried the possibility of disaster, which made me tense, until the chain saws started again.

Then Jack helped assemble the floating log booms. First, balancing on the logs in the water, he created a rectangular frame by connecting logs together, end to end, with metal hooks and eyes. Then the loggers rolled freshly cut logs down an embankment where Jack, with a long, hooked pole, arranged them inside the frame to fit as many as possible, a project that pleased both the rugged outdoorsman and the mathematician in him. The logs were ready for the tugs, which pulled them to the mill in Powell River.

The job required him to balance on the boom frame logs, which—although attached to each other and tethered to an occasional post—still rolled. If he fell, the raucous free-floating logs could crush him. He could get trapped under the logs or knocked unconscious while coming up for air. Once, he mashed his right foot between two logs, and although I didn't see it, he said his foot was pressed flat.

"Flat as a pancake," Janet added.

Jack had pale feet, fine-boned, with hair on his knuckly toes and skin as translucent as skimmed milk, with blue veins pulsing underneath. His second toe was as long as his first, which he said was the proper shape for toes (so I thought my toes, and Janet and Rima's too, descending in size, were wrong). Jack's flattened foot didn't break, because, Jack explained, "Wilsons have flexible bones." But he lost the feeling on the top in a circle about the size of a quarter. I'd try to tickle the spot. "Can you feel that?" I asked again and again, unwilling to believe he couldn't.

Sometimes when Jack was away felling logs, Rima and I walked the empty boom frames ourselves. We'd try to balance, as the logs rolled slightly to the right and left.

"Stop it, you're rocking the log," I'd yell to Rima, half a beam behind me.

"No, you are," she screamed back.

One afternoon, while Rima napped, I decided to walk the boom frames myself, glad for a stretch of solitude. The clouds were thin and high, an even gray. The sun a silver quarter. The first two logs were easy. I held my arms above my head, and then out to the side and nodded to the trees that lined the curve of the bay, a black-green curtain. I was a ballerina. I pointed my toes. I did a little hop. Nothing could shake my perfect balance. I was remarkably agile for my age, I thought.

The next log was dark and floated low in the water, salvaged from the ocean where it had been floating for months. Its bark had melted away.

Arms out. Point toe. Hop. Step, point, hop. Then the shock of cold, which sucked my breath and crushed my chest. Salt in my mouth and nose. My half circle shoreline was broken and bobbing, tipped sideways. I grasped for the slick wall of a log, which only scraped the insides of my arms. I sank.

Underwater, I opened my eyes. Above, sunlight streamed through the waves, a jewel-green broken by undulating white diamonds. The current cradled me from side to side. Seaweed rocked beside me. My feet were suspended above speckled pebbles. A school of small fish, who—as if they had one mind—all changed direction, flashed silver for a moment, then black again.

My chest ached. I pointed my feet. I sank until my big toes touched the bottom, then pushed off as hard as I could. My head barely broke the surface.

"Help," I squeaked, then sank again. I thought my toe-pointing and pushing idea was clever. Point. Push. "Help!"

I don't remember being pulled from the water, except the vague sensation of thumbs pressing against the inside of my elbows. I wasn't, afterward, afraid of the water, nor did I stop walking the boom frames: the ocean had been kind, and Jack could break the laws of time and space to appear instantaneously at my side.

WHAT I FEARED MOST:
FROZEN HEART

It was the happiest day that the Kingdom of Matania had ever known, for it was the <u>fifth</u> birthday of the lovely little princess Charmain, and, as everyone knows, the fifth birthday is always the most important, because it is the one just before you go to school, when you have finished with the nursery, and, after that, anything exciting might happen . . .

"Ah, but I bring you a gift. See here!" The Thunder Witch held up something between her finger and her thumb. . . . "I give thee a hailstone for a heart! Henceforth no heart you'll have save one of ice, and icy cold to love or pity! Be heartless, and loving none, be loved by none! That's my gift! Ha! Ha! Ha! . . ."

"The Little Pearl Heart"
The Kathleen Fidler Omnibus

WHAT I DIDN'T UNDERSTAND: DEATH AND PHYSICS

"Don't get your clothes wet," Janet called out the door after us, dishrag in her hand. She'd just spent the entire previous day learning how to clean our clothes in a hand-cranked wringer washing machine on the gravel in front of our house and didn't want to wash them again soon. At the beach, I took off my halter-top and bell-bottomed corduroys, folded them, and set them on a log Rima tugged off her shorts and red sneakers. Her legs were skinny, but her belly was firm and round. She tried to wiggle out of her shirt by herself, but it got stuck on her head. I pulled. Her head popped out: green eyes, almond-shaped and wide apart. Cheeks smudged with dirt the shape of islands. Fine, blonde hair tangled on the back of her head—her "bird's nest," Janet called it. I folded her clothes and set them, with her red sneakers, on the log next to mine.

We waded. Cold bit our arches and ankles, until we couldn't feel our feet or the barnacles and sharp rocks under them. Cold crawled up our calves and settled under our knees.

We jumped over waves, trying to clear each the moment it broke. When we fell, seaweed strands, red-brown and buoyed by little heart shaped balloons, strangled our waists. We tried to pop the hearts. They felt like slippery chicken skin.

Then we saw our log, with the clothes still folded on top, bobbing in the water, just out of reach and moving farther from us. The ocean, playing with us like a bad, happy dog, had snuck up behind us and grabbed them. I'd betrayed Rima's red shoes by not keeping an eye on them. But I was also secretly delighted by the decadence—whole outfits, freshly laundered and too costly to replace, disappearing toward the horizon— leaving us in bare, seamless skin.

Rima was the one who lunged for the log and lugged it back. She saved our clothes and her red shoes.

A week later, Rima almost drowned.

We were alone again. The tide had pushed in a log. We mounted our sea horse. I held onto a slippery bump that used to be a branch, and in the gentle surge of waves, my toes touched and lifted, touched and lifted from rocks below. Rima sat behind me, gripping my shoulders. Then a big wave broke early, just behind us.

When I stood, I couldn't see Rima.

Then I saw her, on her back, under three feet of water. Her arms and legs bulged and rippled under the waves. Her face was round and featureless, like a dinner plate.

I turned and ran toward the house. The gravel punched the bottom of my feet. The road stretched. I couldn't swallow enough air. A million pins pricked my lungs. If I could bring Janet, Rima would be safe.

Janet sprinted. When we arrived, Rima was standing ankle deep in the water and, crying. Mucous ran over her mouth and chin. Janet reached for her.

Janet's words shot sideways at me.

"Why didn't you pull her up?"

It hadn't occurred to me—but I knew that wasn't a reasonable answer. So I thought of another one.

"She's too heavy."

"People are lighter in the water," she said, as if this fact were perfectly logical, "You could have lifted her easily. You could hold *me* up in the water." She shifted Rima in her arms.

I felt layers and dark colors in her words. It was true sometimes I didn't want Rima with me, following as she did, constantly talking, crying, wanting whatever was in my hand. It was true sometimes I wanted to be alone. But I didn't want her face under the water like a plate.

I followed silently behind as Janet carried Rima, nestled and quiet, back to the house. The back of Janet's knees looked soft. Rima looked at me, absently, over Janet's shoulder, and then closed her eyes. I was afraid to be noticed, to remind Janet of what she believed about me, to think about what I should have done.

Like Jack, I'd keep my mind on scientific facts. "How interesting . . ." I thought, "How strange it is, that people are lighter in the water."

Tarn, Gibsons Bay, just before moving to Pocahontas Bay

Rima, Gibsons Bay

WHAT I LEARNED ABOUT LOVE: SEAWEED MAMAS

The first big storm deposited heaps of Seaweed Mamas on our beach. They were a brown kelp with long, tapered tails that attached to the ocean floor; a hollow bulb that bobbed at the surface; and on either side of the bulb, long blades, which rested on top of the water. The smallest ones, the baby Seaweed Mamas, were only a foot long, while the largest had tails twenty feet long and bulbs as big as six fists.

We knew, from the moment we plucked our first one from her tangled pile, she was called a Seaweed Mama and she was alive. It didn't bother us that her neck merged right into her tail, with no body in between, or she didn't have any arms or legs, for she had a shiny face and hair naturally arranged in ponytails. We liked best the Seaweed Mamas with flawless skin. Although we felt guilty about it, we didn't like as well the ones with mushy white spots or strange bumps or crispy dry tails. And when we stepped on a Seaweed Mama by accident, we felt awful—that horrible pop of a splitting head.

We had a ritual for caring for our Seaweed Mamas. First, we carried them to the water's edge. We rested their heads in the palms of our hands and leaned them back gently into the water to keep their faces dry while we scrubbed their hair— just as Janet did when she washed us in the kitchen sink. Afterward, we wiped their faces with "washcloths," bumpy squares of seaweed, and trimmed their hair by ripping each blade to the same length. Finally, sitting on the sand, our Seaweed Mamas on our laps, we tied their ponytails with green kelp shaped like ribbons.

When we showed Jack and Janet our first Seaweed Mama, they laughed. Jack wanted to carve her a face with his pocketknife. But her face was so smooth and shiny, Jack's knife might mar her. And what if the face he carved didn't look like her real face, the one I could see where Jack saw only a slippery blank?

He held her in his left hand and opened his switchblade. "No!" I cried. "That's the back of her head!" How could he carve her face if he didn't even know what side it was on? He turned her over and brought his knife to her skin. I closed my eyes. When I opened them, the Seaweed Mama had a lovely face: wide eyes like Janet's, a small nose, and friendly smile.

So she wouldn't die, Jack curled her up in a bucket of salt water. Because the heat inside would cause her to rot and smell, we kept her on the steps by the front door. I was sorry to take her from her friends, but glad to have her so close. We took her out to play and changed her water every day to keep her fresh, but she got mushy anyway. Soon we had to let her go to her death, which had already begun before we met her.

Parents are spoiling their children's lives by forcing on them outdated beliefs, outdated manners, outdated morals. They are sacrificing the child to the past.

Summerhill: A Radical Approach to Child Rearing
A.S. Neill, 1960

WHAT I DIDN'T
KNOW THEN:
MANNERS

The dirt road to Pocahontas Bay was narrow and shaded until it emerged from the trees, dropped down a hill into the camp, and turned to the right to pass our house and parallel the bay. Just at the curve sat a white, two bedroom house Rima and I called the Big House. Like a mother at the head of the table, it had a full view of the workings of the logging camp.

Every weekday, just as the pale morning light settled into all the cracks and corners, the loggers barreled into camp, jammed into an extended cab pick-up they called the "crew cab." Rima and I didn't think the loggers had ever been boys; they had always been men with black hair on their arms, red plaid shirts, and stomachs that hung over their pants.

Usually the Big House was empty, but that fall, for a short while, Cassy the Cook lived there. Later, I learned Cassy had been a cook in logging camps all over the Canadian interior, but at the time I didn't wonder about her past or even ask why she was called the cook when all the loggers brought mailbox-sized lunches and went home for dinner. We assumed she'd always returned to that house in that flowered housedress with the apron stretched over her wide stomach, knowing we'd step onto her front porch. She'd kept candy in her drawer just for that moment.

We first met Cassy with Janet, but didn't listen to the words that passed between them at the front door. Instead we fingered the balls of hard candy Cassy had given us, popping them in our mouths, spitting them into our hands, sucking them up again. We didn't think the candy came from a store or Cassy might eat it herself. It grew in her drawer for us.

Another day, Rima and I wanted more candy and asked Janet to take us to the Big House. Janet was on her hands and knees, scrubbing the floor with a rag. Her toes and her knees were red. We whined, pleaded. Rima pulled on the edge of Janet's cut off jean shorts. "Pleeeeeease."

Janet sighed, leaned back on knees. "No, I said I'm not going. You're big enough. You can go by yourselves." With the back of her hand, she brushed away the bangs stuck to her face.

Before we could talk ourselves out of it, we ran toward the Big House. We slowed as we got closer. If we looked at each other or spoke, we might lose our courage. Tingles blossomed in my stomach. Each of Cassy's steps grew taller, so I could hardly climb them. Through the screen door, I saw the dark gray outlines of a stove, a table, and Cassy's wide back, moving. She turned and shuffled toward the door.

From stories, we knew there were words that open doors: "Abracadabra" and, if we were in Arabia, "Open Sesame." But we didn't know the words to say to a proper lady with big, hanging bosom, who wore housedresses. We hadn't planned that far. But it was too late to leave. Cassy pushed open the screen door and looked down. Her hair was in a bun, blonde streaked with gray, strands flying out around her face. She wore house slippers.

"What do you want?" Her tone implied we'd interrupted her. We didn't answer. "Didn't your parents teach you any manners?"

Then I realized—in the way I sometimes understood in a burst—that Jack and Janet knew the words to say before and after asking for candy, but they had chosen not to teach us. I didn't know why.

Cassy half grimaced, half smiled.

"I know. You want some candy, don't you?"

We nodded. She shuffled to the white drawer in her kitchen and returned with two pieces of butterscotch and set them in our hands.

We looked back at her, her wide flat cheeks, and then turned and leaped down the steps.

"You're welcome," she yelled after us. The screen door slammed shut behind her.

We ran almost back to our house before we stopped and I helped Rima tug off her cellophane wrapper.

I slipped the butterscotch in my mouth, but didn't taste it. I was too busy thinking. Jack and Janet had reasons I didn't understand, a life bigger than the one I knew, lives of their own that stretched out before my birth.

An Incomplete History of Jack and Janet

Janet Frances Rusheon	**John Arnold Wilson, Jr.**
Born on October 30, 1947 in Shreveport, Louisiana. Lives in town of Haughton.	Born October 21, 1942 in Pennsylvania. Lives in suburban Glenside.
Two older sisters, Patty and Travis.	One older sister, Gay.
Father is an elementary school principal.	Father is an insurance executive.
Raised a Christian Scientist.	Raised an Episcopalian.
Father dies when she is seven.	Makes his own kit-radio. Listens to *The Lone Ranger, Sergeant Preston in the Yukon, The Shadow, The Green Hornet.*
Age ten, discovers rhythm and blues singer Etta James.	Secret ambition, which never leaves him, is to "know everything."
At the beginning of sixth grade, family moves to Boulder, Colorado.	At seventeen, reads *On the Road.* Afterward, he sometimes hops freight trains. He reads more of the Beats. He and his friends take a road trip for spring break—and don't come back. His parents promise they will ask nothing else of him if he will only return and finish high school.
In junior high, loves rhythm and blues singers Robert Johnson and Howlin' Wolf.	
Her sisters leave home and her mother stops mothering. She hates her mother's noodle and Campbell soup recipes. She's lonely.	In 1960, Jack accepted at CU Boulder with a Navy ROTC scholarship. Pledges Lamda Chi Alpha.

On his first Christmas holiday, secretly elopes with his high school girlfriend. That night they each sneak back to their childhood bedrooms.

As a married man, Jack loses his scholarship and fraternity membership. In Boulder, he and his wife share cheap housing with some hippies.

As a teenager, she bleaches her hair, wears thick eye make up, and talks so much in class that one teacher tells her she has "diarrhea of the mouth."

Jack has a daughter, but not long after, he and his wife divorce, and she takes the child and moves away.

She listens to James Brown, Otis Redding, and B.B. King. She drinks and smokes and dates a greaser, who drives a motorcycle and folds his cigarettes in the sleeve of his white T-shirt.

Jack is in and out of college, but he reads: James Joyce, Thomas Mann, Franz Kafka, Herman Hesse, Aldous Huxley, Dostoevsky, Thoreau's *Walden*.

She waitresses long hours at Bennett's pizza place on the Hill across from the university. One teacher feels sorry for her and lets her sleep through class.

He decides to major in mathematics and works part time at CU's Institute for Behavioral Science, where he programs computers for social science applications. He will finish his degree in eight years.

Janet starts college at CU Boulder. Drops out after one semester.

Jack has a crush on his waitress at Bennett's. She's beautiful and lively and thinks he's brilliant.

Janet is interested in Jack: he's
smart and well-read and rebellious and makes her think,
believes she can think.

Jack and Janet move in together.

Janet's mother sends the ladies
from the church, in flowered
hats, to convince her she is
living in sin with a divorced
Beatnik.

Jack's mother doesn't want
him to him to marry Janet. She
is so young, only eighteen, and
Jack doesn't support the child
he has.

Jack and Janet marry.

On their wedding night, Janet
is hurt because Jack invites
friends to sleep on the floor
next to their bed.

Jack doesn't believe in phony
traditions; he believes in community. On their wedding
night, he asks friends to stay at
their house.

Jack and Janet live in a little cabin without electricity
or running water on Sugarloaf Mountain.

Janet likes the meadow full of
wildflowers. She learns to chop
wood and make bread.

She cuts her hair short, like Twiggy's.

Jack makes her drive to the East Coast,
with him for a family visit, pregnant, in an
open Jeep with no shocks, in the rain.

She is so pregnant the only dress that
fits is a Hawaiian muumuu from
K-Mart. She drives up the mountain.
The brake and gas pedal fall to the floor.
The car rolls backward. She steers around
the mountain curves, gaining speed.
She sees a farmer's field and aims for it.
She smashes into a large rock: the hood
flies up, the horn goes off, and she steps out,
shaken but unharmed, with her Twiggy hair cut,
in her muumuu. The farmer stares.

November 19, 1967
I am born.

STORIES I COLLECTED: JANET

When Janet dropped stories of her childhood in Louisiana, I grabbed them and strung them together like a bead necklace.

When Janet was six or seven, Janet's mother Wuh-Wa (a toddler-warped pronunciation of Mama) caught Janet in the driveway, sitting on her next-door neighbor Diane and strangling her. Janet was big for her age; Diane had bird bones. Someone had to pull Janet off.

I'd only known Janet in gentleness, and this hidden violence thrilled me.

"Why'd you do it?"

"I don't know." Janet stood and wiped the table. "She had a box of one hundred crayons; I had a box of eight. When I went to her house to color, she colored lightly inside the lines. My coloring was dark and messy." Janet grabbed one of my dull crayons and peeled the paper off for me. "She told me not to press so hard because she didn't want me to wear down the points . . . But when she came to *my* house and I told her not to wear down the points on *my* crayons, Wuh-Wa told *me* not to be rude."

"That's not fair!" I said.

Janet smiled, pleased I was on her side. "I've never met a Diane I liked."

I tucked away this warning about Dianes.

When she kneaded her whole wheat bread dough, Janet told me Wuh-Wa had only fed her store-bought white bread. In her neighborhood, mothers would feed any children playing in their yard a slice of white bread with white sugar sprinkled on top.

"Can you imagine?" Janet said. "White bread and white sugar." She folded her dough over and punched it down. I secretly longed for white bread and sugar as much as I knew Janet secretly liked it. Those same mothers made an art of afternoon "visitin'," wearing hats and pantyhose, serving demitasse, telling elaborate, practiced stories. And no matter how close the visit, they drove their cars. Wuh-Wa curled her red hair and put on pink lipstick to drive across the street.

When Janet's hands were busy for a long time, mashing soybeans or rolling out dough for cinnamon rolls, she told me other, sadder stories. Wuh-Wa—whose own father had deserted her family—worshiped her tall, handsome husband. He was the father she never had. She hadn't planned for Janet, her third and accidental daughter; she didn't want her husband's attentions divided again.

But Janet's father had loved her dearly. When he came home from work, he swung her in his arms and called her his Teddy. He died when she was seven. Her words about him were warm, but sparse—her memory so intimate, I could only stand at the edges.

The maid, Gertie, whom Janet loved more than anyone except her father, had to enter through the back door and couldn't drink out of Janet's cup. When Janet asked why, Wuh-Wa answered, "Why, honey, you know Gertie is one of the family. That's why we give her all of our old dresses. But the coloreds are different; they're more like children."

I knew Janet shared this story to show me how different she was from the rest of her family and to rouse in me a sense of justice.

When her father died, a school was named for him in honor of his work as a superintendent. He'd helped obtain books and supplies for black schools, so dozens of black people walked ten miles to town to lay handpicked flowers on his new grave. To Janet, those flowers were more beautiful than all the formal bouquets. Her father was frozen in a perfection he could never lose.

The day of the funeral, when Janet was seven, the house was filled with grown-ups in suits and dresses and heels. She walked invisibly between them, but a young man leaned down to talk to her for a moment and handed her a little card with a game on it. She kept this card, this token of male love, in her wallet until it disintegrated, years later. I felt her grief, still so large it was a presence, a man-sized shadow that followed her everywhere.

After her husband died, Wuh-Wa was too crushed by grief to mother. So Janet was left without an Easter basket to take to school for the Easter egg hunt. So her sister Travis unearthed an enormous fruit basket, filled it with grass from the yard, and decorated it with little animals and a few plastic flowers. Janet was grateful for Travis's effort, but she knew the children would tease her. They did. She was the only child who found not even one egg.

She told the story as if it were funny, but I could hear the edge of bitterness. I loved the story, though, because Janet knew what it was like to be a child moving into the world, ashamed and shy and wrong.

When the family moved from Haughton to Bossier City, Janet stood on the lawn of the house they had to sell, yelling "house for sale, house for sale!" She was helping. No one drove past.

I sensed Janet was still calling "house for sale" on her inside, yet to find the place that felt like home, a place as safe as her father's arms.

*I want to be drippin' in diamonds
and drivin' a bottle-green Cadillac.*

Wuh-Wa, dropped in casual
conversation with me, 1980.

WHAT I KNEW THAT MY MOTHER DIDN'T: BILLY

"I'm not as creative as you two," Janet said, as she swept the floor. Rima and I sat on Jack and Janet's bed, drawing pictures of Seaweed Mamas. Her comment made me feel a little heat-flush of pride.

She paused and leaned on her broom. "I just remembered... After my father died, I did have an imaginary friend."

Rima and I looked at her. We hadn't known she had an imaginary world. She spoke slowly, pulled details from her pockets of memory.

"Billy... His name was Billy. Not creative. Like the names you think of."

"I like the name Billy," I said, trying to make her feel better.

"What did he look like?" Rima asked.

"About this tall." She held up her hands. "Five inches or so. With green hair. And *orange* eyes." She scrunched her face.

Rima and I were silent, surprised by Billy's odd ugliness. We would have chosen a furry, pretty imaginary friend.

"That's creative," I said.

"No, that's ugly. You wouldn't have such a weird imaginary friend."

We didn't answer.

"Whenever I did something bad, I said Billy had done it."

Rima and I laughed. That was a good idea.

"No," she said, "I really believed he did."

Her emotions moved across her face, a pain, then confusion: she was talking about a child she didn't understand.

"Once, when Wuh-Wa was having a party, I set Billy in a tea cup and left. When I walked back in the room, one of the ladies was drinking from his cup. I yelled, 'You swallowed Billy! You swallowed Billy!'"

Her eyes were far away. Then they flashed at me.

"Wuh-Wa always told that story to make people laugh."

I didn't laugh. I felt the loss that had created Billy, the part of Janet that needed to be boyish and bad in a house of women and ruffles and grief.

"What happened to Billy?" Rima asked.

"Wuh-Wa asked her friend to spit him out . . . and she did."

I imagined a lady in a wide-brimmed hat spitting Billy—his green hair wet with tea and saliva—into a saucer.

Even then, I sensed what Janet couldn't see: Wuh-Wa couldn't give Janet what she needed and she turned all her sad stories to funny ones, but she had asked her friend to spit out Billy. She hadn't taken Billy from her.

In my generation, many of us knew we did not want to be like our mothers, even when we loved them. We could not help but see their disappointment.

The Feminine Mystique
Betty Freidan, 1963

WHAT I LEARNED: PRESENTS

Jack, who was full of stories, told us almost nothing about his childhood. Only later did I eke out a few details. He'd been an altar boy in the Episcopal Church. He was a wrestler: considered athletic, good-looking, popular, an "all-American boy." He'd competed on his high school cross country team—in flat black Converse shoes—and won one race. Once, visiting his parents, my Granny and Granddaddy, I found a black and white picture of him, age eleven, in his football uniform: feet together, chest tall, helmet in his left hand, football under his right arm, a big W on his chest—but with a gentle look on his smooth face. Wyncote Elementary, Granny had written on the back in pale script. Jack never told me he'd played football; playing football was against his principles.

I didn't notice an absence of Jack's childhood stories, though, because I was distracted by his physical presence: Rima and I each sat on one of his feet, and he lugged us around, walking like Frankenstein. He threw us upside down, tossed us in the air, spun us, held us over the edge of docks or ferries until we were delirious with the illusion of danger. He carried us on his shoulders, always reminding us to duck when he walked under doorways.

He lay on his back in the main room and put his feet in the air. His socks, black business socks left over from D.C., had holes in the toes. I leaned my stomach against his feet and he gripped my wrists. He had a permanent line of black under his fingernails. "You can tell a lot about a man from his hands," he told me, admiring his calluses. When he straightened his legs, I rose into the air and he made airplane noises. His heels pressed into my gut, which hurt and blocked my breath, but I was having too much fun to stop. He lowered his feet over his head. "Oh no, airplane crash," he said as my head descended toward the floor. He pulled me up just in time. Then it was Rima's turn. "Do again, do again," she bounced.

Sometimes, in evening or late afternoon, Jack and I walked, just the two of us, along logging roads into the bush. Once I found a fern with a stem black and stiff as a wire, a fern he didn't recognize. We looked it up in a book. It was a rare find, and I hoped he thought I, too, was rare for having found it.

In mid-October, Janet took me to town to buy Jack a birthday present. Jack and Janet believed children, not parents, should choose their own gifts for friends and family.

In the window of M and M's Variety Store, I saw a shiny, purple logging truck with real rubber wheels, doors that opened and closed, and wooden dowels stacked in the back. Our house was purple, Jack liked both playing and logging equipment: the gift was perfect. Janet was strangely hesitant.

"Are you sure, Tarn?" Inside the store, she turned the truck over to check the price. She held her breath. "I can't believe they charge that much for a toy."

I was certain Jack would love a purple logging truck above all other possible presents.

After the delicious anxiety of waiting, the unbearable waiting, Jack sat in his purple chair after dinner, looking both radiantly pleased and a little self-conscious to have us all gathered around him. I handed him my present, wrapped in newspaper I'd colored. As soon as he'd pulled off enough paper to recognize a truck, he laughed. He put the purple truck on the table and opened and closed the little doors.

"It's purple," I said.

"Yes, I see that."

"You can dump the logs out."

"Yes."

"It's just like a real logging truck."

"Yes, it is."

"A purple logging truck."

His reaction wasn't enough. I wanted something more, for him to exclaim it was the best present he'd ever received, for him to croon over the little black steering wheel, for him to push the truck around the floor.

"Do you want to play with your truck?" I asked.

"Later. I'm enjoying just sitting right now." He swallowed some coffee and leaned back in his chair. "You can though." He handed the truck to me.

Rima and I poured the logs out, stacked them back in, and then constructed a logging road between chair legs and over a crumpled sweater. Jack's hand rested on the book Janet had given him.

I wondered, suddenly, if I had chosen a present I wanted instead of one Jack would like. It hadn't occurred to me there might be a difference. It hadn't occurred to me there were parts of Jack I'd never know or understand.

It is best to erase all personal history because that would make us free from the encumbering thoughts of other people. I have, little by little, created a fog around me and my life. Nobody knows for sure who I am or what I do. Not even I. How can I know who I am, when I am all this? Little by little you must create a fog around yourself; you must erase everything around you until nothing can be taken for granted, until nothing is any longer for sure, or real.

Journey to Ixtlan
Carlos Castaneda, 1972

WHAT I DIDN'T KNOW THEN: WHAT WAS REAL

I walked alone on the beach. The sky and water were flat, gray sheets separated only by a pencil-line horizon. It was silent. No ravens, seagulls, or growling chain saws. The world seemed pulled back, faded, like a dream. How, then, could I be certain I wasn't dreaming? I'd heard someone say, "I had to pinch myself to make sure I was awake." So I tried. I pinched myself hard on my right thigh. My leg stung, but the dream-like haze still draped everything, smudging the fir trees. Then I reasoned. If I were dreaming, and I pinched myself, wouldn't that be a dream pinch? How, then, could it wake me?

Later, I awoke in the middle of the night to a black so dark it was like a weight on my eyes. But the black wasn't a smooth sheet—it was made of tiny speckles, like the static on our TV in Alexandria. The next morning, I could still see grayish dots. Air molecules. I couldn't wait to tell Jack. He was slurping coffee out of a tin cup and turning the pages of the *Powell River News* when I announced my discovery. Jack looked up from the paper.

"I don't think you were seeing air. Air molecules are too small to see without a special machine."

"But I can see dots."

"The dots are actually inside your eyes. Your eyes have thousands of cells, rods and cones, which collect light. Your mind fills in the spaces in between and creates a picture." Jack turned the page and took another sip of coffee.

I didn't understand what he was saying. He just didn't know how to make his eyes see like mine.

Another night, Jack shined his flashlight toward the bush by the creek. Yellow eyes floated in the black, glowing and without a body. They turned sideways and disappeared. Jack told me they belonged to an animal: a raccoon or a wild cat—some animal with special chemicals in its eyes to help it see in the dark. But I wasn't sure. I felt no connection between the lumbering animals of the day and that unblinking yellow stare.

I liked to press my eyelids and watch the fireworks display, a vibrating night sky, blue flashes, swirling black and white checks. But if I pressed my finger firmly on the side of my closed eyelid and turned my eyes sideways, I saw an animal eye: a round, black, glowing ball with a gold aura. It frightened me. I pushed my eye again and again to see if it was still there. It never left. I didn't tell Jack. Certainly, if he didn't understand I saw air, he wouldn't believe I had an animal eye in a secret, black gap between myself and the outside world.

Sometimes, Janet would pause, freeze. Her eyes, already large, would get even bigger. She wouldn't blink or move her body. It frightened Rima and me a little, for she seemed as if she'd left her body. "What are you looking at?" Rima and I would ask, trying to bring her back. She was silent for a moment, then answered, without blinking or moving, "just staring into space." And then she'd shake herself free.

Other times, she'd fold up her eyelids so the raw, pink insides were on the outside. She'd ask Rima and me an ordinary question, and when we turned to answer, there she'd be, serene and horrifying. We'd scream and scream until she turned them down. Then we'd ask her to do it again. Jack, usually so brave, was disgusted and wouldn't allow her to fold her eyelids in his presence.

Most mornings, I had yellow, crusty chunks growing at the base of my eyelashes. Janet called it "sleep." My dreams were liquid; they oozed out of the cracks between my eyelids and solidified when they hit the air. Rima didn't have sleep on her eyelids, which made her seem more pure. If I had only a few bits of sleep, I enjoyed scraping them off with my fingernails. The flakes had holes in them where my eyelashes had poked through. They tasted salty. Sometimes, by accident, I yanked out my eyelashes too and my eyelids itched. But when the sleep was too thick for picking, Janet heated water and loosened the chunks with a hot washcloth. Every time Janet cleaned my eyes, I thought it would be the last time, she'd wiped all the goop away for good. But the sleep grew back.

One morning, when I awoke before everyone else, my eyes were cemented shut. When I tried to pull them open, all my eyelashes tugged at the roots. I was blind. This both hurt my feelings and fascinated me. If I picked off all the sleep myself, Jack and Janet wouldn't believe my story. I had to show them. So I crawled, sightless, down the bunk bed ladder. One of my eyes pulled open slightly. I squeezed it closed. My story wouldn't be as good if my eye were open.

I felt my way toward Jack and Janet's bed. But Jack and Janet liked sleeping and had told Rima and me, many times, we were not to wake them. So I stood next to the bed, Janet's back toward me. The story of my pitiful blindness grew in my mind. Suddenly, Janet woke and turned, as quickly as if I'd shaken her.

"What's the matter?" The concern in her voice released in me an unexpected, crying hiccup.

"My eyes are stuck."

"Oh, honey," she laughed and pulled off her covers. Her voice was froggy. She pulled on Jack's green flannel shirt over her breasts and started the fire in the wood stove. She dipped the washcloth in the hot water and wiped my eyes.

As she dissolved the last of the sleep, she told me a story: when we were in Washington D.C. Jack read a newspaper article about a man who had a pet monkey named, strangely enough, Rima. When monkey-Rima was tired of waiting for the man to wake up, she crawled on his bed and pushed up his eyelids.

I laughed. I laughed because the story was funny and the monkey was named Rima. I laughed because even though I couldn't always tell if I were waking or sleeping and didn't know if I could see air or if I had an animal eye inside my eye, I knew this moment was solid: my eyes were raw and clean; steam rose from the pot on the stove; Janet's shirt and the skin under her eyes were soft. I could have waited to wake Janet, and she knew it, but she'd risen anyway. I was washed clean by laughter and that love, real: outside of me and bigger than I thought I deserved.

Jack, age seventeen, the year he read On the Road

Janet, age seventeen, a year before she married Jack.

WHAT I KNEW ABOUT HUNGER

Early in the morning, Jack slipped into the rain to work with Hagman's crew. When we awoke, Rima and I crawled onto Jack and Janet's bed and looked for him out the front window. He was gone. Water drops slid down the panes. Slate-gray clouds, heavy with moisture, sank toward the water.

Since moving to Pocahontas Bay, Rima and I spent most of our days outside, but November drizzle had driven us in. All day, it was almost as dark as twilight, so even though we couldn't afford the fuel, Janet burned both a kerosene lantern and the wood stove. "Colorado gets cold," she said, as she stoked the fire, "but it's usually dry and sunny. Not so bone-chilling damp."

As she did every morning, Janet held up a spoonful of cod liver oil and slipped it in my mouth. I scrunched up my face. "I know, it's horrible," she said, filling one for Rima. But secretly, I loved the golden color and the fishy residue, which coated the back of my throat. I liked, too, the rare routine, evidence of Janet's love.

"Want some granola?" she asked. She'd just made a new batch: oats, walnuts, raisins, and honey burned in a frying pan. "You'll like it this time."

Her raisins were as hard to chew as pebbles. I was sure they'd stay in my stomach forever, that I permanently carried what couldn't be digested: pieces of gum, rock-like raisins, and watermelon seeds. "Don't swallow the seeds; watermelons will grow out your ears," Jack had said.

"More?" She waved a wooden spoon at us and Rima and I shook our heads.

"How 'bout some yogurt?" Janet also grew yogurt, white and lumpy, in a container on the counter. The yogurt was alive, she'd explained, which was why she had to save a spoonful: to pass life onto the next batch. I didn't want to eat anything alive—it might wiggle in my mouth or set up house in my stomach. But Jack had said the animals were very small, invisible, and actually helped digestion; store-bought yogurt, on the other hand, was dead. So I let Janet stir in brown sugar. I pressed sugar lumps against my front teeth.

Janet divided her bread dough into three bowls, covered them with damp towels, and set them in warm corners of the kitchen, like sleeping cats. Every several hours, after they'd ballooned again, she poured a little flour on the table, rubbed it on her hands, and then dumped the dough. First, the dough resisted but then exhaled its air.

"Can I try?" I poked a hole in the dough with my finger and then pressed my fist into it, leaving knuckle marks.

"You have to push harder, use your weight, push down with the heel of your hand." Janet took the dough back, rolled and pressed. She was feeling efficient. "Wuh-Wa always bought our bread. It was her life goal to do as little work as possible." Janet was Southern-girl turned pioneer woman.

When she was done, she rubbed some flour on the dough, then slapped it. "Just like a baby's bum."

I knew Janet missed babies, but I didn't like thinking of our bread as bums. The baking bread smelled first yeasty, then sweet-crunchy. In the late afternoon, we finally ate our loaf, warm and with honey. While we snacked, she drained the water off of the soybeans, which had soaked all night, and dumped them in a pot to boil.

Then she started dessert. Peanut butter balls. She mixed the peanut butter with powdered milk, powdered sugar, and corn syrup, then rolled them in her palm. Then she coated them in coconut or powdered sugar. She handed me one. Then she lined the rest on a cookie tray and put them in the purple cooler to chill.

I held my peanut butter ball in my hand until it was oily. Then I ate it. The peanut butter clogged the back of my throat. I asked Janet for another one. The big one. The biggest one. The one without coconut. One with coconut. Another one. Janet realized I had a hunger for peanut butter balls that could never be satiated, so she put them away.

"It's not fair. How come you can have a peanut butter ball whenever you want, but I can't?"

She was too tired by this point to argue—and it was against her and Jack's philosophy to answer "because I said so"—so she wiped the powdered milk off the counter and didn't answer.

"And you ate my best Halloween candy," I added.

"That was a month ago," she said. "I told you I was sorry."

Janet squashed the soybeans, first with a potato masher and then with a fork. Then she stirred in peas, grated carrots, wheat germ, and onion flakes. She let them sit to absorb the flavor.

Just as Rima and I were getting restless, tiring of the long, warm sameness of the day, Jack pushed open the front door. Cold air rolled in behind him, carrying the smell of trees and sweat and damp clothes. Our house was Janet-sized, and Jack seemed too tall for it. Rima and I tumbled off the bed toward him, toward his differentness. Our crayons fell to the floor. Rima and I took turns grabbing his cold hands, walking up his legs in our bare feet, and flipping backward.

Janet patted the soy mush into burgers, doused the burgers in Worcestershire sauce, and dropped them in the frying pan. When they were almost done, she melted a slice of cheddar cheese on the top of each. We sat in our purple chairs at our purple table. I stabbed my burger with a fork. Her burgers satisfied even the hunger that lingered at the far bottom of my stomach.

Jack grabbed the ketchup bottle and whacked the back until his burger was smothered. Janet pulled in her chair and stared at Jack's plate.

"You could at least taste it first." She sounded as if she'd been holding the words for a long time and they had finally escaped in a hiss.

We were all silent.

Jack looked at Janet.

She looked everywhere but his eyes. Her fork clicked on her plate as she cut herself a ketchup-less bite. "Is that good, girls?" Janet looked at me but not really at me. "Do you like it?"

"Actually," Jack said, "I taught Janet how to cook."

"You cook?" I asked.

"Sure."

"What?"

"Spaghetti, scrambled eggs, beans and wieners. Somato toup."

Rima giggled, "somato toup." She sat on a stack of books, which looked precariously balanced.

"That's a Spoonerism," he explained, "named after a guy named Spooner who talked like that all the time."

"On purpose?" I asked.

"No, I don't think he could help it."

"But I didn't put ketchup all over *your* food," Janet said, but no one was listening.

The next morning, Janet asked Jack to put honey on our oatmeal. He squeezed the plastic bear and sprayed the last of the honey over Rima's bowl.

"We're out, I'll get more," Jack said, and headed to the shed where we kept the bulk food.

He returned with a white five-gallon bucket. He pried opened the lid with the end of his spoon, then tucked the bucket under his arm.

The honey, dribbling over my raisins and walnuts, was mesmerizingly beautiful: liquid amber, slowed sunlight. A gentle weight pressed my head, as if Jack were laying his hand there, spreading his fingers over my scalp and into my hair.

"Ja-ck!" Janet said loudly, in a voice part correction, part self-righteous anger, "the bucket!"

He jerked the bucket back up as the honey began to crawl down my forehead toward my eyebrows and the bridge of my nose.

The unexpected sharpness in Janet's voice made me cry.

"Jack. You've made her cry."

Janet was defending me, so I couldn't tell her I thought honey-on-my-head was funny. I was crying because of her sharp voice and Jack's stunned silence; because my allegiance was stretched equally between them; because of the vague sense I'd done something wrong.

Jack took me by the hand and walked me through the rain to the loggers' bathhouse. I closed my eyes to keep the honey out, but I liked the feel of the raindrops splashing against my skin. I liked being outside where emotions couldn't settle and fill up a room. Jack scrubbed me through five showers in the loggers' bathhouse before I was cleaned of so much sweetness.

How Janet liked her coffee
Lots of milk and sugar

Janet's favorite tobacco
Export A

Janet was proud she
Was a good seamstress
Marched in anti-
    war demonstrations
Rolled her own cigarettes

People told Janet she looked like
Goldie Hawn

Janet liked
Calico fabrics
The color purple
The color yellow
Daffodils
Daisies
Embroidered ribbons
Sewing

How Jack liked his coffee
With condensed milk

Jack's favorite tobacco
Export A

Jack's favorite beer
Labatts Blue

Jack's favorite drug
peyote

Jack's favorite foods
Spaghetti and meatballs
Beans and hot dogs
Sardine, cheese, and onion
    sandwiches
Clam chowder

Jack's favorite palindrome
kinnikinnik (a Colorado
    desert plant)

Jack loved
Art of M.C. Escher
Binoculars
Constellations
Chopping wood
Crossword puzzles
Gargoyles
Go, the ancient Chinese
    strategy game
Graph paper

Harmonica
Monopoly
Ravens
Recorder
Trains
Whittling

WHAT I DIDN'T UNDERSTAND: THE SOLAR SYSTEM

Just before sleeping—right after I'd come back from the outhouse and sipped some water and heard a story, just as Jack was tucking the covers around me and giving me a kiss, his scratchy face brushing mine—I asked questions. Jack accused me of avoiding sleep. Sometimes I did want his attention a few moments longer; sometimes I wanted to watch the way his mind puzzled, arranging answers into words I could understand; but, most often, as I sank into the warmth of the covers, my thoughts from the day would break into fragments, and the questions would rise: "What number comes after infinity?"

The afternoon after I'd asked Jack why the moon got bigger and smaller, he took me into the shed with a flashlight and an orange.

I loved the moon, whose path of light on the waters of Pocahontas Bay always ended at my feet, who followed me, peeking through the darkness of the trees when we drove at night. The pattern on the moon was as comfortable and familiar as the vein on the backs of Janet's hands. I liked the moon best when it was full. When it became only a shaving of itself, Rima and I imagined we saw a giant who'd sprayed himself with invisible potion and missed only the tip of his fingernail. Imagining his size sent us screaming back to the house.

Jack stepped on a chair in the middle of the shed and held the orange at arm's length. "This is the moon." The room smelled musty. He'd stuffed rags in the cracks in the walls to keep the light out, but it sneaked in around the edges.

"Why doesn't the moon fall?" I imagined some sort of string coming out the top, but I couldn't guess to what it attached.

"Gravity. Gravity is the same force that causes the rock that you throw into the air to fall to the ground."

I imagined a world in which there was no gravity, in which my rock, thrown into the air, floated above my head just out of reach. I didn't understand how a force that made my rock fall held the moon in empty space, but I didn't know how to ask my question.

Then Jack held his flashlight in his other hand. "This is the sun shining on the moon." The moon was like a ball, he explained, and only appeared to be getting bigger and smaller because part was in shadow. "Now walk around the orange and look at it." I walked, stepping on bits of old kindling. "You're the earth. Actually, the earth revolves around the sun and the moon revolves around the earth and the moon and earth are actually rotating, but I only have two hands."

For a moment, I could almost picture Jack's description of spinning spheres rotating around spheres, but the vision slipped away. Walking around the orange, I only saw an orange. I couldn't see the fingernail moon blowing up into a circle and then disappearing again.

"Do you see?" Jack said.

I wanted to, but I couldn't. My mind wouldn't open any farther. My legs were tickly. I wanted to run fast and get the tickles out. But I knew Jack's mood of concentrated enthusiasm. If he knew I were befuddled, he wouldn't stop explaining. He wouldn't believe I couldn't understand.

"Yes," I said, "Yes, I see."

And although I couldn't understand the relationship of sun, earth, moon, light and shadow, when I next looked at fingernail moon, I no longer saw a giant's fingernail. My eyes could fill in the dark places, could see the dimpled sphere, lighted on one side, suspended and rolling in space.

I have, as it were, my own sun and moon and stars, and a little world all to myself.

Walden
Henry David Thoreau, 1854

WHAT I DIDN'T UNDERSTAND: THE BALLOON

The latest storm had left behind new driftwood, heaps of sea-weed, plastic bags, decomposing fish, a dead seagull, and a single yellow flip flop. Jack and Janet strolled together, hands in their pockets, while Rima and I dodged back and forth, looking for surprises. The clouds were still low and blue-dark, and the wet beach shone black and silver.

In a mound of seaweed near the water, Rima spotted an unused white balloon with an unusually large opening. The ocean licked at it, pushing it toward us.

Rima ran to Jack and Janet, holding it up. "A balloon! Blow up my balloon!" Jack had just read us a book about pioneer children who had inflated up a pig's bladder for a ball, so we were glad to have found a real balloon.

Jack and Janet were silent, in an awkward sort of way. They looked at each other. Jack rarely deferred to Janet, but, in this case, he seemed to need her reassurance.

"What do you think?"

"I don't know. . . I guess it's okay." Janet pulled her coat around her. The wind lifted the hair around her face.

"It's been in the water a long time," Jack reasoned. "Salt *is* a disinfectant."

I thought Jack and Janet's reaction peculiar—odd enough to store it as a memory, a puzzle to be solved later. But at the time, I was too focused on my desire.

"Pleeeeeaase." I jumped up and down for added effect.

Jack squeezed the opening smaller and blew hard. His face turned red. Finally, the rubber yielded to his breath. He tied it. Rima and I tossed the balloon back and forth between us. It looked extra white against the dark sky. Hitting it into the air, we watched it wobble down in unexpected ways.

The problem child is the child who is pressured into cleanliness and sexual repression.

Summerhill: A Radical Approach to Child Rearing
A.S. Neill, 1960

WHAT I KNEW ABOUT LOVE

On weekend mornings, Rima and I ran to Jack and Janet's bed, and they hauled us up by our underarms. There we'd loll until late morning. Rima and I crawled over the mountains of Jack and Janet's bodies and burrowed into the dark caves between them.

One Saturday, Jack lay on his back next to the window with his hands behind his head. Janet lay on her side, facing him, and Rima rolled back and forth between them.

I was on the outside, on the other side of Janet's wall of a back. The blanket draped from Janet's shoulders and hips to the edge of the bed, so I couldn't wrap myself. Gusts of cold air circled me. My strip of bed was so narrow, I had to cling to the sheets to keep from falling off.

I cried silently, but I let my body shake—just a little—because I both wanted and didn't want Janet to notice I was on the outside. If she included me because she felt sorry for me, then her love wasn't love, but pity. If I were Rima, I'd crawl over Janet's hip and throw myself in the middle, sure I was entitled to love.

Janet turned over, the warmth of her body opening toward me.

"What's wrong, honey?"

I tried to stop crying, shocked a real voice had entered my story.

"Are you sad you're on the outside?"

I nodded.

"Here," she said, "crawl over me," and she lay flat on her back, opening the middle. Rima crawled on Jack's bare chest.

Then I was embarrassed to have imagined I wasn't welcome. But it was too late. Rima's bones were poking me and Jack and Janet had finished laughing and it was time for French toast, and Jack and Janet got up, leaving their warmth and smell in the covers, and the bed was hard on my back, and Rima stepped on my leg. I felt hollow with loneliness, with the longing for love.

Later that week, after Jack left for work, Janet made her bed, tucking the blue and red patterned Indian spread into perfect, inviting tidiness. While Janet worked in the kitchen—the house warmed by the wood stove and the smell of rising bread—Rima and I sat on her bed and spread out pads of paper and our new picture books which had been mailed to us from the library in Vancouver. Rain speckled the window, then ran in rivulets down the panes; moisture condensed on the inside and made a little puddle on the windowsill. Outside, loggers passed by in yellow coats and black rubber boots.

Then I saw Eno, leaning into the rain, his dark hair rain-slick on his forehead. Eno was a bachelor, older and smaller than the other loggers, with an odd, distant look in his dark eyes, as if he were thinking in another language. The other men found Eno aloof and strange, but Rima and I loved him.

After we'd first been introduced to Eno, Rima and I made up a chant about him: "Uh-oh, En-o, Uh-oh, En-o." We sang it and marched around the house and yard. We weren't afraid of him; we just liked the sound of his name and our clever rhyme. Janet told us not to sing it to him—it might hurt his feelings—but the next time he greeted Jack on his way to work, we ran out the front door and marched around him, "Uh-oh, En-o. Uh-oh, En-o." His stiff face cracked into a grin. At that moment, we loved him: we loved we'd made him laugh. Later, we loved him because he thought it was an honor we'd chosen him above all other loggers. We had never known such power.

That morning, Eno walked a little behind the other loggers. The rain streamed down his yellow jacket. "Uh-oh, Eno, uh-oh Eno," Rima and I bounced on the bed and chanted and waved at him through the window. He looked up and saw us, smiled, lifted his arm. In that moment, equally unbidden as my earlier loneliness, was a sudden, perfect fullness of love: the bed, covered in books and smelling of cedar and wool; the roar of the fire in the wood stove; and through the window, Eno, his wrinkled hand waving.

Eno, far right in suspenders.

WHAT I LEARNED ABOUT LYING

Rima giggled easily, but was also prone to temper tantrums. She'd writhe on her back, flail her arms and legs, and scream. Jack was uncomfortable with her trombone emotions he said she'd inherited from Janet. He believed that I, on the other hand, had inherited his own even-tempered reasonableness. (While in Washington D.C., Jack had watched Star Trek and decided he was really a Vulcan, an alien race governed almost entirely by scientific logic.)

When I asked Janet why Rima had temper tantrums, she explained Rima was born in January; she was a Capricorn, a goat, so she was stubborn and angered easily when she didn't get her way. Although part of me felt superior for being more in control of myself, I also secretly admired her. I loved the words *temper tantrum*, the sound of them, and the wild way Rima threw herself about. I was in awe of her as if she were a little storm.

When Jack had finished building our bed, both Rima and I wanted the top bunk. Jack gave it to me because I was older. Rima had a temper tantrum, which only convinced Jack he'd made the right decision. I didn't think Jack's reasoning was fair, since Rima couldn't help being younger, but I liked being seen as more mature than her. Even more, I loved being able to look at Jack right in the nose, loved the way the heavy scented cedar smoke floated toward the ceiling and settled around my blankets. So I kept quiet. After several days, Rima forgot her anger. She decided she liked having her own personal roof over her head and the way we all gathered on her mattress for bedtime stories.

Neither Rima nor I liked to wake up in the middle of the night with the darkness pressing on our eyes like water, so Jack left a kerosene lamp burning on a small table under the window. The light flickered patterns on the walls, long skinny animals, dancing. They chased the shadows out of the corners. I was a little afraid of the lantern, the heat and flame, but Rima liked to twist the knob on the side to make the flame bigger. Jack told her she had to stop because she was blackening the chimney and burning too much kerosene.

Every morning, Rima and I crawled out of bed and huddled over the lantern. In the gray light, the flame looked pale, exhausted. Since my hands were bigger, I pulled the chimney from the metal clips and set it on the table. Because I was afraid of the flame, Rima blew it out. Sometimes she had to try twice. I turned my head and closed my eyes so as not to see the fire near her face. As unsettling as this ritual was, I was addicted to it, addicted to the way the glass felt in my hands, full and fragile as an egg, addicted to the risk of danger and the relief when it was over.

Usually Jack read us stories while Janet cleaned the kitchen, but one night they cornered us in the bedroom next to the lantern.

"Girls," Jack said. He sounded as if he were apologetic. He didn't like to give us any rules. "We've talked . . . and we don't think you should blow out the lantern in the morning anymore." The hair in his face was growing in fuzzy patches.

I thought that was odd, as Jack rarely forbade us to do anything.

He lifted up the chimney and held it in his hand. "These are fragile."

"And expensive," Janet added.

"They break easily."

"You could cut yourself."

"How come *you* can hold it then?"

"I'm a grown-up."

That was an unfair answer. I crossed my arms over my chest.

"But more importantly, if you knock the lantern over, the house could start on fire."

"We're careful."

Janet added softly, "I know you're careful, Tarn, but we have to be extra safe because the house is made of wood. The whole house could burn down."

"Tarn, do you understand?" Jack asked.

I nodded. I didn't want to give them the satisfaction of a verbal answer.

"Rima, do you understand?" She giggled and tried to escape between Jack and Janet's legs. Janet repeatedly caught her. "Rima, do you understand?" Jack asked. She barreled into Janet and swung on her arms. Jack looked at me and I knew I was responsible for both of us.

Then Jack read us our story on Rima's bed. Afterward, he turned down the flame on the lantern, tucked our covers tight around us, kissed us, and whispered goodnight as he left the room.

Then we started to giggle, the same giggling that started every night in the same way, over nothing, over the memory of the giggling from the night before. Rima stood up on her bed and pressed up on my mattress, bouncing me. I hung down by my waist from the top bunk to look at her. As usual, her fine, white hair matted on the back of her head in a fuzzy tangle. I loved her ski-jump nose, which looked even more pronounced upside down in the yellow light. She laughed and pointed at my face, which was getting hard and red.

"Girrrls," Jack warned from the other room, making his voice deep and gruff.

We tried to stop, but the giggles were like the bubbles of the ruby red soda pop in the glass bottles at Mary's Cafe in town.

"Girls, no more talking."

We were still. We held our mouths closed, but the bubbles filled up our stomachs, filled up behind our mouths. We held our breath. We held our bodies rigid. The bubbles pushed our mouths open and squeaked out.

"Girls, do I have to come in there?"

The floor creaked outside our room. Jack was heavy. He could make the floor bend underneath him.

We were silent and he stepped back. We would have giggled again, but we were worn out from the way our stomach muscles had seized up. Finally we were still, then sleeping.

The next morning—moved by habit—I crawled down the ladder and stood next to the lantern. Rima still slept, small and dense under her covers. Cool air pressed my skin.

Inside the glass base, the kerosene looked like melted diamonds, flashing all colors. I held my hand over the opening until my palm burned. Then I tugged the chimney from the base and set it on the table. The naked flame rose and then sank into itself. I had to act quickly before the memory of what Jack and Janet had said crawled into the front of my mind.

I blew. The flame bent away from me. The heat burned the underside of my nose. I closed my eyes and blew harder. When I opened them, all that was left was a crunchy wick.

Then I heard Rima's even breathing and the memory of Jack and Janet's words.

All four of us stood around the lantern. Rima held onto Janet's little finger. The warmth of sleep still radiated from her body.

"Who blew out the lantern?" Jack didn't sound apologetic this time. He was holding back an animal who lived in his chest.

Then a new thought came to me, fully formed: my words didn't have to tell the truth. How did I know, as if I'd been doing it all my life, that I must be careful with my body and my voice? I kept my back straight, looked Jack in the eyes, and spoke clearly.

"Rima did."

I was only thinking of saving myself for the moment; I didn't believe I could fool Jack, who knew everything.

"I didn't do it." Rima began to cry,

Jack put Rima back on her bunk and told her not to get out. She had to stay there for her punishment. Suddenly, my mind doubled in size: I contained the truth of everything I knew plus the lie I could tell about it.

Rima sobbed and beat her arms and legs against the bed. "I didn't do it." Then she let out a piercing, angry scream.

Rima seemed frantic enough Jack asked me again, the one to whom he had given the top bunk, "Are you sure?"

He'd never questioned me before. I wanted to undo the doubling, but I had already slipped away into a place numb and gray and far away. I didn't know how to pull myself back.

I nodded my head and left Rima sealed in the prison I had created for her with my story.

Tarn, Pocahontas Bay

Rima, Pocahontas Bay

STILL LIFE: CHRISTMAS

"I bought these for our first Christmas tree—the one we had on Sugarloaf Mountain before you were born." Janet hung tin solders with tall red hats and purple and gold coats on our little tree. "We cut it ourselves. It was skinny and almost bald, but it had a bird's nest in it. I loved it."

I was jealous of the time Jack and Janet lived without me; I didn't want us ever to have been apart.

"Your Granny and Granddaddy don't put up their Christmas tree until Christmas Eve." She handed me some tinsel. "Then they pretend Santa Claus decorates it Christmas night." I knew this was a criticism of Jack's parents: the holidays made her feel irritable about Jack's family and her own. "I like to enjoy my tree longer than that." She was teaching me the traditions she was inventing.

Granny hadn't wanted her son to marry Janet—she thought she was too young—and she'd corrected Janet's word usage. "Not *purse*, dear, *pocketbook*. Not *silverware*, dear, we reserve that for the silver; this is *cutlery*." Janet couldn't forget how small Granny had made her feel.

Janet draped cedar boughs over shelves and doorframes. She nestled three red candles into the cuttings on the table. She made us stockings out of red, fake fur and sewed ribbon around the top—white with red ladybugs for Rima, red with black ladybugs for me—and hung them on nails behind the stove.

Most nights, Jack disappeared into the logging shed at the top of the hill by Janet's garden. Janet wouldn't tell us what he was doing and wouldn't let us follow him.

Jack and his mother, January 24, 1943

I drew pictures of well-dressed, upright rabbits in Christmas scenes. Jack asked me to reproduce a sketch on the front of a shelf fungus he had plucked off of a fallen log. He carved around my drawing until it stood out in relief and set it on the table for decoration.

Granny mailed us a box of presents and home-made treats: candied orange and lemon rinds, cookies cut into stars and folded over a date, snowflake-shaped cookies that smelled like licorice. Tucked in the box was also an envelope for Jack, the same kind she sent him throughout the year, newspaper clippings on the garden show, local high school sports, and the recent successes of former neighborhood children. Jack and Janet laughed at her dull suburban-ness.

She also sent an advent calendar with numbered windows to open each day of the month with pictures inside from a story we didn't know: mules and camels and men in dresses and crowns, and a baby sleeping in a bed of straw. Rima and I agreed to alternate opening the windows, but sometimes one of us couldn't resist temptation and opened a window out of turn and then tried to close it again so the other wouldn't notice, but the other always did, and then we'd fight and cry.

Granny's presents were wrapped in silver paper with swirly patterns and tied with stretchy gold cords. The wrapping paper was perfectly folded with no extra creases or stray pieces of tape.

"Granny didn't wrap those presents," Janet said "a department store did. I wish she'd just sent us money so we can get what we need rather than expensive gifts we don't want."

I touched the packages over and over, tracing the letters of my name on the tag, written in my grandmother's own delicate, light blue hand. Although I didn't remember Granny well, it seemed to me everything about her was light blue: the tint of her hair, her seersucker blazer, the sketches of birds in her books with the smooth pages, the flowers in front of her brick house. Jack and Janet said, out of all the grandchildren, with my thin bones and thick hair, I looked the most like Granny.

The night before Christmas, Rima and I asked questions about Santa Claus.

"How does Santa get around the world in just one night? How will Santa fit down the stove pipe?"

As Jack invented answers, Janet's face turned more and more into itself. When Janet's older sister Patty was twelve years old, Wuh-Wa finally had to tell her there was no Santa Claus. She was devastated.

Finally Janet blurted, "You know there isn't any Santa, right?"

"Yes," we blew out our breath. She'd interrupted our pretending.

On Rima's bunk, just before we went to sleep, Jack read us *The Night Before Christmas*. I imagined Santa's stomach jiggling like a bowl full of jelly and, although I had no idea what sugarplums were, I looked forward to visions of them dancing in my head. In the picture, the man looking out the window for Santa wore a long pointed hat. When I asked Jack about it, he said before central heating, people wore night-caps to bed to keep their heads warm. Because we lived the old-fashioned way, I thought I should have a nightcap too, a striped one.

Christmas morning, Rima and I carried our stockings to Jack and Janet's bed and sat between their feet. Our stockings were lumpy and stuffed. Jack and Janet moved slowly, pushing themselves to sitting position. Their hair stuck up as if they had been wrestling in their sleep. Janet watched as we pulled out each item she had carefully packed: a candy cane; a net sack of gold-foil-covered chocolate coins; lilac flavored candies in a tin from England. A thin metal egg on the end of a stick. When I pushed a long button in and out, the way Jack started the fuel on the Coleman stove, the end spun faster and faster and blue and red sparks flew from the bottom and the egg opened to a spinning, plastic Santa Claus.

"I never had anything good in my stocking," Janet said, drawing on her cigarette she'd just rolled. "Just some cheap candy and an old orange stuck in the toe."

Rima pulled out two naked plastic trolls, about an inch and a half high, one with glowing green hair, the other with red.

"Indian Go Go!" she exclaimed with both surprise and love, as if she recognized them. We all laughed. Rima looked a bit like a troll with her fuzzy hair, turned up nose, and the way she planted her feet wide apart when she was feeling stubborn.

Jack's sister, Gay, sent us floor length, deep red velvet dresses with gold trim, queen dresses.

When we unwrapped Granny's silver packages and saw the dolls through the plastic windows of their boxes, for a moment Janet didn't speak.

"Oh. Dolls. What do you think, girls? Do you like them?" Her face was tight. I didn't know if she was disappointed, or if she didn't want us to be disappointed.

Janet and Rima and I had previously agreed we didn't like dolls. We liked stuffed animals. (Earlier I asked if we liked Raggedy Ann; we all agreed we did because she was soft and had mismatched clothes.) But plastic dolls were hard and cold, their arms too stiff for hugging, and they had sharp fingers and toes. Their faces, frozen in stiff half-smiles, were like the women from Jack and Janet's childhoods. Stuffed animals, on the other hand, were soft and warm, like Janet, and we could nuzzle our faces in their stomachs. The expression on their faces changed: the corners of their mouths tugged upward a little when they were amused.

We'd asked Janet once if she'd ever owned a doll. She had, several, and had pushed them around in a baby carriage. She seemed embarrassed by this.

"Wuh-Wa loved dolls." And then her voice changed, mocking her mother's Southern accent, " Baby-dolls. I just *love* baby-dolls."

Rima and I pulled our Christmas dolls from their boxes. They wore pleated plaid skirts, white tights pulled over realistic knees, buckle shoes, white shirts with Peter Pan collars, and velvet jackets with gold buttons. Rima's had bouncy-shiny brown hair; mine had bouncy-shiny blonde hair. They were pretty. If they were real girls, they might not play with me because I was dirty and looked like a boy. If my Granny saw me, she'd be embarrassed because, with my stretched, ripped clothes and my messy hair, I didn't look like a Christmas doll.

After all the other presents had been opened, Jack carried in the gifts he'd been building for us every night in the shed. Mine was an almost exact replica of Janet's stove—with an oval plate which opened to a wood compartment, a shelf above the stove top, and a black oven with white speckles. Rima got a plywood steam shovel, like Mike Mulligan's in

Mike Mulligan and the Steam Shovel with working levers, a bucket, and a twisting seat. It was yellow, just like the logging equipment in Pocahontas Bay. We took it outside and Rima scooped the white powder from the oyster shell pile.

By Christmas afternoon, we had taken our queen dresses on and off several times. I loaded my new stove with kindling and decorated my shelf with Texada rocks, wood chips, drift wood, polished glass pieces, ceramic animals which came as prizes in the Wade Red Rose Tea box, and Christmas candy I knew Janet would eat when I wasn't looking. Rima and I stripped the Christmas dolls' clothes and tested them on various stuffed animals. The clothes looked especially nice on Beary, Rima's bear with the jointed arms and legs, who could even wear the shoes.

Not long after Christmas, the naked dolls sank to the bottom of the purple toy box. Rummaging for a missing toy, I'd see them there, scuffed, upside down, a leg turned backward. They'd been hopeful dolls, hopeful of being loved and attended to, set on a shelf in a neat girl's room; I'd betrayed them by taking their clothes and by not loving them. I closed the toy box lid and tried not to think of their loneliness.

During the "Christmas Bombings," from December 18–30, 1972, the U.S. dropped 20,000 tons of explosives on cities across Northern Vietnam. 1,318 died in Hanoi.

On Christmas Eve, after Rima and I had fallen asleep, Janet listened to the CBC radio reports of the blitz and cried.

WHAT I KNEW
ABOUT DESIRE

Jack and Janet's kisses were different. Janet's kisses were soft and frequent and flowed into me and through me, a part of my own body. She lifted our T-shirts and blew on our stomachs; we rolled on our backs on the big bed under the window and laughed. She nuzzled the soft spot on our neck just below our ears. Her kisses could come at any time during the day. They were skin and movement and warm smells.

Jack's kisses, on the other hand, came only at bedtime after he had told me to go to sleep and not ask any more questions. He leaned over me. His eyebrows made a little shelf over his eyes. I scrunched my eyebrows and tried to look like him. The air around his face was tingly. His scratchy kiss felt awkward and important.

The first time Jack kissed Janet, they hadn't even had a date: she was eighteen and a waitress at the Bennett's pizza parlor on the Hill across from CU Boulder. It was a funky place, with purple and green murals on the walls. Janet's sister Travis, with her voluptuous curves and cat-shaped eyes, was so admired on campus she was painted on one of the panels.

Jack and his friends—who should have already graduated, but were extending their stays because they refused to jump through graduation requirement hoops—ate pizza, drank beer, debated the virtues of socialism, and predicted computers would revolutionize the world, reducing the work week and creating more time for art and gardening and making music together.

Janet poured their beer behind the counter, a black line drawn across the top of her eyelids, her blonde hair teased on top of her head in a soft poof. Jack jumped over the counter and kissed her right on the mouth.

The first man, besides Jack, I hoped would kiss me was David, a fifteen-year-old boy—our first and only babysitter in Pocahontas Bay.

Janet was happy that night, as she and Jack got ready to see a band at the pub in Vananda. She wore a white gauzy shirt with an open neck. Her skin, freckled from Colorado tanning, stretched tight across the top of her chest, over her ripples of bone. She didn't wear any make up—Jack didn't like it—or any perfume because, she said, it reacted with her skin and turned to "bug spray." But she seemed scrubbed clean and held herself differently—taller, fuller, more gracefully. She wore a necklace of intricately connected wire circles, like delicate chain mail, with bright beads. She talked to us, but there was warmth in her eyes not directed at us.

David, the babysitter, was quiet and thin with black hair curled behind his ears. He'd never been a babysitter, and we'd never met a teenage boy. He didn't know how to play with little girls, so as soon as Janet and Jack left, Rima and I took charge. We told David what to do and he did it. Rima and I would begin a game, but unused to such undivided and tentative attention, we'd quit and make up a new one. We were too loud and quick and self-conscious.

When darkness seeped under doors and through windowpanes and into the corners of the house, David told us to go to bed. Rima and I felt frayed from being too "wound up," as Janet would say. We crawled under our covers. My bed was cold. I felt Rima's anxiety in the bunk below me.

Jack and Janet, before we went to sleep, always read us a story and gave us a kiss, and Rima needed routine and ritual. If I touched her on one shoulder blade, she asked me to touch her on the other. If she ran her hand over the back of one kitchen chair, she had to run her hand in just the same way over the backs of all the chairs.

"Jack and Janet always read us a story before bed," I yelled to David in the other room. We all sat on Rima's bunk and he read us the big picture book version of *Three Little Pigs*. The familiar rhythms soothed Rima. She breathed evenly.

When David returned to the main room, I yelled, "Janet and Jack always give us a goodnight kiss."

He stood in the doorway. Jeans. Flannel shirt. He smelled like the promise of something, like the air vibrating, like wind and trees.

"Jack and Janet always give us a kiss goodnight."

He didn't move.

I wanted him to kiss me. I thought his kiss would be different than Jack or Janet's kisses, a little exciting and dangerous.

He didn't come any closer, and I thought Rima would cry.

"Rima can't go to sleep without a kiss," I said.

"Not just me," Rima said.

I thought we could make him do what we wanted. He moved towards us, but then suddenly I knew he was moving against his will.

Then I was ashamed I asked David for what he didn't want to give. I didn't want a kiss anymore, but it was too late. He gave us each a dry peck.

The next morning, David had evaporated. Jack was already out. Janet stirred condensed milk into her coffee and told us about her evening at the pub. The band was so-so. Young Mr. Hagman and his wife Roxy had been there. Roxy was outrageously sexy, as usual: tight dress, make up, a perfume that smelled like tropical flowers. Men flocked around her.

"Roxy," Janet said, speaking in a tone part gossip, part condemnation, "wore red high heels." I imagined them: bright pumps with curvy lines, three-inch heels, and a slight sheen. Janet wore only flat sandals, hiking boots, or the gumboots Jack had found for her at the dump. She didn't approve of high heels in a place with so much mud and work to be done. But I heard something else in her voice too, a tinge of admiration, maybe even envy.

Years later, I can still recall in perfect detail those red high-heeled shoes I never saw.

T.V. shows Janet had watched
All in the Family
Laugh In
Mod Squad
Star Trek

T.V. shows Jack had watched
Star Trek
Reruns of *The Twilight Zone*

Movies Janet liked
The Graduate
The Pink Panther

Movies Jack liked
2001: A Space Odyssey
Cat Ballou
Easy Rider

Books Janet read for fun
Agatha Christie mysteries
Nero Woolf mysteries

Books Jack read for fun:
Cowboy books by Louis
    L'Amour

Janet's favorite musician
Etta James

Books Jack loved
Alice in Wonderland
The Lord of the Rings

**Musicians Janet loved
but couldn't listen to in
Canada because we had no
electricity or record player**
Aretha Franklin
Tina Turner
Otis Redding
Marvin Gaye
James Brown
Stevie Wonder

Other books on Jack's shelf
Catch 22
*Bury My Heart at Wounded
    Knee*
How to Survive in the Woods
*Operating Manual for
    Spaceship Earth*

Musicians Janet liked

Beatles (mid career)
Joe Cocker
Creedance Clearwater Revival
The Doors

Musicians Janet didn't like

Joan Baez
Janis Joplin
Joni Mitchell
Carly Simon
James Taylor

New writers who influenced Jack

Carlos Castaneda
Buckminster Fuller
Allen Ginsberg
Jack Kerouac
Ken Kesey
Timothy Leary

Jack's favorite comics

Asterix
Pogo
Tintin

Jack's favorite musician

Bob Dylan

Musicians Jack liked

Arlo Guthrie
Woodie Guthrie
Pete Seeger

WHAT I KNEW ABOUT JANET: LONELINESS

Jack carried a harmonica in the front pocket of his shirt or jeans. When he played, he covered it with his hands and flapped his fingers like bird wings. Janet told him he sounded as good as Bob Dylan. Rima and I grabbed it from him and ran naked around the house, sucking in and out of the holes and making noises like a horror movie organ. When we handed it back, Jack knocked out our spit onto his hand.

Jack also played a recorder made of red wood. He could hum a song, experiment for a few minutes, and then make those same notes come out the bottom. He let me try. I couldn't stretch my fingers wide enough to plug all the holes and made a goose sound.

Janet didn't play an instrument, but she wanted to make music. She knew she had a sense of rhythm—she was a good dancer and could shake the tambourine—so she thought she'd try the washboard. She and Jack could play music together— or with their new friends who played banjos and guitars and handmade drums. They could even be in a band.

She took the ferry to Powell River where she purchased, in the hardware store, a wood-framed washboard with ripply glass. At the sewing store she bought silver thimbles of all different sizes, one for each finger. I turned the pinky thimble upside down and pretended it was a drinking cup for a glass animal. Janet practiced running her thimble-covered fingers up and down the glass ridges, louder, softer, faster, slapping the edge. Rima and I jumped up and down and danced along. But Jack and Janet never played together, never played with friends. "I never finish anything," Janet said and kept the thimbles in her sewing box.

Janet sang to me as she rocked me on her lap:

Hush little baby, don't say a word,
Mama's going to buy you a mockingbird.
And if that mockingbird don't sing,
Mama's going to buy you a diamond ring.

I loved the warmth of the word Mama, the promises in the song, and the string of odd things to buy children: a bottle of wine, a horse and cart.

To Rima, Janet sang, "Pickin' up paw paws, put 'em in your pocket . . . way down yonder in the paw paw patch." I'd never seen a paw paw and didn't think to ask what one was—although I knew they came from the South, the storybook place of Janet's childhood, where Brer Rabbit lived and people stretched their words. I imagined Rima underneath a tree picking up spiked green balls and filling the pockets of her dress.

To both of us, Janet sang, "Two little babies lyin' in bed, one of them's sick and the other's half dead, Mama's little baby loves shortnin', shortnin', mama's little baby loves shortnin' bread." Since I was older, I thought I was the first, sick child and Rima was half-dead. But Janet saved us with shortnin' bread, which I assumed must be like those Scottish shortbread cookies sold in plaid packages in Vananda.

As Janet worked in the kitchen, she sang a song from the radio that wasn't for us, but for herself, "Country roads take me home to the place I belong." I knew a man named John Denver wrote the song, and Denver was a city in Colorado, so I thought Janet was singing about her Colorado mountains. She sang the song over and over, adding her own interpretation—lengthening or adding notes. She thought all music should have "soul."

Rima and I thought Janet sang well enough to be on the radio.

"No" she said, "I used to be able to sing . . . but smoking ruined my voice."

She wouldn't sing in the pub, for friends—for anyone but us. I loved her song, but it also made me sad. She sang as if she missed the mountains, a mama. All her songs sounded lonely.

We announce the birth of a conceptual country, NUTOPIA. Citizenship of the country can be obtained by declaration of your awareness of NUTOPIA. NUTOPIA has no land, no boundaries, no passports, only people. NUTOPIA has no laws other than cosmic. All people of NUTOPIA are ambassadors of the country. As two ambassadors of NUTOPIA, we ask for diplomatic immunity and recognition in the United Nations of our country and our people.

YOKO ONO LENNON (with signature)
JOHN ONO LENNON (with signature)

Nutopian Embassy
One White Street
New York, New York 10012
April 1, 1973

WHAT I LEARNED ABOUT INSTINCT AND GRIEF: BLUE

"Why'd you name him Blue?" I asked Jack. I was confused because our dog wasn't blue. He was white—not the kind of white so pure it's almost blue, like footprints in the snow—but a ragged white, with gray tips. Blue was fond of rolling in dead fish, after which Jack would say dead fish is dog perfume and he should bottle it.

Jack explained he'd named Blue after a cowboy in a movie. But I'd never seen a movie, and a human named Blue seemed almost as odd. We had a cat named Rabbit, but that made some sense because she was fat and lost her tail.

"It's time the girls had a dog again," Jack explained to Janet when he brought Blue home, but really, I believe he missed our old dog Gandalf and wanted another male to keep him company, one who would love him without complication. But Blue wasn't like Gandalf, a white German Shepherd, who, without any training on Jack's part, grew from a puppy into gentle, self-contained maturity. Jack believed dogs, like children, should be raised without restrictions.

"Samoyeds never grow up," people told us too late. Blue frightened Rima and me a little: he was tall as our chests and leapt on us with sharp toenails. His favorite game, which he invented, was "bite-the-back-of-people's-ankles-and-make-them-jump." When we screamed and ran away, he chased us—a large, inescapable, smelly ball of fur with needle-like teeth.

Janet scooped Rima into her arms, "No, Blue. No."

He smiled. No rebuke, no matter how harsh, could ever wipe the grin off his face.

But I did love his wide, rough pink tongue, and the way his tail curled into a circle. When I pulled his tail straight, it bounced back like a rubber band. I'd memorized the difficult name of his breed and could repeat it to people I met, "Blue is a Samoyed." Jack said Samoyeds came from the snow and that's why Blue had so much fur. "Do you think he's too hot?" I asked Jack.

"Probably," he said, so I worried about his temperature, but Jack said Blue was tough.

I knew Blue was tender, too. When Rima or I cried, Blue dropped presents at our feet—a rock, a balled sock, one of our favorite toys he had stolen and chewed. Then Rima and I would laugh and wrap our arms around his smelly neck. He smiled and swung his pink tongue.

Blue was often the main character in funny stories Jack collected to tell friends: one day Jack took Blue to town in the back of a truck, and as they drove, Blue snapped at the cedar branches which dangled over the truck bed. Once he caught a large branch in his mouth and forgot to let go. Jack looked over his shoulder just in time to see Blue pulled from the truck and swinging by his mouth from the tree. Afterward, Blue was so embarrassed, he slunk along the ground and wouldn't look Jack in the eyes.

One morning Janet made French toast and Jack tossed a piece in Blue's bowl, just outside the front door. Just as Blue was about to bite, a raven swooped down and stole his slice. He flew above Blue's head, dangling the French toast just out of his grasp. Blue barked and leaped. The raven led Blue toward the water—and then along the old logging road that ran the length of the bay. When we could no longer see them, but could only hear barks echoing off the wall of trees, the raven turned back. Blue followed, hoarse, panting, and leaping only half-heartedly. Finally, having experienced for the first time hopelessness, Blue sank to the ground in front of the house. The raven dropped the French toast between Blue's front paws and flew away.

Jack explained that the raven, clever and playful, was a sacred bird to the Northwest Indians and Jack's own totem animal.

One day a man visited us who had three lean dogs, slick brown dogs, who didn't stick around to socialize, but took off into the bush, with Blue bounding behind them. All four returned late in the day, muzzles wet with blood.

After that, Blue would disappear for an afternoon, an evening, several days. Janet, Rima, and I would worry. Jack never worried. "That's what male dogs do," he said in a knowing way, as if he understood something we couldn't.

One day a ranger pulled up in front of our house; Blue rode in his truck bed, smiling. Blue hopped out as the ranger stepped from his cab. Younger than Jack, the man wore a brown suit with no wrinkles and a thin brown belt. He told Jack, as we stood behind him, if he ever found Blue chasing deer again, he'd have to shoot him. He couldn't allow dogs to kill the deer on the island, especially out of season.

"Certainly. Sure, I understand completely," Jack soothed him.

After the ranger drove away, I was confused. Why didn't Jack talk back to the lies? How could Blue, who was smaller than a deer, kill one?

Jack explained a dog can leap on the neck of a large mammal, severing an artery. But I couldn't, in my mind, connect the Blue who brought us toys when we cried with one who tore into the necks of deer.

"We should feed him more food," I said.

"It's not about food, honey," Janet said. "Those other dogs taught him to hunt for fun. He thinks it's a game. He doesn't know he's doing anything wrong."

"He's not actually doing anything wrong," Jack explained, "Carnivores have a natural hunting instinct."

"If we got Blue neutered . . ." Janet introduced cautiously, knowing Jack's feelings on the subject.

"Neutering is unnatural. It changes a dog's personality not to be able to fulfill his biological purpose. Besides, now that Blue has tasted blood, nothing will stop him."

"Then we'll just have to tie him up," Janet said.

The next day, Jack tied Blue to the chopping block with a long rope. First, Blue wiggled his head out of his rope collar. Jack tied the rope tighter. Blue chased Jack, who was leaving to work with the loggers, and yanked his neck so hard he wheezed. Then he wailed. He ran zigzag through the objects in the yard, shortening his rope. By the end of the day, he had wrapped his own legs and tripped himself.

"I can't stand this," Jack said that evening and let him go. Blue took off into the bush without looking back.

Several weeks later, early evening, we heard a knock at the door. Jack stepped outside to talk to the ranger and closed the door behind him.

Inside the house, I didn't move, but sat poised, tense and listening: the ranger's truck humming, the ranger's voice low "another deer . . . pregnant," Jack's voice rising louder and higher. Fragments from Jack, "the f—king establishment . . . out to get us . . . No, you didn't *have* to shoot him."

Janet was frozen also. It frightened us all to hear Jack angry, the Jack who prided himself on reasonableness, and to feel his raw loss.

Tarn and Blue

WHAT I LEARNED ABOUT TIMING: THE OCTOPUS

Rima and I waited on the shore for Jack to return with his prawn trap. I felt the same excitement I did at Texada Days, the celebration on Shelter Point, when Janet paid a quarter so I could go fishing: I hung a fishing pole—a yellow trowel with a string and bent wire hook—behind a booth. When I felt my pole tug, I pulled up my prize, a little green plastic man with a parachute. Rationally, I knew every child who paid money caught a prize and a grown-up hid behind the booth to hook them, but I couldn't help being surprised anyway. I didn't even mind when my green man's parachute failed to open and he careened to the ground; it wasn't the prize that mattered, but the tug on the end of my string, a secret swinging on the end of my pole.

Jack's trap, which he dropped from his rowboat into the middle of the bay, was a wire mesh box with a funnel entrance on one side. The prawns, Jack explained, crawled through the funnel to eat the bait, but couldn't crawl back out. I couldn't visualize the prawns, pink and orange with feathery legs, climbing up the side of the cage, but they must have, because the trap, which descended empty, always came up full.

Jack hauled his rowboat, the Raven, onto shore. We ran toward him. "Go get Janet," he called to us. "I want to show you something. When we returned, his trap was on the ground and stuffed with curling legs—wet-black and bruise-blue with white edged suction cups. I wanted to look, and I didn't want to look.

I imagined the octopus pulsing in the water just under Jack's boat—in sight of my own house. How had a creature so close, so large, so strangely shaped, been invisible to me and me to it? How had it snuck through that small funnel into my world? Jack explained octopus love prawns and have no bones—they can squeeze through a hole as easily as silly putty. I worried about those wires pressing into the octopus' flesh and didn't like that it couldn't stretch its legs.

"Spread out, I'll bet it's ten feet long!" Jack said. I felt embarrassed for it—for its size and nakedness.

I was comfortable only with sea creatures who seemed defended: purple crabs who backed into crevasses, waving their pinchers in front of them; barnacles, like the heads on suits of armor who opened their crusty mouths to brush out feather-plume tongues. I liked oysters, clams, and mussels—but only when they were closed. I didn't like shells even partially opened to wet bodies, skin-colored and smooth as internal organs. Rima loved to touch sea anemones and make them curl into themselves; I liked how they waved their protrusions like princesses with handkerchiefs, but their softness made me want to cry.

Janet averted her eyes from all that purple in a trap, purple just a little deeper than our house trim. "Can we take her back? Is it too late?"

"She's probably been dead for hours."

I was surprised Jack didn't know how to bring her back to life.

Jack seemed disappointed we weren't acting more excited.

"Can I touch it?" Rima asked.

"Sure," Jack said, glad for some enthusiasm. I hoped he didn't notice I wasn't brave enough.

"Oooooh," she said, a word that combined disgust and delight.

"What does it feel like?" I asked.

"Soft, but the circle part is hard."

Jack decided we should eat the octopus. He believed we should use what we kill; death can be redeemed if we "keep energy moving through the system." Janet was reluctant, but agreed eating the octopus was better than its life going to waste. She looked through her copy of the *Joy of Cooking* and told us she'd found recipes for rolling homemade candy on a chilled marble slab, but no directions for preparing an octopus.

On his next trip to town, Jack asked everyone he could find for cooking instructions. "I hear octopus is great," each person said, but no one could tell him how to prepare one. Janet wouldn't experiment, saying an improperly cooked octopus could make us all sick, but I think she didn't want to see all those legs sticking out of a pot of boiling water. Secretly, I was relieved. I didn't want a suction cup sticking to my tongue.

Jack decided, then, we should feed the octopus to Rabbit-the-Cat. Janet worried octopus would make her ill, but Jack sawed up the legs anyway. He put some chunks in a bowl and set them on the dirt next to the front door. As squirmy as the octopus had made me feel, I was sad to see her in pieces.

"What's that black juice?"

"I broke the ink sac by accident. Octopuses are shy. When they're afraid, they release a cloud of black ink to hide themselves."

I felt a sudden warmth of understanding, a feeling almost like friendship. The octopus understood something about me and me about it: I, too, was shy and soft and wanted to hide from what made me afraid.

Rabbit touched her nose to the bowl and then waddled away.

Afterward, Jack told the story to people on the island. It was a funny story, well-paced, but Janet never laughed. When Jack finished, someone always added, "I love octopus. You should've asked me. I know how to cook one."

This seemed to me the worst possible ending. Before this, I had thought the world moved in harmonious and meaningful rhythm. I didn't know plots could turn on accidents: misplaced and mistimed messages.

On page 412 of Janet's edition of *Joy of Cooking* is a recipe for preparing and cooking octopus.

WHAT I LEARNED ABOUT SHAME: MY THUMB

When we walked through Vananda, the town people gave unsolicited advice to Janet and Jack about how to make me stop sucking my thumb. One woman suggested painting my thumb with Tabasco sauce. A man at the counter in M and M's Variety Store swore by iodine and held up a small bottle. It had worked on his daughter. "But put it on both her thumbs," he said, "or she'll switch on you."

I tried sucking my left thumb, but it seemed dry and obtrusive, like someone else's finger. My fingernail jabbed the roof of my mouth. My right thumb, however, fit as perfectly as a snap.

I couldn't sleep without sucking my thumb and nuzzling Soft Blanket. Soft Blanket wasn't a baby blanket like other children's, but queen-sized, white with blue flowers, edged in light blue satin, and grayed from being dragged on the ground behind me. Janet cut off one edge of satin when it unraveled and the other side when she'd accidentally burnt a hole in it with her cigarette. Sucking my thumb with Soft Blanket was as relaxing as gentle kisses on my eyelids and either side of my nose. My breathing slowed and my thoughts curled into a warm, light-blue place.

"Her teeth will grow in crooked," a woman warned.

I listened absently, as if the town people were talking about someone else. I felt pleasantly invisible and shielded. Jack and Janet were raising us differently than other children: we called Jack and Janet by their first names, as if we were equals; Jack would answer any question, and with grown-up words; he expected us to pick ourselves up after we'd fallen, without tears or complaint; Janet didn't believe cold or wet weather made us sick and didn't run after us with warm sweaters. We wandered where we wanted, ate when we were hungry, took naps when we were tired. Jack and Janet didn't take the parenting advice of town people, their own parents, or anyone who owned a TV or ate white bread. I was proud of their philosophies. I believed they had made Rima and me brighter and braver than the average child.

One Saturday morning, before driving to town, I sat alone on Jack and Janet's bed, not thinking or doing anything in particular, just noticing the bumpy paint on the windowsill, the mildew in the cracks and dents.

"Tarn," Janet said. She sat down on the edge of the bed and Jack stood behind her. "We need to talk to you about something."

Jack or Janet had never prefaced a conversation before. Janet's lips were gray; Jack shifted his weight and looked above my head.

"We were talking . . . " Janet looked at Jack and then back at me.

I was suddenly aware they'd had a conversation about me the night before and had planned their strategy. Heat rushed to my head and pulsed in my face. It had never occurred to me Jack and Janet might discuss me when I wasn't there. That seemed to break some understanding of equality and openness in our family.

" . . . that it's probably best you stop sucking your thumb."

Janet tried to explain herself in fragments of "Don't want them to think you're a baby. Not what we think, of course. When you go to school . . . "

But I was made deaf by shame. I wanted Jack and Janet to think of me as bright and advanced for my age. I wanted to please and impress them, but instead I'd embarrassed them. I wanted to be so good I was never in need of correction. I was confused they were suddenly concerned with the opinions of other people, even for my own sake. They'd changed the rules.

I must have looked stricken, because I could hear through my deafness Janet stumbling for words.

"Well, just in town. You can still suck your thumb at home." Janet looked for support at Jack, who looked back at her, uncertain.

Rima crawled onto the bed. "I don't suck *my* thumb." She started a somersault and then rolled over onto her side.

I pulled the Indian spread over my head. Pinpricks of light pierced the dark patterns. It smelled warm and salty, like Jack and Janet's sleep. I wanted to be invisible again, with neither the town people nor Jack and Janet's attention on me. I wanted to be in the dark-blue quiet until the rushing stilled. Tears itched my eyes. I sucked my thumb until I felt quiet and empty.

"Tarn?'

Janet took the spread off of my head. "You okay?"

I nodded.

"Were you sucking your thumb?"

I nodded.

She pulled me into her lap. "Oh honey, you can suck your thumb at home. I didn't mean to upset you. I just thought . . . "

I put my head against her chest but couldn't melt into her.

I didn't suck my thumb in Vananda that day, but on the way home, in the dark of the back seat, I put my thumb, unwashed, in my mouth, in a sour tasting mix of rebellion and need. Afterward, I couldn't stop sucking my thumb, but neither could I shake the shame, so I turned my head away from Jack and Janet so they couldn't see me, and they never spoke of it again.

I believe that to impose anything by authority is wrong. The child should not do anything until he comes to the opinion—his own opinion—that it should be done.

Summerhill: A Radical Approach to Child Rearing
A.S. Neill, 1960

STILL LIFE: MARY'S CAFE

Either Rima had entered a more severe stage of imitation, or I felt a sudden, fiercer need for independence. She followed me everywhere: to the edge of the water, to our marsh grass house, to the log stack, to the outhouse. When I wanted to draw, she drew too. If I drew a rabbit wearing clothes, she drew a rabbit wearing clothes. If I drew a tugboat, she drew a tugboat. If I looked at a book, she wanted the same book. When I yelled, "Stop copying me," she yelled back, "Stop copying me." If I told her I didn't want her to come with me, then she cried, and Janet told me I had to let her. Janet had work to do, and she didn't want Rima to feel that same, left-out way she had as a child, rejected by her older sisters. This copying made me feel as if I were covered in cobwebs I couldn't wipe off.

During this period, we took a trip to Vananda to restock supplies. As usual, we ended our day at Mary's Cafe, where we sat in the red vinyl booths. Rima and I sat across from each other, next to the window, overlooking a paved road lined by blackberry bushes. Down the hill were small wooden houses with overgrown gardens and behind them tall, dark trees and the thin line of gray ocean. The sky hung down, wet and heavy. When a few miners and loggers opened the door, cool air puffed in. The loggers seemed to carry a permanent breeze with them, a smell of cedar and salt. The air around the miners was more still and smelled of lime.

The Formica table came to the top of my chest. The waitress, in a pink uniform with white trim, brought Rima two phone books for a booster seat. Because Rima's veins were close to the surface, her cheeks were always pink and her eyelids a sweet, pale blue. Waitresses always thought Rima was cute, which annoyed me.

We ordered a chocolate milkshake, as we always did, to split between the four of us. I asked Jack why the silver shake container had water droplets on the sides. He began an explanation I didn't understand about humidity and temperature differentials. I put my hand on its side, and the cold made my palm ache. Nothing at our house was that cold.

Jack poured the shake into four glasses. He always left behind a ball of vanilla ice cream the machine hadn't mixed, so we all raced to finish our milkshakes first so we could have that last lump.

"I get the lump!" I cried, thumping my empty glass to the table. Jack plopped the ice cream into my cup and it oozed to the bottom. My chest burned from drinking too much cold, too fast.

"I want the lump," Rima cried.

Janet looked at Jack. "Tarn *did* have it last time."

Jack scooped out half of my lump and put it in Rima's cup. Rima giggled, bounced on her phone books, and swung her spoon around, not caring in the least I had won, fair and square.

The waitress took our order: batter-fried shrimp, batter-fried sole, a grilled cheese sandwich—all with fries—and an extra plate for sharing with Rima. Usually, Rima and I ordered milk with dinner: real, cold milk so different from the lukewarm, bluish powdered stuff we drank at home. Then we'd hum while blowing bubbles in our milk with our straws. When the bubbles rolled over the top of the glass and everyone in the restaurant was looking at us, Janet would whisper at us to stop.

But that day I didn't want to drink what Rima was drinking. While Janet helped Rima find her spoon she'd dropped next to her phone books, I leaned over to Jack. "I don't want Rima to copy me. Can I whisper my drink to the waitress?"

"Okay."

"Anything to drink?" asked the waitress, ready to write on her pad.

I looked at Jack, "Rima can go first."

"What would you like, sweetheart?" the waitress cooed at Rima.

"Mi-wk," Rima said, looking especially small and button-nosed.

The waitress looked at me. I stood up and whispered toward her, "I'll have iced tea." She scribbled on her pad and turned back to the kitchen.

I sat down and didn't look at Rima.

"What'd you say? What'd you say?" Rima didn't like to be left out of anything.

"She ordered iced tea, honey," Janet explained.

Rima began to cry, "I want iced tea. I want iced tea."

"But you like milk," Jack said, "You always get milk. You don't like iced tea."

"I want iced tea." She was starting to hiccup between her cries.

The waitress came back. "Is something the matter with your order?"

Janet looked at Jack and then back at the waitress," Yes, can she have an iced tea too? I hope it's not too late."

"Oh, not at all. You'd like an iced tea, sweetheart?" Rima nodded sweetly.

I huffed and crossed my arms.

"Tarn . . . " Janet warned.

Usually, while waiting for our food, Rima and I would take all the sugar cubes, double layered in their cardboard box on the table, and build houses. Jack would show us how to build a castle wall; then he'd try to build a vaulted arch, which would teeter for a moment, then fall. Afterward, we'd build sculptures out of silverware, which would collapse with a clang. Canadians are a quiet people, and we were noisier than the shake machine and the buzzing soda pop cooler and all the other people murmuring at their tables.

But that day I didn't care about sugar cubes or silverware sculptures. I was too busy disliking everyone. Janet dipped her paper napkin in our water cup and rubbed off the chocolate around our mouths. When I tried to turn my head, she held my chin. The napkin was cold and she rubbed hard enough to leaves little balls of paper on my face.

Jack, who was so handsome to me at home, didn't seem so handsome in Mary's cafe with its clean tables edged in chrome. His jeans hung too low, were covered in grease spots, and had that fruity, salty smell of dirty denim. His hair was greasy around the temples. He had wanted to grow it long, but had only managed a few wisps, of several inches, which he tried to hold back with a rubber band. His teeth, peeking out from under his mustache, seemed gray around the edges.

He was telling the story again about the time he was hitchhiking in Virginia, wearing striped pants and a flowered shirt from the thrift store and was arrested under suspicion of being an escaped convict. He had to spend three days in jail until the police were convinced he really was a computer programmer at the Brookings Institution. He was proud of this story. I wasn't sure what I thought of it. I wasn't sure I belonged to these people.

I was trapped between Jack and the window, trapped across from Rima, stuck to my hot seat. The skin on my face tightened and I barely breathed. Most of all, I knew I was trapped inside my own selfish self.

The food came on thick white plates. Jack dribbled ketchup all over his food. Janet poured the ketchup in deep pools on the edge of her plate, so she could dip each piece individually. Jack ripped the paper off the end of the straw, and then blew, sending the paper wrapper flying across the table. Rima wanted to try. Jack said he could show us how to make spit wads, but Janet said she didn't think that was a good idea. I didn't answer. I was too annoyed.

At first, my food tasted salty and rich, but then grease started to coat my fingers and the inside of my mouth, clog up the back of my throat, congeal in a ball in my stomach. I didn't want any more. I felt hot. I put my head down on the seat. Neither Jack nor Janet said anything to me, not wanting to feed my needy irritability. The vinyl was cool against my cheek. I pulled at the edge of a piece of duct tape mending a hole in the seat.

The waitress asked Jack and Janet if they wanted more coffee.

"No!" Rima and I said in unison. I sat up.

"Sure," Jack and Janet said.

Rima and I knew time would stretch long and thin and our legs would get itchy with waiting.

I wanted to stay distant and cold and angry, but boredom won. I gave in.

"Want to make a mixture?" I asked Rima.

In the bottom of a milkshake glass, we mixed all the condiments on our table: four creamers; a dash of ketchup, mustard, vinegar; a shake of salt and pepper; and a blob of grape jelly. We stirred until the liquid turned pinky-yellow with black specks. Then we each dipped a spoon.

"You go first."

"No you go first."

"We'll go at the same time," and we eased our spoons into our mouths, tasting first the cold of metal, and then the strange sweet-sour.

"Eeuuuuuuuuuu." We scrunched our faces.

"Look what we made!"

Jack and Janet nodded and looked, but didn't see. They were talking grown-up talk.

"Do you want to taste it?" They didn't answer. "I like it. I think it tastes good," I said.

"Yah, it tastes good," Rima said. She swung her spoon in the air and we laughed and laughed.

Because eating provides a great deal of pleasure in childhood, it is too fundamental, too vital, to be marred by table manners.

Summerhill: A Radical Approach to Child Rearing
A.S. Neill, 1960

WHAT I FEARED: DRUGS

At Rima's feet, on the car floor, sat an old battery. Jack told us not to touch it: the acid oozing from the top could burn us, even kill us if we swallowed some. I got a little on my finger while crawling in the Volvo, but was too afraid to tell. Driving to Vananda, I forgot and put my finger to my mouth. It tasted bitter and metallic. I sat, silent, and worried about my death. Then I forgot, worried again, and then forgot.

At my feet was a large hole in the floorboard, edged in mildewed carpet and splintered plywood. Janet had put me on the side with the hole, because I was older and would remember to follow her instructions. But still, she worried and, every few minutes, turned her head back to us.

"Stay away from the hole, girls."

I wasn't afraid. I loved the hole, a window to the world under us: racing sticks and gravel, winking puddles, and best of all, when we made it to town, the smooth race of road and, when Jack changed lanes, the flash of yellow.

After the winter rains when the road was furrowed and trenched, we played the rag doll game: we held our bodies as if we were Raggedy Ann, loose and floppy as possible, so when Jack hit a pothole, we'd fly off our seats. The seat springs squeaked when we landed. "Stay away from the hole, girls." The more relaxed we were, the higher we'd bounce, so we tried to ease the tension even from our faces and joints. Rima won when she bumped her head on the roof.

After a day of laundry, restocking supplies, dinner at Mary's Cafe, and a quick stop at the pub, we drove home, our trunk full of folded laundry, boxes of powdered milk, and white buckets of honey and flour and oatmeal. Rima slept, slipping lower in her seat with each bounce. I sat in the middle of the back seat so I could see out the front window.

By the time we turned off the High Road onto the road to Pocahontas Bay, the darkness was so thick and heavy, I thought it might dent the doors. The darkness swallowed even the headlight beams, so they were but pale circles passing over tree trunks. The trees looked as if they had been caught naked by a flashlight and seemed to start and twist away.

Sometimes, driving home, we surprised deer crossing the road. The headlights would freeze them and they'd stare at us, unblinking. We'd watch for a moment—antlers balanced on the head of a buck, a shiny doe eye, spots on new fawn's back—and then turn off the headlights, releasing them.

That night, Jack drove more slowly than usual and laughed more often. "This drive is much longer tonight," Jack said. Janet laughed and agreed.

"Why is the drive longer?" I asked, not understanding how the road could have lengthened.

They laughed some more. "Smoking grass can alter your sense of time and space," Jack explained.

I didn't like Jack and Janet in a different time and space than me. Their place stretched long and thin; mine was black with a few clear outlines. I'd have to stay extra alert for all of us, smelling the decaying fabric of the car seats and the spilled battery acid, following the circle of headlights. If I could stay awake and watch everything, I might get us home safely.

A buck and a doe froze, midstride, in our headlights. Jack stopped. The deer flared their nostrils. Fur tufted out under their tails. We watched. We watched. We watched.

"Turn off the headlights, Jack," I said.

"I forgot." He laughed. He turned off the headlights and turned them on again just in time to see the deer bound into the bush.

Finally, the canopy opened a little to night sky, the air smelled cool and salty, and I could hear the murmur of ocean waves: splish, splish, splish. The headlights rounded the corner and hit the grove of short alder trees, white with black lines, some trunks straight, some bent at odd angles, all of them familiar. Down the hill and around the corner and we'd be home.

Only when we were parked in front of our house did I notice I was tired. Usually, I'd pretend I was asleep so Jack would carry me, but that night I wouldn't let myself rest. Janet lifted Rima out of the car and handed her to Jack. Jack stumbled, almost fell, then hoisted Rima up on his shoulder. Jack and Janet giggled. I walked ahead of them. I'd lead the way into the dark.

Nakedness should never be discouraged.

Summerhill: A Radical Approach
to Child Rearing
A.S. Neill, 1960

WHAT I LEARNED
ABOUT NAKEDNESS:
BREASTS

In anticipation of summer, Janet bought calico fabric, yellow with small red flowers and little green stems, and sewed herself a halter-top. She modeled for me. Her hair, brown and shiny from a winter without sun, was twisted under a leather barrette. She spun. Her shoulders were broad, her waist narrow, and in the triangles of fabric, her breasts were full and heavy as grapefruits. I admired her curves and firm softness.

I noticed my own body only when I injured it. In bare feet, Rima and I stepped on gravel, barnacles, and rusty bits of metal. We fell off logs and driftwood and slipped down hills. Wearing my yellow boots with Big Bird on the side, I jumped onto an old board and a rusty nail pierced all the way through my toe. Jack and Janet argued about an important sounding word: tetanus shot. Janet wanted to take me to the doctor. Jack told me to soak in the ocean; the salt water would heal me. I believed him. I liked to watch my blood swirl in the water and disappear. The salt stung in a satisfying way, as if it were cleaning and sealing the cut.

The scar on my knee was shaped like a smile. When I bent my leg, it was a mouth of straight, white teeth, but when I straightened my leg, the scar wrinkled into the ripply grin of an old, toothless man. Every time I looked at it, I couldn't believe it was still there, like a bad dream, this marred, wrinkliness I'd have to carry with me forever. Who would marry me with such a scar? I alternated between trying to pretend the injury hadn't happened and bending my knee over and over, straight and wrinkly, straight and wrinkly, equally shocked every time I looked. I didn't want to believe in permanent damage.

With Janet's leftover calico, she made me a matching skirt. It was short and full like a buttercup. When I put it on, I was the center of a flower, the center of a sun. I wore it when I dressed up to wait for Ishkin and Bishkin, on top of all my other clothes so the elves would see it first.

The first sunny day of spring, Janet put on her halter-top and headed toward the pile of logs to sunbathe. I put on my calico skirt and followed her. She leaned against the logs, and closed her eyes. In the sunshine, her whole face seemed to release. She took off her top and laid it on the log next to her. I squatted in the dirt at the base of the logs, collecting cedar wood chips.

The Crew Cab bounced down the road toward us, six of Hagman's loggers stuffed in the extended cab of the pick up. Behind them, dust rose from under their tires and settled on alder leaves, making the trees look like concrete statues.

Janet trembled as she tried to tie her halter behind her back, her neck. She was only loosely covered when the truck stopped in front of us. It made growling noises and bounced a little as if it were getting ready to sprint away. These loggers, who had talked easily to Janet before, now talked in a different sort of way, like a rumbling coming up from their stomachs. They laughed, but Janet didn't laugh back. The loggers didn't seem like themselves, like the men who waved at us, who sat on these same logs and ate out of big silver lunch boxes. They seemed instead like a single six-headed creature, with many-arms.

When they were gone, having left behind the sour taste of their exhaust, Janet tightened the knots on her halter.

"Why'd you put your shirt back on?" I crawled up on the log beside her.

She didn't answer. She was still inside herself, and I wanted to bring her back.

"Do I have to wear a shirt?" I knew I'd been invisible, but still I was worried.

"No." She wrapped her arms around herself.

"Jack doesn't wear a shirt."

"No, he's a man."

"Why don't I have to wear one?"

"You're a little girl."

I was sad for Janet, for her trembling. I was angry she had to wear a shirt while Jack didn't, but I was also glad my chest looked like Jack's, flat and smooth. She'd chosen to grow into something vulnerable. I'd make a different choice. My body would stay a little girl's, invisible and stringy and not quite so soft.

Gradually, I came to realize that the problem that has no name was shared by countless women . . . Just what was this problem that had no name? What were the words that women used when they tried to express it? Sometimes a woman would say "I feel empty somehow . . . incomplete." Or she would say, "I feel as if I don't exist."

The Feminine Mystique
Betty Freidan, 1963

STILL LIFE:
THE SLOW FARM

We first discovered the Slow Farm while driving home from Vananda on the dirt High Road. We'd stopped to feed the sugar cubes we had pilfered from Mary's Cafe to two horses in a field. We leaned over the split rail fence and let the horses' crusty lips skim our palms. The horses, who belonged to someone in town, were well cared for: their muscles rippled under smooth, brown coats.

But on the property across the road from the horses, unfenced animals roamed freely. Chickens with bent feathers and bare, pink spots nested in the grass. Goats with matted fur gnawed tin cans and licked bumper stickers off cars. Cats gave birth to kittens; kittens disappeared into the bush. The animals deposited their droppings everywhere.

The property, originally a homestead built by Scandinavian settlers in the late 1800s, included a three-roomed cabin built of notched logs, an outhouse, a barn, a chicken house, a few fruit trees, two walnut trees, and a small grove of pines. Over the years, someone had added an outdoor kitchen and an extra bedroom, both made primarily of tarpaper.

Jack introduced himself to the residents. Lynn and Len were transplants from Toronto with six children, ranging in ages from five to twelve, all pale with dark, wavy hair. Thereafter, we made regular visits. Rima and I liked to talk about Len and Lynn because it was a tongue twister to say their names fast: Lynn and Len, Lynn and Len, Lynn and Len.

Len used to be the editor of a major Toronto newspaper. To me, he looked like a scary Santa Claus with his long, gray beard edged in white. Sometimes his long, wavy hair sprung out behind him and other times was tied back in a ponytail. Although children and animals spun around him, chasing each other and screaming, his movements were slow, as if he were moving under water—or as if the objects around him seemed to him to be vibrating or fuzzy or changing shape. Sometimes he wore clothes, biblical-like robes, but more often he was naked, his big penis flopping, his private skin loose and soft.

Lynn was skinny, high strung, with narrow hands and a drawn face. With her wild, curly black hair, she looked like a witch. Although she was young, some of her hairs were already white and wiry. To protect the children and animals from barreling logging trucks, Lynn painted

SLOW
FARM

in drippy yellow paint on a sheet of plywood. She nailed the sign to a two-by-four and pounded it into the ground next to the road. Soon the loggers driving past started to call the property The Slow Farm, a name that soon spread island-wide.

The back to the earth movement was one aspect of a New Age Movement that was predicated on the belief that people were able to attain an increased level of awareness by communing with nature. On 24 February 1977 the prestigious Rand Corporation described the shift from urban centers to rural areas in 1970-75 as one of the most important trends in recent American history.

American Decades: 1970-1979
Gale Research, Inc.

WHAT I DIDN'T UNDERSTAND THEN: JANET'S TEARS

On the way back to Pocahontas Bay after a visit to the Slow Farm, Janet looked out the passenger-side car window and didn't speak. She'd spent the afternoon inside, alone with Lynn, and now her shoulders were tight and she didn't seem to be breathing. I was used to reading her thoughts and feelings, but her mind was racing along an unfamiliar trail.

Rima and I sat quietly in the back seat playing with Purple Lion. Lynn had made Purple Lion for her children. He had a velvety purple body, an embroidered face, and a yellow yarn mane. Since Lynn's children had abused Purple Lion—stringing him from a tree with a rope and hitting him with sticks until his seams burst—Lynn gave him to us. We put his body in a purple Crown Royal bag and pulled the string tight around his neck so he wouldn't lose any more of his foam stuffing.

Janet turned to us and spoke in a low voice. "When Lynn finds *her* children's toys on the floor, she puts them in a box. If she finds that same toy on the floor again, she throws the toy away." She announced this like the final, winning point in a debate I didn't know we were having. "That's what I'm going to do."

I thought Janet loved our stuffed animals. She talked to them; she held them over her shoulder and gently patted their backs as if they were babies; she held her fingers, invisible to us, on their backs and made them dance to music. When Rima left Beary in a restaurant during a road trip, Janet didn't question we should turn around and drive the several hours to get him. When Rima and I found a stuffed dog, Sleepy Doggy, at the dump, Janet washed him and sewed up all his holes.

Rima was already certain she'd lose her toys. "No, no," she cried.

Jack drove silently, staring ahead, as if he were trying to make himself invisible; if he were still enough, maybe Janet wouldn't turn her splintering irritation on him.

First, I felt indignant. She'd complained about our toys before, but never threatened them. Even more, I was afraid of Janet's anger, which I rarely saw and which I didn't understand. I feared it came from a deep, invisible well.

"No, no, no . . ." Rima cried.

"Rima. Stop it. I want to, but I won't. I won't . . . I won't be able to do it." She put her face in her hands and cried.

Children accept swearing as a natural language.

Summerhill: A Radical Approach to Child Rearing
A.S. Neill, 1960

WHAT I BELIEVED
ABOUT GROWN-UPS

I wanted to become a grown-up so I could take care of myself, but I worried I wouldn't be ready in time. I didn't know how to start a fire or drive a car or tell time or count out money at the grocery store. I imagined myself bigger, but just as raw and trembling "How do you know when you're a grown-up?" I asked Janet.

She answered differently on different days. "Some people say it's when you turn eighteen, some when you turn twenty-one. I don't know. Maybe people never grow up. I don't feel like a grown-up yet." She was confessing something I didn't want to know. I wanted her to be a grown-up so she could take care of me. I wanted her answer clearly defined; otherwise how would I know when I had arrived—and how much time I had to learn?

On another day she answered, "When you have children." She said this as if she believed it, but her answer didn't seem to contain all the truth. The Texada hippy men—with their long beards and sour breath—had no children, and they certainly seemed grown up to me.

When Jack and Janet were not watching, Rima and I pretended to be fancy, grown-up women putting on make-up. We plucked pink thistle flowers, which grew by the road below the oil and gas tanks, and used them as make-up brushes. With the large flowers, we brushed rouge on our cheeks; with the small ones, we dabbed scent behind our ears and colored our lips. I thought lipstick was beautiful, the way the color slipped on shiny, sometimes missing the lines. But it made women seem vulnerable too, bright and overeager. With the thistle flowers already turned to gray seed and soft and thick as Jack's shaving brush, we dusted our eyelids and then powdered each other's faces, closing our eyes and yielding to the soft sweep across our noses and foreheads.

Generally, grown-ups were cleaner than we were, but while we could scrub ourselves pink with soap and water, grown-ups seemed as if dirt had been ground into their cracks. Like old white T-shirts worn too many times. They were oily. Their fingers and teeth were yellowing. They had big feet, took big breaths, and had wide pores on their faces. While our bodies seemed as light as our minds, grown-ups lugged theirs along like inconvenient and rumpled sacks. Grown-ups smelled different than children too, a musky smell, underarm odor mixed with something else, a smell that seemed to confuse them.

I wanted to grow up, but I was afraid. I didn't want the swear words, the heavy smell of alcohol and cigarettes, the slurred voices, the haze I could see floating in the air when I peeked in the pub, the way grown-ups sometimes looked at each other with heavy eyelids.

Jack and Janet could sprinkle swear words in almost every sentence. One evening, trying to impress Jack and Janet, I told them I didn't understand how words could be "bad."

"Words are just words."

Jack nodded in agreement and passed the joint to Janet. But that wasn't the way I felt. Bad words were *not* like other words. Grown-ups said them differently: sometimes a little softer, as if they were curling back from them; sometimes louder after which they looked as if they had surprised themselves; sometimes spitting them out as if they were hot. Most of all, when they said the bad words, they suddenly seemed conscious of themselves in their own bodies, of the words coming out of their mouths.

Jack drank Labatt's Blue beer from brown bottles. I collected the caps, which were blue and painted with a white happy face. When Jack finished his beer, he blew in the top of the bottle and made a sound like a fog horn or tug boat whistle. I didn't like beer—the sharp bubbles crawled up the back of my nose—but I did want to make a bottle sound like a foghorn. Rima, on the other hand, grabbed Jack's beer bottle and gulped gulped gulped before Jack laughed and grabbed it from her. "That's enough." She kept swallowing, trying to get all the foam down.

Grown-up-hood came easier to Rima. We both liked to sit on Jack's lap and steer the car while he was driving, but I was always afraid while Rima didn't want to stop, not even when Jack told her the RCMP might not like a three-year-old driving. She watched Jack's feet on the pedals and hands on the gearshift, memorizing, preparing.

Jack and Janet rolled their own cigarettes with tobacco from a big green Export A can. They held a thin paper in a "V" between their fingers, stretched the pieces of reddish tobacco, licked the paper, and then rolled the cigarettes until they were the right shape. The cigarettes didn't light easily. They lit a wooden match, cupped a hand around the tip of the cigarette and sucked. I didn't like the sound they made with their breath; what if they sucked too hard and the fire went down their throats? The fire ate away at the match until it twisted like a deformed bone. The fire sometimes touched their fingertips and they didn't even notice. Their ashes stayed longer than seemed physically possible on the end of their cigarettes and then, with one tap of a forefinger, fell to the ground or into an oyster shell ashtray. The skin between Janet's first and second finger looked indented and had the sickly, yellow-green of a healing bruise. She coughed regularly, from deep inside, as if her very center were clogged.

Rima pretended to smoke. She used the horsetails that grew in the shade next to the creek. The plants had hollow, segmented stems easy to pull apart, and each section was ashy gray on the end, like the tip of a cigarette. Rima held her horsetail section between her first and second fingers, dropped her wrist in an elegant way, brought the cigarette to her mouth, sucked in, dropped her wrist again. She shook her head as if she had long hair. Then, like Janet, blew smoke out over my head. She looked like a grown-up. She looked like Janet.

In 1960, Texada had the highest per capita beer consumption in the province.

Texada Island
Bill Thompson, editor

WHAT I LEARNED ABOUT GIRLS

One day we had visitors in Pocahontas Bay: the whole buzzing hive from the Slow Farm and other men with stringy hair and sunken chests. The few women gathered in the kitchen. The men sat outside, on stumps, or leaned against the house, bottles of beer in their fists.

The older children climbed to the top of the gravel pile and pushed each other off. The winner, whose victory lasted only a moment before a violent dethroning, yelled, "I'm the king of the castle, and you're the dirty rascal!" Rima, who wanted to play with the big kids, scrambled her way through the long legs and pokey elbows, to the top: she was the smallest, but the scrappiest. Her knee bled. She lifted her arms. Having misheard the line, she screamed in victory, "I'm the king of the castle and you're the dirty assholes!"

All the men laughed. Confused, she confronted them, hands on her hips. "What's so funny?" They laughed some more. She screamed, "*What* is so funny?" When they wouldn't answer, tears welled her eyes. She ran inside to complain to me and found me just pulling my Queen Dress from the toy box to show Tristan.

Tristan, the youngest of the Slow Farm children, just my age, reached his hand toward the gold lace, the dark red velvet folds; the dress still had the feeling of Christmas clinging to it. Rima and I had decided to wear our dresses only in the house, to keep them clean. The dresses transformed us into wiser people: royal sisters who smiled lovingly, wisely on our subjects. Rima pulled her dress over her head. It was too long and dragged a little behind her. She lifted her chin and adjusted her face into a serene, benevolent expression. Her job as a Queen required she set aside her personal problems.

"Can I wear it?" Tristan asked, rubbing the velvet between his dirty fingers. I was afraid he'd rip or soil it, but there was such longing in him. I understood the desire to be inside that Christmas beauty. I held my dress for him as he pushed his pale face through the neck. His dark curls smelled of grease, wood-smoke, the distant scent of rotting fruit. I pulled his sleeves to his wrists then fluffed out his skirt. He looked strange, not queenly like Rima, but a little disoriented, his face smudged, his features slightly askew. But he was happy, and even after playing Queen, Tristan didn't want to take off my dress. I let him wear it when we went outside to push our Tonka truck through the oyster shell pile.

The other children had jabbed and tumbled their way to the beach. But Jack and the other men still leaned against the house, passing a joint in a roach clip I called Jack's crocodile because it was pointed with sharp teeth.

One of the men nodded his head toward Tristan and then all the men started laughing.

"Queen dress," I heard Jack say.

"Queen dress . . . get it? . . . queen dress," a man repeated and they leaned over with laughter. Men, with bare, skinny chests.

Tristan didn't notice. He'd disappeared inside the sensation of red velvet and was humming to himself, his face blank and young.

The men were bent over laughing. I was mad at them, mad at the laughing. Then I was mad at Jack. He had given Rima and me Tonka trucks. He had told us there was no difference between boys and girls. He was proud of Rima and me when we looked and acted like boys; he laughed when Tristan acted like a girl. I sensed then Jack thought boys were just a little better, and I could never grow into what he admired most.

If a child's questions are answered truthfully and without inhibition on the part of the parents, sex instruction becomes part of natural childhood.

Summerhill: A Radical Approach to Child Rearing
A.S. Neill, 1960

THE SECRET I SENSED BUT DIDN'T UNDERSTAND: TRISTAN

Even before our kiss, Jack and Janet and other grown-ups said Tristan was my boyfriend. This made sense. Our favorite color was dark blue. Both our names were unusual, started with a "T," and had an "r" and an "n" sound in them. We were the same size, the same age, and had the same kind of too-long limbs spurting out from our torsos. Our bones stuck out.

On Recreation Day at Shelter Point, we won the three-legged race together. The competition was held next to the beach on the stretch of grass between the swing set, the horseshoe pit, and the shuffleboard. I was afraid of other children, the competition, the yelling grown-ups lining the sides, but someone tied a bit of bicycle tire around our legs, plopped us on the starting line, and whispered some advice about counting as we walked, one-two, one-two. Tristan and I wrapped our arms around each other's waists and started slowly, one two one two, and then faster and faster until we were running. Other children stumbled. We glided across the finish line.

The judge, a tall man with a buzz cut and a big stomach, whispered to the man next to him they were out of prizes. I wondered if they didn't want to give us an award because we were hippies with messy hair. But both men dug in the front pockets of their jeans and gave us shiny quarters we liked better anyway.

But Tristan was different from me, too. He was gentle, yes, but there was something urgent and disorganized in him, a fast and jerky way of moving. He didn't draw or write neatly; he lost his toys, his train of thought. I felt a little sorry for him, but I didn't know why.

I wasn't sure what I thought about boyfriends. I wasn't sure what one did with a boyfriend, besides letting him wear your queen dress and winning the three-legged race with him. I didn't feel with Tristan the same swallow-my-breath way I did when our babysitter stood in the doorway. Mostly, I thought Tristan was my best friend. He was my first friend who belonged especially to me.

The day of the kiss we had been put down for an afternoon nap in the same sleeping bag. We were at the Slow Farm in the back tarpaper room, dark even in the middle of the day—the kind of darkness that incubates moss and mildew and invisible, secret organisms. The sleeping bag, with its balled flannel inside, which had probably never been washed, smelled sweet-sour. Tristan himself smelled like pee and the black grime under fingernails. He moved his body close to mine, greedy for hugs.

I lay on my back, stiff and straight, and didn't hug him back.

Rima and I didn't even cuddle that close. We wrestled and pushed, fell together in the car, jostled against each other as we each rode on one of Jack's feet, but I didn't like her sweetness sleeping against me. "She kicks me," I said to Janet when she made us sleep in the same bed—and she did, throwing her limbs in her sleep, jerking—but really I was afraid our skin would melt and we'd become one person. I'd lose my separate thoughts and become that baby softness.

I wasn't afraid of becoming Tristan. His thoughts didn't seep into mine, were ordered in a different way from my own. But I was cautious about something else I couldn't identify.

Tristan nestled down into the sleeping bag and curled up by my right thigh. He tugged my arm, trying to pull me under. I didn't understand why he wanted his head where it was hot and damp and dark. I needed cool air around my mouth and nose.

"Come down. Come with me," he whispered. I didn't answer or move.

I felt his lips against my bare right thigh.

"This is my first kiss," I said to myself. "I must remember." And so I do. My body remembers, so that I can, even now, put my finger on the exact spot. But the memory of my first kiss is tainted with shame, a numb, almost frozen sadness.

I wanted to ease Tristan's longing, but I didn't know how to open the door he was asking me to open. And even if I had, I sensed that inside was a darkness in which I'd be lost.

I do not think that seeing intercourse would have any bad effect on a self-regulated child.

Summerhill: A Radical Approach to Child Rearing
A.S. Neill, 1960

THE STORY I NEVER TOLD

Peter was the oldest of the five Slow Farm children, twelve years old, very old—already in the double digits. Like the others, he was lean and strong with dark curly hair; unlike the others, he talked too fast. All his words hinted meanness. Once, he bragged, he'd caught, cooked, and eaten a garter snake.

One afternoon when the grown-ups and Rima were who-knows-where, Peter called all the children into the tarpaper room. I was nervous, but the others giggled. The room had no windows and smelled of mildew and dirty sheets. Pale light filtered through the Indian spread hung in the doorway, outlining a bed.

"Take off your clothes!" Peter demanded.

The other children flung them off as eagerly as if they'd been invited to swim. I slowly slipped from mine.

"Your underwear, too!"

The Slow Farm children giggled again, nervous. They'd played before. I could barely see Peter's frame as he bent to take off his jeans, but could feel a jangled buzz emanating from him.

"I'm going to fuck you!" Peter yelled to everyone.

I hated the sound of the word "fuck." Jack and Janet said it all the time: when they were angry, when they talked to friends; when they listened to the news on the radio about Vietnam. With Lynn and Len, they use the word to modify almost every verb and noun. I never got used to the sound, so sharp and breathy, a rock against a garbage can lid. When I asked Janet what fuck meant, she told me "to have intercourse, to make love." But I couldn't hear any love in that word with the sharp, mean "k" sound at the end.

Peter chased us around the room. "I'm going to fuck you!" Children scream, leap over the bed, hide behind each other. It's terrifying and thrilling to be in such a small room with such a big boy, where we have to be quick and there is no easy escape. My feet tingle. I squeal as he moves toward me; I duck and he lunges toward someone else.

Peter seizes his sister, flattens her against the wall and pushes his penis against her. I stop watching—he makes me feel warm and rotting. I want to leave, but I don't want to disappoint the other children. And part of me likes rush of danger. Besides, he'll never catch me.

Then he's behind me. I push my stomach into the wall to protect myself. He presses against me. Being caught feels like my mind shooting down a long, black hole. Everyone else is gone. First the children. Then Peter. Then the tarpaper room. I'm in a black room inside myself. Silent. Empty. Safe. I stand on an invisible floor and lean against the wall of my skull.

I bury my story deep in my memory and never speak of it to anyone.

The child must never be made afraid, must never be made to feel guilty.

> *Summerhill: A Radical Approach to Child Rearing*
> A.S. Neill, 1960

WHAT I LEARNED
ABOUT SHAME:
THE ROOF

At the Slow Farm, Tristan and I hunted for eggs. Most of the chickens nested in the chicken house, but some preferred secret spots in the dry grass. Those eggs, by the time we found them, could have been months old. They were cold and had bits of grass glued to them. "Don't crack them," Tristan said. "Peter throws them and they smell bad. Like the paper mill." I was fascinated and frightened by secret rottenness.

Afterward, we joined Rima and some of the Slow Farm children who were scrambling up the cherry tree next to the house. The tree was over a hundred years old, with a trunk twisted like taffy, and leaning, so the older children could walk up it without using their hands.

I climbed until the branches got too thin. Then I lay on a limb and let my arms and legs hang down on either side. My heart beat against the wood. I swung my feet and hands and they grew heavy as the blood settled into them.

Someone suggested we jump from the tree to the tarpaper roof on the addition to the house. Rima and I watched the other children fling themselves into space. We wanted to jump too, but we were scared. So together, we crawled to the end of the jumping branch. Underneath us, the roof was covered with cherry pits speckled with dried bits of flesh. We dropped. Woomf. The tarpaper roof bent a little under us. We crawled down the wall, up the tree, and jumped again and then again—quicker and bolder—in a dizzying circle.

Just before a jump, Jack materialized under our tree. He seemed small and his words came from a long distance.

"Don't jump on the roof any more. It's made of tarpaper and you're going to put a hole through it."

We were all still and quiet—until Jack was out of sight. Then the Slow Farm children started jumping again.

Rima and I rarely disobeyed a direct order. But I wanted again that sensation of flying—that leap into the gap where everything stopped, my thoughts, my breath, my memory of Peter and cooked snakes and rotten eggs—all my senses closed off and shut down, until I was jarred open again by my landing. I had to move fast, faster than the thoughts only a head-length behind me.

The skin around my temples shrunk, hot and tight. Delight and fear in my freedom grew in the back of my mind, like an overly perfumed flower.

Half a beat ahead of me, Rima jumped, then ripped through the tarpaper. Her feet disappeared into the dark, and I felt her pain on my own body: the crossbeams scraped her sides then, when they caught her, bruised her underarms. All the children froze. Someone remembered the grown-ups and went to get one.

Afterward, with Rima safe and small in Jack's arms, I—who had been growing bigger and bigger, bigger than Jack and Janet—shriveled back to my usual size.

These old white rulers . . . in their lust for control, they have set up systems of compulsory education to coerce the minds of the children and to destroy the wisdom and innocence of the playful young.

The Declaration of Evolution
Timothy Leary, 1968

WHAT I WANTED MOST: THE SCHOOLHOUSE

I wanted to go to school so I could learn to read and write. I wanted to read books and billboards and powdered milk packages. I wanted to write my stories so they would stay on the paper where I put them instead of always changing or evaporating like the stories I told. I wanted to know what words Jack and Janet spelled above my head at Christmas time. "Did you get the C-A-N-D-Y?"

"You don't need to know how to read yet," Jack said. I'll read to you." But I didn't want him to be my key: I wanted to open the words myself. Jack was always reading, going places I couldn't follow: *Scientific American*, Westerns by Louis L'Amour, theoretical books with equations and graphs and musty, yellowed pages. I tried to convince Jack to send me to school by telling him Tristan, who was just my age, was almost finished with kindergarten "In kindergarten, you only draw and sing songs and play games. Real learning starts in first grade. Grade one, they call it in Canada." I wanted to trust Jack as I always had, but my desire to read was like a horse at a starting gate, ready and pushing.

I checked with Tristan and was relieved that he was learning what I already knew: basic colors and shapes, the alphabet song, counting to ten. I could count to a hundred— except I sometimes got lost in the middle. But Tristan was also learning to read and write some words: cat, boy, his own name. As far as I could tell, all the other children my age on the island were in school. I didn't want to be behind before I even started. So I asked Jack to read the same story over and over until I had memorized each word, trying to teach myself. Soon, I could recognize simple words and would point them out to Jack and Janet in books, and then, when we drove to town, on shop signs, the sides of trucks, bumper stickers.

Janet seemed worried for my worry, my anxious begging, which, unlike earlier obsessions—such as my plan to sew an entire cave-shaped room out of scraps of dark blue calico— didn't pass.

Before Jack and Janet married, Janet rarely read. Wuh-Wa bought only *Reader's Digest* condensed books, four novels in a book, four books to a hardback set—and then only for decoration. In high school, Janet found her English books boring—besides, she was usually too busy to read them, working late nights at Bennett's, catching up on sleep, and riding on the back of her boyfriend's motorcycle. Her first semester at CU Boulder, she procrastinated on her homework and then tried to read all of *War and Peace* the night before the test. She didn't go back to that class, or any other, and forgetting to withdraw, took home a semester of F's, for which she never forgave herself.

The first Christmas after they were married, Jack gave Janet a box of books, individually wrapped in newspaper, classics she'd never read by Hemingway, Steinbeck, Hesse. Reading those stories she'd always assumed would bore her, she laughed and cried and, afterward, didn't stop reading.

One evening, from my bunk, I overhead fragments as Janet tried to argue my case.

"She really wants to go . . ."

" . . . any of that middle class bullshit . . ."

" . . . has to go to school sometime."

" . . . she can learn from me . . . apprenticeship . . . Indian children . . . selling out to the system . . . "

The next day, Jack explained we lived too far away from town to drive me to school every day, but he'd decided he'd be my teacher. This seemed to me the best possible solution: I loved being with Jack's entertaining mind, I wouldn't have to meet other children who made me shy, and Jack and I would have time alone together every day. When I was feeling generous, I'd let Rima join us.

Jack said he'd convert the wooden building by the outhouse into a schoolhouse. Before Jack's plan, Rima and I had mostly avoided the long, narrow structure. The front windows were coated in grit and spider webs. Inside was perpetual twilight, an otherworldly stillness. Someone had used the space to store old planks and paint buckets, half-filled with chewy, white skin.

Jack and I surveyed the room to decide how to arrange it. Under the front window, I found a dead bird the color of dust with shriveled eyes. One wing twisted at an odd angle. I squatted next to her and stroked her forehead with a finger. Her beak had splintered like a broken pencil.

"Birds trapped in buildings fly toward the light." Jack's voice echoed above me. "They beat against the windows until they die."

Jack picked her up by the wing, carried her outside and flung her into the bushes behind the woodpile.

Jack brought home a freestanding chalkboard and put it in the Schoolhouse. Rima drew pictures on it with white and yellow chalk—people with potato heads sprouting arms and legs. I tried to write letters. We both pretended to write in cursive. I waited for school to begin, but for Jack every day was a too-busy day. Jack felled trees, walked the boom frames, cut salal, ran errands in town.

Old Mr. Hagman paid Jack to paint the words *oil* and *gas* on the raised tanks in front of the garden. The words were beautiful, bright blue block letters shadowed in black against the silver tanks, and I memorized them. I was proud of Jack's way with words and how useful he was—no one would get the oil and gas mixed up—but I wanted his words to become smaller and sit on my chalkboard. I tried to sweep the schoolhouse with a broom, but couldn't figure out a system for gathering the dust into a pile and pushing it out the door, so I just swirled it around and imagined Jack standing at the chalkboard writing words or numbers I'd pencil into my notebook.

America is moving out of Vietnam after the longest and most divisive conflict since the War Between the States. But Vietnam is not moving out of America, for the impact of the war there is likely to influence American life for many years to come. Though it is probably too early to distinguish between the temporary and enduring consequences, one thing is fairly clear: There has been a sharp decline in respect for authority in the United States as a result of the war—a decline in respect not only for the civil authority of government but also for the moral authority of the schools, the universities, the press, the church, and even family.

"War Leaves Deep Mark on U.S."
James Reston, *New York Times*,
January 23, 1973.

WHAT I LEARNED ABOUT JANET: DIRECTION

Because I thought we were enough for her, I didn't know Janet was lonely for the friendship of women. Usually, the only visitors to Pocahontas Bay were the loggers. Occasionally, Jack would invite some hippy men he'd met in town, who sometimes brought women. These women, though, didn't have children and were interested mostly in the other men. But once a woman with a child Rima's age came to Pocahontas Bay to spend the day with Janet. In celebration, Janet planned to take us all to Palm Island Cove.

I rarely saw Janet when her hands were not busy—sewing, weeding, kneading bread or forming soy burger patties, searching for potatoes, pulling carrots, planting marigolds or daffodil bulbs—so the idea that her hands would pause and we'd all walk together seemed like an adventure.

Palm Island Cove, just to the northeast of Pocahontas Bay, was a curve of beach with a miniature island in its bay. Jack had discovered it while exploring the coast in the Raven and then had rowed Janet, Rima, and me there for a picnic. I wanted to trust Jack—his arm muscles flexing so beautifully as he pulled the oars through the water—but the Raven seemed dangerously low with all of us in it. Water seeped through the bottom. When it got to my ankles, I asked Jack if we were going to sink. He looked annoyed, handed me the green coffee can, and told me to bail.

Jack was bundling salal behind the house when Janet told him we were ready to leave. He paused, placed his hands on his lower back, and arched.

"I don't have time to take you. I need to finish these by the end of the week. Just stay here."

"I thought we'd go by ourselves." She shifted the blanket in her arms.

"You can't take the Raven. She has a leak. I don't think you could row that far."

"I was planning to take the trail."

Jack had recently discovered a path between the two bays.

"It's not easy to follow. Most sections are no wider than a deer trail." Jack tightened the string around the branches and tied it.

"I'll keep my eyes on the water. I won't get lost that way."

Jack didn't answer, but walked to the side of the house to grab another bundle.

Whenever we'd left Pocahontas Bay before, Jack was the one who led the hike, drove the car, rowed the boat, or figured tide charts and ferry schedules. He always knew where we were going, for how long, by what route. He wouldn't always tell us, but assured us, when we asked, he had all necessary facts. He could even tell the time by the angle of the sun or, when cloudy, by the quality of the light.

Janet carried blankets under one arm and held Rima's hand with the other. The other woman carried a bag of food and ushered her daughter along ahead of her. I felt as if I were following, not grown-ups, but well-meaning older sisters. This added the thrilling possibility of danger, mishap, or surprise. I tried to stay alert so as not to miss it.

Next to the trail grew mushrooms I'd never seen before, bright contrasts against decaying leaves: small red ones, clustered, with white stems; single big red ones with chalky polka dots; pale yellow ones jutting from rotting logs. I was amazed these spongy surprises lined the trails so close to my house. I wanted to show Jack. Maybe I'd discovered new kinds of mushrooms and would have to tell the scientists, who would put them in books.

I showed them to Janet, who told me never to eat mushrooms I found in the woods unless I was with a grown-up, because many mushrooms are poisonous, especially brightly colored ones. "On second thought," she said, "don't eat them even if you are with a grown-up. Some grown-ups think they know what they're talking about when they really don't." There was a surprising anger in her voice. I didn't want to eat mushrooms anyway, with their slime, bumps, and secret underflaps like feathery sea creatures.

Janet chatted nonstop with her friend. "I have no sense of direction. It runs in my family. My mother gets lost just coming out of a department store and trying to find her car!"

I didn't like Janet saying bad things about herself to her friend, and I didn't like hearing about any feminine deficiencies I might have inherited. I assured myself I knew my way around Pocahontas Bay. I was like Jack: we both liked to explore, had flat chests, and pushed our long sleeves up to our elbows.

In spite of Janet's sense of direction, we found the beach easily. Instead of silt and sand speckled with rocks like Pocahontas Bay, this beach was covered entirely in large gray pebbles, which sounded like broken plates when we stepped on them. Janet and her friend stretched out on a gray wool blanket.

Rima played with the other child, carrying sticks and rocks from one place to another, games too young for me. Although I thought I was tired of Rima following me, copying everything I did, I felt at a loss without her behind me, as if

I were a balloon and didn't know how to keep myself on the ground.

I sat down on Janet's blanket and looked at her new friend. She had red highlights in her hair and soft white hairs along her jaw line.

"Why don't you play with the girls?" Janet asked. I glanced at Rima and her friend, peering into a hole they had just dug.

"I don't want to."

"Tarn," Janet paused, "we're talking."

Janet had never asked me to leave a conversation before.

I wandered to the edge of the water where I found a long piece of seaweed shaped like a feather boa and dragged it behind me, back and forth along the water line.

Palm Island shimmered in front of me, kept from me only by a narrow strip of water. It was the perfect size for children, tall with protruding rocks and yellow grasses and wide enough only for its three arbutus trees, with naked-red trunks. Rima and I knew the island belonged just to the two of us. We had named it Palm Island because we kept forgetting the name arbutus and because, although we didn't know exactly what palm trees looked like, we knew they grew on perfect islands.

"Don't go in too far. Remember the rip tides." Janet's voice barely punctured the silence that swirled around Palm Island and hung heavy over my head, but I obeyed the warning about invisible currents. When I looked back at Janet and her friend, they'd already sunk into conversation again, their heads bent together, their mouths and faces tight and quick. They seemed to have an impenetrable sphere around their heads, large enough only for two.

Hiking back was harder, an act of endurance rather than anticipation. We were slowed by moss-covered logs across a trail that no longer seemed familiar.

"I don't remember that log," I said to Janet.

"I know," she answered.

The trail seemed higher. I could see the ocean far below us, could see past Palm Island to the grown-up islands beyond. Then there didn't seem to be a trail at all, but just salal bushes, which scratched our arms and legs, leaving numb, white tracks.

"My man's waiting," Janet's friend said. She sounded irritated, which made me sorry for Janet.

"If we can't find our way home, will we spend the night in the woods?" I asked. I imagined sleeping on a moss-covered rock and pulling ferns over myself. I'd like sleeping under the trees with Janet beside me. We could eat huckleberries.

"We are not going to spend the night in the woods."

"Jack'll find us," I said.

"Maybe. I don't know. I don't think so. I know where I'm going."

Rima trudged behind Janet, too tired for tears or complaining.

A damp chill soaked into our clothes, then into the center of our joints. Yellow banana slugs glowed against the twilight dark of the trail. But instead of slowing, Janet's body seemed looser and more vigorous, as if she could emanate enough energy to move us all.

Just before dark, we popped out of the woods on the road by the vegetable garden above our house.

Janet's friend carried her stuff to a car with a man waiting in it. Jack didn't react to our arrival, but continued to walk between the buildings, carrying his ax, as if we hadn't crossed his mind. But his face looked whiter than usual. Janet bubbled out her story to him of how we were lost and how she had figured the way, the clues she'd noticed, the landmarks she'd followed. "And you know I have a terrible sense of direction," she added like an exclamation mark.

Jack didn't answer. Rima was already moving toward sleep.

But they couldn't take away Janet's satisfied and energetic flush, and I wanted to stand in the glow of it.

The heterosexual men didn't want you to be smarter than them, didn't want you to have spiritual ideas, didn't want you to be equal.

Interview, 2006, with Fayette Hauser, member of the Cockettes, the 1960's psychedelic gender-bending San Francisco performance troupe.

WHAT I LEARNED
ABOUT JANET:
MAGIC

Janet was more sensible than Jack, a quality Rima and I didn't admire. Jack's interaction with us was always touched with magic: elves arrived in silver airplanes, birthday weasels delivered gifts, fairies carved apartment buildings in mushrooms. A penny, tossed in the ocean from a ferry, would make a wish come true.

On trips to the mainland on the ferry, Janet sat in the car while Rima and I ran between the parked vehicles—under the lingering smell of salt air and motor oil. Jack met us at the boat's railing where we stood on the bottom rung and pressed our faces into the wind.

"Make a wish," Jack said, handing Rima and me each a penny, warm, from his pocket.

A wish seemed to me a weighty responsibility. I was sure Jack, his own penny in his hand, was wishing an important, grown-up wish. I knew Rima, being young and still fascinated by the bright color of things, would wish for something she could see and touch. I thought I might wish for the happiness of everyone in my family. But that seemed too small. I'd heard grown-ups talking about world peace. I'd wish for world peace—that everyone in the world would love each other and that there would be no more war.

Jack tossed his penny.

I tossed my penny and yearned earnestly, my heart muscles straining. The future of the world rested on the quality of my wishing.

Rima didn't want to toss her penny at first, torn between the certainty of that penny in her hand and the vague promise of future reward. But she let it go, wanting, like me, to watch her penny whirl in the air currents, seem to hover for a moment, then shrink until it disappeared in the wake of white foam.

I wanted Jack to ask me about my wish so I could tell him and he could be impressed with my mature generosity.

"Can I *please* tell you?"

"Nope." He put his hands in his jean pockets and looked out over the water.

"But I *want* to."

"No."

"But *why*?"

"I told you." He looked down at me and then back to the islands slipping by. "If you tell your wish, it won't come true."

"You tell me yours then." I wanted to know his secret thoughts.

"Nope."

In contrast to Granny and Granddaddy, who kept track of every cent, Jack was consciously careless with the pennies loose in his pockets or scattered on the table, in saucers, on windowsills. Janet claimed them and Rima and I dropped them in an empty apple juice jar—clonk tinkle—and watched them rise.

Rima and I dumped the pennies to play with them: line them in rows and squares, circle them in flower patterns, or have a contest to see who could stack the highest tower. Rima lay on her back and I covered her stomach with them. She put a penny on each nipple.

But Janet didn't want us to play with the pennies without her watching because Rima and I had each swallowed some. She worried about us choking. She added, "Just think of how many hands have touched those pennies and what those hands may have been doing." I imagined pennies passed from fingers to fingers, from island to island, like a connect-the-dot picture in my coloring books.

I didn't swallow pennies on purpose, but I couldn't help putting that-which-I-wanted-to-know-more-intimately in my mouth. The penny tasted like rust and dirty fingers before it slipped, involuntarily, down the back of my throat to lodge by my collarbone. The quick pain frightened me, so I swallowed hard, and again. The penny moved down my chest and out of the range of sensation. I imagined the soft landing in my stomach—into a dark soup surrounded by pink light. My swallowed pennies would be in my stomach forever, piling up, weighing me down. So with my throat still bruised on the inside, I'd vow I wouldn't suck on any more pennies—or buttons, or salty bits of shells, pebbles, or worn beach glass. But the next time I had something small and smooth in my hand, I told myself, "Just for a moment," and, "I'll be more careful," but the object would jump backwards again into my dark passages.

One day Janet counted all our pennies. She poured them on the purple table and stacked them in piles, ten pennies high, then clustered them in groups of ten. We had over twelve dollars. She announced she'd take Rima and me to the store and we could choose something to buy.

"You can buy something too," I said to Janet.

"No."

"Yes, we want you to. We want you to buy something too." I said. Rima nodded.

"No, it makes me happier to buy something for you."

I didn't understand this sentiment, so my excitement was tinged with a sudden weight of responsibility, as Janet's happiness seemed to depend inexplicably on mine.

I assumed we'd go to M and M's Variety Store which sold, in addition to nails and chain and ropes and other hardware supplies, pencils and gum boots, but instead Janet wanted to take us on the ferry to the real toy store in Powell River.

Jack didn't understand our excitement. "I could have given you money to buy toys for the girls if you wanted to so badly," he said to Janet. He didn't go with us.

Leaning against the railing on the ferry on the way to Powell River, Janet seemed smaller than she did at home. She wrapped her arms around her body to keep warm.

"Don't step up on the railing, you might fall."

"Jack always lets us."

She didn't answer, but looked over the water.

"Can we have a penny?'

"Why?"

"To make a wish."

Her face was blank.

"To throw a penny in the water and make a wish. Jack always gives us a penny."

"I know you can make a wish when you throw a penny in a fountain, but not in the ocean. I think Jack made that up."

"No he didn't."

She stuck her hand in her floppy leather purse, looking for strays. She gave us each a penny, absently, like one who doesn't believe in wishes. They had lint on them.

"Aren't you going to throw one?" I asked her.

"No, I'll save mine."

"Don't you want to make a wish?"

"I'm not sure it's good for the ocean to have pennies in it."

I hadn't thought of that before, but I wanted so much to see shrinking copper against the water and feel again the strength of my hope. I made my wish, that there be world peace and no more wars.

Janet didn't watch our pennies drop, but stared at the horizon.

I then imagined what I hadn't considered before, what happened to my penny after it broke the surface of the water. I pictured a fish nudge the penny with its nose and then, thinking it was food, swallow it. Like me, that fish would be weighed down by a penny in its bowels, having swallowed what he shouldn't have.

A bell jingled when we pushed open the door. The store was narrow, only two aisles, with tall shelves neatly stacked with Spirograph sets, Tinker toys, Lincoln Logs, Etch-a-sketches, model train cars, and boxes of Pick Up Sticks and Tiddlywinks. Near the front counter, at eye height: Slinkys, Silly Putty, and bags of jacks and swirly marbles. The stout woman behind the register nodded at us but didn't smile. She was brown all over: brown eyes, limp brown hair, a light brown sweater, and a dark brown skirt.

On a shelf above her I saw a bear with jointed arms and legs, and a tweed suit. I took Janet's hand and pointed to him.

"He's a Steif, from Germany," the woman said, taking him down gently. I hadn't realized some bears had names grown-ups said with reverence.

"I think Granny has a Steif," Janet said.

"Can I hold him?" I asked.

"We can't touch him, dear. He's very expensive." The woman didn't believe that we, in our jeans and uneven haircuts, could afford him.

"We have twelve dollars," I said.

"He costs much more than twelve dollars."

"How much?" Janet asked. I could see her mind clicking, trying to figure out a way to get him for me.

The woman squinted at his tag. "Twenty-five."

I wandered away from the counter, hoping to distract Janet from her disappointment and me from my embarrassment of wanting for more than we could afford.

I found on a shelf, about eye height, a small, stiff lamb with scratchy white hair. She seemed almost alive, as if she were waiting for me, hoping. I carried her around the store, cradled in my hands, wondering if the naturalness of our togetherness would wear off. It didn't.

"I want Binky," I told Janet.

"Are you sure? It's pretty scratchy." She knew I loved to touch anything soft: flannel blankets, velour shirts, animal fur. "You have more money to spend."

But I couldn't put Binky, who had chosen me, back on the shelf.

Rima cried because she couldn't decide between three toys. I assured her I liked the Etch-a-Sketch in her hand. Janet told her any of the toys she liked would be fine. But she wouldn't be settled. I knew she believed only one toy was the *right* toy and to choose wrongly could cause unforeseen suffering.

Janet poured the jar of pennies onto the counter, piles of them. Two pennies rolled off the counter and onto the floor. The woman exhaled loudly and leaned over to pick them up. I worried there might be some rule against buying toys with too many pennies.

Janet acted as if she hadn't seen the woman's expression: her thin, straight lips, and the tightness across her forehead. Instead, Janet chatted as if the woman had been smiling back at us. "The girls have been saving for so long . . . months really. . . so looking forward . . . counted them so many times." Her hair she'd recently washed bounced up and down.

Slowly, the woman's face began to ease and open. She started to help Janet stack pennies. Finally, she smiled and pulled all pennies toward her.

"Go on then. I trust you. I'll finish counting . . ."

We left the store, and I was satisfied. I had a lamb cradled in my arm, Rima, although still uncertain, had a new Etch-a-Sketch, and I had seen a new kind of magic, Janet's magic, subtle but real, a magic which could soften the world through which I moved.

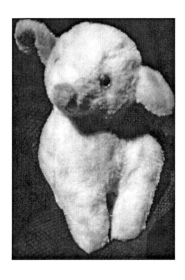

Binky

WHAT I DIDN'T KNOW THEN: WHAT WAS REAL

Early in the spring, Lynn left the Slow Farm and her family and checked herself into a mental institution in Vancouver. When she emerged, she'd changed her name to Lark and become a radical, political lesbian. She sent for her children. Len drifted away from the Slow Farm to Vananda, leaving the animals behind. Janet found him once, later, wearing a black leather jacket and telling her that if he turned the radio dial to the static between the stations, he could hear *them* talking.

The rent at the Slow Farm was affordable, a dollar a year, so Janet argued that, since the Slow Farm was closer to town, we should move there so I could go to school.

Jack finally yielded, and we planned our move for the beginning of the summer. I was frightened. I still wanted, more than anything, to learn to read and write, but I worried about starting grade one. All the other students had attended kindergarten and Tristan wouldn't be there to teach me. They'd be able to count higher, read bigger words, and recite the alphabet backward. But since Jack and Janet were moving to the Slow Farm for me, and had even fought over the decision, I kept my fears to myself.

One night, just before we moved, we returned late to Pocahontas Bay from a trip to town. Jack struck a match and lit the kerosene lanterns. His face was specked with dark shadows and yellow strips of light.

"Hey, what's this? He picked up a piece of crumpled paper he'd found on the table. "Girls, did you see this?"

My hands were cold and I was drifting toward sleep. I tried to focus my eyes. I recognized our names at the top, written in wavy, capital letters, but couldn't read the rest.

"I think it's a note from the elves," Jack said.

"Read it, read it!" Rima looked as if she might wiggle out of her skin. Jack read it silently to himself and then looked down at Rima.

"Are you sure?" he said. "Maybe I should read it to you in the morning."

"No, now!"

"Tarn?" Jack asked.

I was tired and grouchy and felt an unfamiliar anger. I didn't want to have to wait for Jack to choose to read the note to me. Jack had promised to teach me to read but hadn't given the words to me.

Still, I was curious. So I tried to sound indifferent.

"You can read it now."

Jack used his storytelling voice, wide and magic:

Dear Tarn and Rima,
We stopped by in our silver airplane to visit you.
Sorry we missed you. See you next time.
Ishkin and Bishkin

Ishkin and Bishkin, who had been fully alive only in our minds had become solid—walking and writing on our own purple table. Rima breathed out an "ohhhh" and ran her finger along the edge of the paper.

"The elves didn't write that, you did." My voice was part question, part pleasure, part anger.

"Look at the handwriting. Does that look like my writing?" Jack asked. Although Jack also wrote in all capitals, these letters were wiggly—the writing of an old man with shaky hands.

"Why are the letters all wiggly?" I'd catch him with my surprise questions.

Rima looked at me, puzzled I was trying to break the magic. But Jack was unshaken.

"Elves don't write very well with big people's pens."

I did agree being the size of an elf and holding a pen might be awkward and could account for wiggles.

"Besides," Jack added, "when would I have done it? You've been with me all day."

Rima nodded. Jack was a convincing arguer.

I had no answer. So I stood silent, suspended equally between my belief and disbelief.

THE SLOW FARM

SUMMER AND FALL 1973

STILL LIFE: THE SLOW FARM WITH SHADOWS

In some ways, I was proud to live on the Slow Farm. Our address was the High Road, and obviously, the High Road was better than other roads because it was higher. Rima and I sang, "I'll take the high road and you'll take the low road, and I'll get to Scotland before you." I loved that our farm had a name on a sign. I loved the yellow letters and the two colors of plywood and the rusty nails holding it together. If I announced in town, "I live on the Slow Farm" everyone would know just where I meant.

At the same time, I missed Pocahontas Bay. I missed our small, dry house and the smell of salt and the way my thoughts couldn't stay too busy or bothered—they were always evaporating over the horizon or being blown thin by wind.

The Slow Farm, surrounded by a ring of Douglas firs, felt closed in: bad thoughts could settle and linger like stagnant puddles. My mind was more cluttered, my voice smaller, and Jack and Janet seemed farther away. The Slow Farm was quieter without Len, Lynn, and their children, but not silent; they seemed to have left behind some of their motion and noise. The chickens still scratched through the grass, building nests in secret places; the goats still had long hairs growing out of their chins and pulled up clumps of grass by their roots; and Zanzibar the pig lay heavy on her straw and sighed.

Janet was swallowed by the dark hole of a house and only came out to feed the animals. Inside, she began a cleaning attack, scanning for hidden mildews and sweeping the mortar dust, which chipped from between the log walls. Unlike Pocahontas Bay, The Slow Farm didn't respond to her scrubbing, but continued to be as damp and flakey and saggy as it had always been. Sometimes Jack worked for Old Mr. Hagman, but usually he stood on the patch of gravel in front of the barn, tweaking the engines on several old cars.

As we had in Pocahontas Bay, Rima and I set clear, unstated boundaries for ourselves. We didn't go behind the house into the tangle of salal and firs, except to follow the trail to the chicken house. We played in the meadow to the west of the house—really just dust and dried yellow grass—but didn't pass the outhouse at the far end.

In the beginning, Rima and I spent most of our time in the sand pit, digging with a bent metal spoon and sifting through dusty sand, rocks, twigs, dirt clods, and burnt matches in search of treasure. We found old British coins, plastic bits of broken toys, bent jewelry—even a dark blue pendant with an inlaid gold knight on a horse trampling a dragon—and more chipped Red Rose Tea ceramic animals: the owl, hippo, and giraffe. Jack stopped by and asked us if we were digging a hole to China. I asked him how long it would take and if we'd be standing upside down when we got there. He tried to explain to us about the core of the earth, how it was hot enough to melt us, and how the people in China think they're right side up and we're upside down.

We didn't cross the road and jump the split rail fence into the pasture defended by the town-person's horses, but we did play in Twelve Acre Wood, a small grove of about ten pines, which we named after the forest in *Winnie-the-Pooh,* and which hid our house from the road. One of the trees in the Wood had been cut, and Jack showed me how to find its age by counting the rings on the stump—and how to tell which years were rainy and which were dry. I tried to count myself, only the rings were covered in moss and kept squeezing and expanding. Sap oozed out the top and dried in amber drops. Jack said sap is a tree's blood, which flows to its own damaged parts, then crusts over like a scab. I pushed my finger into it. This stump didn't know it was already dead and was still trying to heal itself.

I put my finger in my mouth. The sap smelled sweet, but tasted bitter and cooled the back of my nose. A little stuck to my front tooth. Janet didn't like us to get sap on our clothes—the spots only got stiffer and blacker with washing. So I tried to roll it off my fingers, but my fingers stuck together. I tried to scrape it off in the dirt, but the dirt stuck and left behind a faded tattoo. I knew Janet would scrub me with turpentine until my hands and arms were red and raw. To her, all the dirt at the Slow Farm seemed sticky and impossible.

We didn't crawl around in the stinging nettles behind the barn east of the house, but we did follow the High Road a short distance toward town, past the Slow Farm sign and just over the Three Billy Goats Gruff Bridge, but never farther than the Rock. The Rock was twice my height and covered in dried moss. Out of the top grew a stunted pine tree. I knew trees need soil—so this pine tree growing from a rock seemed a miracle. Even stranger, instead of being green, its needles were pastel: pink, pale yellow, lavender, minty green, dusty blue. When I told Jack about the different colored needles, he didn't believe me. I took him to the Rock to show him.

"How about that," he said, and was speechless for a moment. "It must be . . . the chemicals in the rock . . ." He didn't sound sure. I loved that the tree had puzzled him.

But even more, I recognized the pine tree. It seemed like my own insides turned out, the part of me that was serene and beautiful and odd. Every time we drove to town—toward the reminder of my fear of school, toward the too-loud, too-large, too-complicated world of grown-ups—I watched the tree until it disappeared.

The word "utopia" derives from two Greek words, meaning respectively "good place" and "no place."

Dictionary of the History of Ideas
Philip Wiener, Ed., 1973-1974

WHAT I LEARNED ABOUT POWER: THE BILLY GOATS GRUFF BRIDGE

Under the Three Billy Goats Gruff Bridge, the water was shallow and smelled metallic. Algae grew at the edges. Silt clung to our ankles. We were afraid something was hiding in the mud—leeches, biting worms, pieces of broken beer bottles—but we couldn't resist looking at the wooden bridge from underneath.

Rima and I acted out the story of the Three Billy Goats Gruff. I was the troll. I imagined myself stout, with thick feet, hair on my toes, and hairs in my nostrils. My eyes were small and far apart. I wanted to be left alone and I wanted attention and I wanted to startle people. Rima was the goat—trip, trip, tripping across the stream. I shouted, "Who's that walking over my bridge?" When Rima got tired of being a goat, we both ended up under the bridge, yelling in unison at invisible goats.

Besides the logging trucks in the morning and late afternoon, traffic on the High Road was rare, but one morning, when we were under the bridge, we heard a car crunching gravel. We looked at each other without speaking. My heart beat faster. As soon as we heard the tires rolling on the wood above us, we shouted, "Who's that walking over my bridge?" Toward the end of the bridge, the car slowed almost to a stop, paused, then kept driving past the Slow Farm. We crawled out from under the bridge and saw only dust. We ran to confess to Jack and Janet.

Jack and Janet said the car was a green Pontiac carrying a young couple, strangers, probably tourists. The windows were rolled down and they were driving slowly, looking around as if confused. Jack and Janet laughed and said they must have been surprised to hear high-pitched voices coming from nowhere. No, we had deep, troll voices, Rima said. We asked Jack and Janet to tell us the couple's reaction again and again, hoping that in the retelling the story might get even better, the couple might be even more frightened. We were amazed we had the power to alter the world of grown-ups—to confuse, confound, or distract them.

The heterosexual men I met all wanted to take me into the woods—to reduce me to a pioneer woman. I never wanted that. That's why I went with the freaks instead.

Interview, 2006, with Fayette Hauser, member of the Cockettes, the 1960's psychedelic gender-bending San Francisco performance troupe.

WHAT I OVERHEARD

I'd first met Zanzibar when she still belonged to Lynn and Len and had just had piglets. I stood on the edge of her pen. She lay on her side on mildewing straw, surrounded by gnawed corncobs and rotting apples. She was bigger than my parents, bigger than any animal I'd ever seen, too large for her pen, too large for the Slow Farm.

Her skin was bare like mine, but rubbery with bristly hairs. But her ears were delicate, large flower petals so thin I could see the veins right through them, branched and overlapping. Her twelve babies burrowed into her, trying to find her finger-long teats. The babies didn't look like Piglet from *Winnie-the-Pooh*, upright and wearing little striped shirts, but they did seem scrubbed pink-clean. I thought Zanzibar's nipples must be sore from so much hunger.

I admired Zanzibar's end-of-the-alphabet, African-princess name. I loved the rhythm of it, the bounce of the two z's." (I pronounced the letter "zee" instead of "zed." This set me apart as American. I wanted to be Canadian, because Janet had taught me Canadians were more peaceful and sensitive. Americans were great balls of bossy, blind energy, invading people's space like large, enthusiastic dogs. Janet had seen herself as understated and shy until she moved to Canada, where her voice was too loud and expressive, her handshake too hearty.) But I did love the sound "zee" like "whee," a silly word I could stretch as long as I liked. Zed, on the other hand, ended with a dull thump. Zanzibar had two "zeeeees" in her name.

My family said I was good with animals, and they saw this as a sign of my good character. I wanted Zanzibar to like me, to let me put my hand on top of her head and scratch her bristly hairs. She lifted her head and looked at me, grunted, and dropped it to the straw. Zanzibar was too busy and tired with so many children.

By the time we moved to the Slow Farm, the piglets had been sold. Even so, after several weeks of trying to care for the animals, Janet complained to Jack, "I can't do this all by myself." Jack didn't understand the fuss.

"The goats take care of themselves."

"I have to milk them everyday. And they destroy everything. They ate my sheets right off the line."

"You can just throw food at the chickens."

"And collect the eggs and figure out what to do with the sick ones . . . and Zanzibar is so hungry, all the time. We don't have enough to feed her."

So Jack sold Zanzibar to the Fast Farm, a new farm on the other side of the island, where the pens were straight and clean and cows milked by shiny machines. (I was proud the Slow Farm was so well known, the Fast Farm named themselves in relation to us—I liked the joke—but I worried the Fast Farm felt they were better. I knew Jack had chosen a slower life on purpose, but I didn't want them to see us as dirty and backward.)

A truck from the Fast Farm with tall plywood sides backed up to Zanzibar's pen. Jack and the two men discussed how to get Zanzibar into the back of the truck, then manufactured a ramp from plywood and planks. They tried to push her. Zanzibar rocked and surged like a boat in a storm.

As I watched, I remembered the fragment of a conversation I'd recently overheard between a hippy couple I didn't know at the Laundromat: "The Slow Farm is hard on women."

The men yelled instructions to each other. Their voices were loud, urgent, slightly fearful. Zanzibar might escape, crush someone against the pen wall, break a foot with her pointed hoof. The pen smelled especially sour, as if Zanzibar's fear were escaping into the air.

I secretly hoped Zanzibar would escape; the men would lose their grip and she'd trot down the road and over the bridge in a puff of dust. But they herded her into the truck. As they drove away, the truck swayed back and forth as Zanzibar slammed against the walls.

Rima and Tarn at the Slow Farm

WHAT I FEARED: BEING A DIRTY GIRL

The peach tree, which grew next to the outhouse, had almost no leaves and was covered in lichen. Its one peach hung from the tip of a branch just out of our reach. We asked Jack to pick it, but he said it was too small and hard and not worth the trouble. "Besides," he said, "I never eat fruit which grows next to outhouses."

The outhouse at the Slow Farm wasn't as frightening as the one in Pocahontas Bay. It was shallower and not as dark. The inside walls were lined with newspapers, and although I couldn't read, the words were comforting. An ash bucket stood in the corner. A little ash sprinkled in the hole neutralized the smell, Jack explained. Rima and I dropped big scoops so we could hear the "whump" when they landed. After we emptied an entire bucket in one day, Jack told us we could only sprinkle ashes when he was with us: we'd fill up the hole too fast and he'd have to dig us another one.

Just before bed, Jack would escort us to the outhouse. Outside the circle of Jack's lantern light, the blackness in the meadow seemed to press on us, filled with tall, flat night creatures. I never dressed warmly enough. Once a visitor dropped his flashlight down the outhouse. It glowed eerily below us until the battery burned out.

But during the day, Rima and I were supposed to go to the outhouse by ourselves. We preferred to stop and pee wherever we were at the moment. Finally Jack gave up trying to enforce his outhouse rule, but asked us, please, not to go next to the house. Since we usually had to pee at the same time, Rima and I invented a peeing contest. Although the game could take place anywhere, except in front of Jack and Janet, our favorite spot was a patch of dirt, well-packed and dusty, between the house and the pines. The ground sloped a bit, and we started our contest at the top of the incline.

First we made sure our feet were behind a line we drew in the dirt. Then we squatted. "Pretend you're a boy," I said, and then we pressed the pee out of us, as hard as we could, squeezing our eyes and making fists. Pssssssst. It sounded as if someone were hushing us. It was satisfying to push that hard, to feel our abdomens drain and then the cool air between our legs.

There were two ways to win. The first was to see whose pee flew the farthest through the air before landing. Secondly, we judged whose pee rolled the farthest down the hill before soaking into the ground. As it traveled, the pee, bright translucent yellow with a hint of green, picked up dust, which floated on its surface. When we peed in the morning, the pee steamed a little.

I usually won. I knew the game wasn't fair because I was bigger and had more volume and strength. But Rima never complained. I told her she could stand with her feet in front of the line, but she didn't. Sometimes, by accident, we stepped in our pee. It was warm and collected dirt.

I looked at Rima with her yellow-brown skin and her yellow-white hair. I'd be going to school without her at the end of the summer. I imagined the town children. They had all gone to kindergarten. They had manners and clean clothes. They didn't have peeing contests and step in their own pee. I was a dirty girl. And I was ruining Rima.

Old Mr. Hagman, filling bulldozer radiator, 1970

WHAT I LEARNED ABOUT NAKEDNESS: OLD MR. HAGMAN

Almost every day Old Mr. Hagman, who was driving to Pocahontas Bay to supervise his loggers, paused for a few minutes in front of the Slow Farm. Hearing the clang of his truck as he hit potholes, Rima and I stopped whatever we were doing—digging in the sand pit, climbing the cherry tree, or playing Pooh-and-Piglet-in-the-Twelve-Acre-Wood—and ran to meet him.

He'd open his passenger door. Old Mr. Hagman was smaller than most loggers, but trim and strong with clean white hair. He'd been a jazz musician in Vancouver but had immigrated to Texada during the Depression to make his living as a logger. On the seat next to him sat his shiny, metal lunch box. "Let's see what the Mrs. sent today." He'd unhook the latch to search for his dessert then hand us an apple, or on lucky days, a chocolate bar.

We were usually naked because it was too much trouble to pull on clothes between waking and playing, too much trouble to pull down our pants to have a peeing contest, too much trouble for Janet to wash our clothes in the creek between monthly visits to the Laundromat. But the first time we appeared naked at the door of Old Mr. Hagman's truck, he frowned.

"You girls shouldn't be outside without your clothes."

Rima pushed her way in front of me so she could see him. "We aren't cold."

He sucked his lips into his mouth. He handed us his apple. "Put some clothes on," he said. "People drive down this road."

As his truck disappeared in billows of dust, I felt, for the first time, bare. Slowly, bodily shame hollowed me out, then filled me up like water, hot, from the toes up.

I promised myself I'd be wearing clothes the next time Old Mr. Hagman drove by, both to please him and to save myself that sudden, sharp awareness of my body, an oyster out of its shell. But I always forgot until it was too late, until we heard his gears grind down and his tires crunch the gravel and I had to be naked or miss him. So Old Mr. Hagman gave up trying to civilize us.

One day, Old Mr. Hagman couldn't find a treat in his lunch box, on the seat, under the seat. He leaned forward, and behind him was his missing banana. The skin had cracked open; semi-transparent banana mush had oozed onto the back of his pants.

"Sorry girls, no treat today." He was genuinely sorry.

This time, as he drove away, we made up a chant about Old Mr. Hagman:

"Old Mr. Hagman sat on a banana. Old Mr. Hagman sat on a banana."

We sang it all day. When we screamed our song, a heavy bird lifted from my chest.

"Old Mr. Hagman sat on a banana."

We sang it in the sand pit and in the cherry tree and that night at dinner as we all sat around the table.

"Old Mr. Hagman sat on a banana."

"What's so funny about that?" Janet asked. She didn't like our edge of meanness. She didn't understand why we were singing that same song so long and so loudly—and about such a nice man.

Then we started giggling. When I could almost stop to answer Janet, I looked at Rima, fork in her hand, her naked belly round and firm as a puppy's, and our giggling began again until our stomach muscles ached and we could barely breathe.

Carl Hagman Sr., with his wife Virginia and two children, moved to Texada in the 1940's to work in the huck brush business. Eventually he began logging with the Woodhead brothers. In 1964 Carl brought Cap' Harrison's logging company situated in Pocahontas Bay. Times were tough in the logging business. Carl not only had the vagaries of the market to learn and contend with, he also had to learn all aspects of the logging business, especially those tasks he had never performed before, such as rigging a standing tree, raising a spar tree, climbing and topping a spar, splicing a cable, driving a truck and falling. Throughout those early years, because he was operating on a shoestring and couldn't afford help, he worked alone. He simply had to figure things out, persevere and succeed, or the job wouldn't get done. Those were the times of long days, dawn to dusk, seven days a week. When they did manage to hire a crew, and in order to meet the payroll, he and Virginia would be out in the bush picking huck.

Texada Island Lines, summer 1996

In 1964, Carl and his father, Carl Hagman Sr. purchased H and H Logging to form their present company, Hagman Logging . . . finally achieving financial success in the early 1970's.

Texada Island Lines, fall 1988

WHAT I FEARED:
WATER SNAKES

Before the Slow Farm children moved, Peter caught a snake and showed us how to hold it—one hand just behind the head so it couldn't turn and bite, the other hand supporting the body. He let us touch it. Instead of scaly and cold, it felt so silky I worried it might snag on my rough fingers. The movement of the muscle under its skin startled me, and I drew my hand back. Peter told us all snakes have poison in the tips of their tongues. The most poisonous snake of all, he said, is the Water Snake, which can swim.

When we told Jack about the poisonous snakes, he argued all the snakes at the Slow Farm were harmless garter snakes. "Garter" sounded like "gardener" and since I knew gardeners were peaceful and vegetable-loving, I believed him.

Still, I was both fascinated and frightened by snakes. Like characters in dreams, they were both familiar and unfamiliar. They had a head like Rima and me, like animals I'd known, with two eyes on either side, small nostrils in the right places, a mouth and a tongue. But their limbs had been smoothed down, swallowed, absorbed—their bodies squeezed so thin they disappeared at the end. That almost human face with a disappearing body made me nervous.

The first time I caught a snake, I was so surprised to have it writhing in my hands, I dropped it—and was sorry because it had no legs to catch its fall. Rima captured the next snake and I gave her advice: grab it closer to the head, support its body. But when she handed it to me, I didn't slip my fingers far enough up its neck and it twisted its head toward me and flashed its tongue. I thrust it back at Rima. But several catches later, I let the snake wrap its body around my arm and squeeze. I ran my finger along its racing stripe. I almost stroked the top of its head.

While holding a snake, Rima discovered a thin, brown liquid staining the creases of her hands; it smelled animal-strange and bitter. "It peed on me!" she yelled. When Rima showed Jack, he explained garter snakes release the liquid to ward off predators. Afterward, we turned snakes over to find the oozing slit.

I knew girls were supposed to be scared of snakes, and although I was still startled by their sudden movements, I hid it. Jack would be proud of us for being like boys. Rima and I wiggled a snake toward Janet's face while she sorted vegetables in the kitchen. She turned her head.

"Take it away."

"But it's pretty. Look." We held it closer. "Look." We laughed. "It can't hurt you."

"I don't care. Take it away." We didn't stop until she was almost in tears. "Take it away. Now!"

I was braver than my own mother.

After the town-person relocated the two horses, Rima and I explored the pasture across the road. Under a pine tree we found a garter snake nest, a hole about a foot and a half across in which about fifty snakes of different sizes slowly intertwined. In the shade, the snakes seemed black and shiny. We stepped back and screamed, looked again silently, and then stepped back and screamed, stomped our feet and shook our hands, and then looked again. It was horrible and mesmerizing, this layering and wiggling of the legless: too slippery and sensual for children to see.

We waded in the creek that was the back boundary of the horse pasture. When the hovering dragonflies and long grasses had grown too familiar, we trudged upstream toward the shadows. With every step, frogs the size of our fists, frogs who'd been invisible moments before, exploded out of the water. A few brushed our thighs; their smooth skin against our own made us shriek.

Once under the cedars, the creek, which had been shallow and free flowing, gathered instead in black pools. Eddies ate away at the banks, carving out caves where pale roots fingered the air and water.

"Look!" Rima pointed. A Water Snake swam straight toward us, undulating though the water as naturally as if it had been on land. We screamed again, scrambled to the bank, ran in our bare feet through thistles and stinging nettles, over awkward fallen logs, to the meadow, to the sunlight.

Then Jack told us there were no dangerous water snakes on Texada and garter snakes can swim. We wanted to believe Jack, the even spoken wisdom of grown-ups. We wanted to contain our fears, hold them in our hands behind their heads so they couldn't bite. But we couldn't let go of the whispered warning of older children. Of hidden poisons. We wanted to believe, but we sensed something dangerous under even surfaces.

Janet's religious beliefs
Agnostic

Jack's religious beliefs
Atheist

Janet's mother's politics
Republican, pro-Vietnam War

Jack's parents politics
Father - Republican, pro-Vietnam War
Mother - Democrat, pro-Vietnam War

Janet's political beliefs
Left, socialist;
Empathy-driven

Jack's political beliefs
All governmental systems are corrupt;
Intellectually and philosophically
driven

Janet's secret ambition
None

Jack's secret ambitions
Be a literary writer
Earn a PhD

Janet's secret fantasies
Be a singer
Be an artist

Be a professor
Be a famous mathematician

Janet's hero
Martin Luther King

Jack's hero
Flash Gordon

WHAT I SAW: THE SLOW FARM IS HARD ON WOMEN

I watched Janet from a distance. By herself, she'd lugged our carpet from the house and draped it over a rope strung between two walnut trees. Then she whacked it with a paddle she'd made from a bent hanger. With each strike, puffs of dust expanded into the air, lazily overlapped, then faded. The sunlight, a late summer yellow, illuminated the floating particles and softened the outline of Janet's face and hair, twisted in a bun.

The rug was Persian, which meant it could be magic, a flying carpet. In our dark living room its intricate patterns had seemed cozy, but now, in the midday sun, it looked filthy and threadbare.

Janet tried to hit harder, but the rug was so big, so heavy, so full of dirt, it barely stirred and made only a dull thud. It swallowed her strength. It swallowed her sounds. And still, the dirt didn't stop coming.

Suddenly, I felt as if I were inside Janet's body. The hanger in my hand was first cold, then warm, then cutting my palm.

My upper arm was weary. Dust clogged my nose and the edges of eyes and crawled between my toes.

Then Janet hit the rug harder, harder and faster. She threw her shoulder into the carpet, turned her face into it. Her knees buckled. The paddle fell from her hand to the ground. Her back heaved with sobs.

I felt the water well up in her nose, slosh around in her head, seep out her eyes. It was murky water, with indefinable shapes floating in it. She was so filled with water, there was no room for breathing. When she breathed, she swallowed her sorrow.

It confused Janet when Jack talked about his "Master Plan" but wouldn't explain it.

It confused Jack when Janet cried.

WHAT I FEARED:
WORMS

"There're worms in my oatmeal," Rima said.

That sounded like something that would happen to Rima. She pointed to the edge of her bowl where a worm, about half an inch long and tapered at both ends, curled in the milk.

That Saturday morning Jack had made us breakfast while Janet worked at her new job as waitress at the restaurant next to the pub. Jack hadn't wanted Janet to work—said he could earn more money any time he wanted—but Janet worried about supplies for the winter.

I was sorry for Rima there were worms in her oatmeal but grateful there were none in mine.

I didn't like worms, not even earthworms. Earthworms had skin the same color as people, but had no bones. They looked easy to stretch. They washed from their homes and drowned in rainstorms. Without eyes or fur or crust or legs, they groped through the soil. Their blindness bothered me, and their vulnerability.

But the worms in Rima's oatmeal didn't look vulnerable. They had crunchy suits of sectioned armor. They matched the color of the oatmeal.

Then I saw the line of a worm in my milk, and then more ends poking out of the oatmeal, dozens of them. Janet had told us, that in the South, where she was raised, she couldn't go barefoot because hookworms could pierced the skin and burrow into the bloodstream. These oatmeal worms might bore through my insides, leaving complex tunnels like I'd seen in driftwood.

"I ate worms!" Rima said, with an enthusiasm that could have been horror or joy.

I put my spoon down and refused to admit to myself I'd swallowed some.

Why had Rima seen the worms while I hadn't? Jack and Janet described me as "ethereal," which they explained meant gentle and sometimes in another world, like a fairy. Jack said this with admiration and Janet with concern. They described Rima, on the other hand, as having street smarts, common sense—she was sturdy while my mind floated in fuzzy places.

Jack theorized about how the worms got into the oatmeal. "They must have burrowed through the bag of oats."

Why hadn't Jack seen the worms? How had they snuck by him? He should protect me even from the invisible.

Jack modified his theory. "Since the oats have been stored in a plastic bucket, an insect must have laid eggs in the oats *before* we bought them and they have recently hatched." He seemed pleased with his reasoning.

I wasn't pleased I'd been eating bowls of worm eggs for weeks.

"Worms are good for you. They're protein," Jack said.

Rima and I looked at him.

Seeing our faces, he added, "They've been boiled, which kills and sanitizes them." He took two bites of his oatmeal to demonstrate.

I wouldn't eat anymore.

"I'll make you some toast," Jack said, taking bread to the stove.

"Not so black, please."

His toast was always burnt.

"Carbon is good for you."

I believed him and usually ate toast as burnt as I could bear. But that day, contrary to his philosophy that he should not accommodate any softness in us, he scraped the blackest parts into the sink. Then he slathered the toast with butter, which moistened it a little and covered the taste.

In order to build a great socialist society, it is of the utmost importance to arouse the broad masses of women to join in productive activity. Men and women must receive equal pay for equal work in production. Genuine equality between the sexes can only be realized in the process of the socialist transformation of society as a whole.

The Little Red Book
Mao Tse Tung, 1965

WHAT I DIDN'T UNDERSTAND: MY PARENTS' SILENCES

After doing errands in town, Jack and Janet stopped for an afternoon drink at the pub attached to the hotel The Texada Arms, the only building on the island that didn't allow children. The pub frightened me a little, with its loud twanging music and the sad stories of what happened there: women who didn't love the men who loved them, men punching other men.

We all stood at the open side door. The room had the feel of dim night, thick with cigarette smoke. The carpet, brown with big swirly orange and gold patterns, smelled vaguely of spilled beer and vomit. The people inside moved heavily—tilting at the edge of the bar, moving in slow motion at the pool tables, tipping their drinks on the way to their tables.

Recently, Jack had told me a story about a man, a well-liked logger, who, drunk at a party, had climbed to the top of the garage roof to crow like a rooster. The man fell and broke his back. I didn't want Jack and Janet drinking in the dark pub where I couldn't get to them.

"Just one drink girls. Don't be silly," Jack said.

Janet followed him through the door. Rima cried a little and then bolted through the wall of smoke for Jack and Janet's table, where they had just sat down with mugs of beer. Jack carried Rima back and told us to move away from the door.

We leaned against the wall, on either side of the door, not speaking to each other, looking down at the cigarette butts smashed into the concrete. Then we kicked the limestone gravel in the parking lot; the dust whitened our toes, which had outgrown the end of our sandals. Finally, we wandered around the other side of the building and peeked through the sheet glass windows into the closed restaurant. Pink paper place mats with scalloped edges were already set at each table.

Next to the restaurant, thick blackberry bushes rolled down a hill. We plucked a few berries. They were large and sweet, warmed by the sun. We ate some more; we ate so many that by the end we could predict—by a berry's color, size, location on the bush, and the ease with which it released into our fingers—just how it would taste, whether it would be juicy or dry, syrupy or tart. "I think this is a good one," one of us would call, and if it were perfect, we'd split it in half to share. Our fingers and lips turned purple.

We wanted to bring the berries home, but we didn't have buckets, so we folded up the bottoms of our T-shirts and filled them. We'd give the berries to Janet, who'd serve them back to us on granola, in yogurt, in pancakes, or with condensed milk on top. The thorns scratched our legs and arms; invisible needles worked their way under the skin of our fingertips. But still, we ate and filled our shirts and dumped our shirts by accident and filled them again until our berries were as bulky as a small puppy in our arms.

"Uh-oh," Rima said, looking down. The purple juice had stained our shirts and dripped onto the dusty tops of our feet.

"Think Janet will be mad?" I asked. We laughed and laughed. We thought she would be, but we were pleased to be bad together, even by accident, and the suspense of her reaction added a tingle to our waiting. Besides, we'd give her the berries and she'd forgive us.

When Jack and Janet finally found us, they didn't seem as if their eyes, or minds, had adjusted to the brightness of afternoon.

"Time to go, girls," Janet said absently as she turned for us to follow her toward the car, as if she'd not even seen our purple faces, our purple shirts, our purple feet.

We'd have to provoke a reaction.

"We got blackberries," I said.

"Hmmmm."

Rima and I looked at each other.

"We stained our shirts."

In the car, Janet looked out the window as Jack started the car. Rima told the story of how we found the berries, thought to carry them in our shirts, had spilled them and picked them up again.

"Do you want one?" I asked Janet.

"Oh," she jerked as if awaking from sleep, "No, thank you, honey."

"They're really sweet."

But Jack and Janet didn't answer; a weighty, metallic-tasting silence hung between them.

At this most critical time, we slap the child into the anxiety-ridden and frightful experience of schooling. For the newly born individual system, this is the equivalent of a violent birth, and the results are pretty much a repetition of that earlier trauma: brain damage, shock, intellectual crippling, and an overall depression that becomes permanent. The great promise with which the child was born is now shattered completely. Each generation produced under schooling proves more shocked, more crippled, violent, aggressive, hostile, confused, defiant, despairing, and the social body crumbles faster and faster.

*Magical Child: Rediscovering
Nature's Plan for Our Children*
Joseph Chilton Pearce, 1977.

WHAT I LEARNED ABOUT NAKEDNESS: THE FIRST DAY OF SCHOOL

A few weeks before school started, I finally confessed my growing terror to Janet. She assured me Ingrid, my teacher, would help me. I'd met Ingrid several times at parties where she discussed politics, smoked grass, and wore jeans with brightly colored patches. Janet told me it was Ingrid's first year teaching, so we'd be new together.

Late in August, Janet took me to M and M's variety store next to the post office in Vananda to buy my first pair of school shoes. M and M's only sold two kinds of shoes, white Keds or navy blue Keds. "These are the same shoes I wore when I was a little girl," Janet said. "I thought more would have changed by now."

Janet thought I should buy the navy because they'd stay clean longer. I agreed because navy blue was my favorite color—the color of the center of the ocean or the night sky the moment before it turns black, a color like both infinite space and a blanket wrapped around me.

She bought my shoes one size too big so I could grow into them. I didn't like that I tripped over my toes, but I did like my white shoelaces, the brightest white I'd ever seen. All my other whites, underwear and shirts, were tinged with gray. I didn't want even my white soles to get dirty.

On the first day of school, I wore my Keds, a pair of pale blue corduroy pants and a pale yellow T-shirt: my softest and most comfortable clothes.

After Janet had greeted Ingrid and left, I stood by myself near the grade one portable.

The town girls, who all went to kindergarten together, gathered in clusters to talk. They were wearing dresses—dresses in pastels, dresses with pale flowers, dresses with satin ribbons that tied in the back—and Mary Jane shoes. Their hair was woven into braids, held back with ribbons, curled at the shoulder. Their hair had no frazzled pieces.

We had no mirrors at the Slow Farm, so I rarely had the chance to look at myself. But going to school, I suddenly noticed I had a body. I was taller than the other girls. My hair was short, uneven, clumpy. My eyes still had sleep on them and my eyelids were puffy from rubbing them.

The boys ran around on the asphalt, chasing each other, tagging each other, weaving in and out of the swing set, under the slide. Their screams and slapping feet echoed off the buildings. It was unusually warm—a late heat wave. Some of the boys took off their shirts and tossed them on the ground or tucked them into the back of their waistbands like rooster tails.

Ingrid greeted parents, moved busily. Instead of jeans or an Indian skirt, she wore sturdy-looking heels and a straight skirt that ended at her knee.

The chubby principal stood on the steps of the main building and shook a brass hand bell over her head.

Ingrid yelled, "Time to line up!" Her eyes scanned the playground and didn't rest on me.

"Time to line up. Boys on the right hand, girls on the left."

I couldn't remember which was my right hand and which was my left. I couldn't remember my trick for remembering. My chest squeezed around my heart.

The town girls floated toward Ingrid and she shepherded them into the right line. I followed and stood behind. I was quiet like a thin tree and hoped no one would notice me.

Rising heat settled around my neck and behind my ears. Even the metal button on my corduroys was warm. I pulled off my shirt and folded it over my arm.

A group of town girls in front of me began to whisper and glance at me. Finally, one girl, small, with a pointed chin and thin, honey colored hair broke from the group and stood in front of me. She had lace around the top of her white socks.

"Are you a girl?"

"Yes." I didn't meet her eye.

She looked at her friends and then back at me. "Why do you have your shirt off then?" There was an edge in her voice I didn't understand.

I looked over her head to the metal vents on the side of the portable. "I was hot."

Ingrid saw something was wrong and took long strides toward us. My breath came back.

"Ingrid . . ."

"You can't call me that anymore," she whispered, "You have to call me Miss Sorensen."

"She doesn't have a shirt on, Miss Sorenson," the town girl reported. I looked up at Ingrid, knowing she'd explain we were only little girls and our chests were the same as boys'.

She bent down toward my face. "This is school now, Tarn. You need to put your shirt back on."

The girls slid closer together to whisper. The boys jostled each other as they finally lined up.

I began to pull my shirt over my head. I liked the way the light shone through the yellow fabric. It felt soft on my face, like sleep. I could disappear into the yellow and the softness. I didn't want to pull my shirt back down and see those girls in their dresses and their buckled shoes. But beyond that classroom door were the words I wanted, and there was no other way but to push my head through and walk.

To read well, to read true books in a true spirit, is a noble exercise . . . it requires a training such as athletes underwent, the steady intention almost of a whole life to this object.

Walden
Henry David Thoreau, 1854

WHAT I NEEDED: THICKER SKIN

The air was damp, my paper damp, so my pencil marks were pale as I copied sentences off of the board into my red, Indian Chief, newsprint notebook. I copied slowly, forming each letter as neatly as I could, lightly touching the bottom line, the top line, crossing my A's on the dotted line. I didn't want to reveal I'd never been to kindergarten by writing my S's backwards or making the legs of my K's kick into the air as if they were wild dancers.

Judy sat next to me. Because her parents were hippies too, she was my only friend. She had tangly brown hair; in fact, it seemed to be actively knotting itself, even as she copied her letters. Her pencil marks were darker and messier than mine.

Every day Judy wore a red coat with fake fur around the hood and let it hang off her shoulders, casual and rebellious. So I wore my coat off of my shoulders. Janet informed me my coat was falling off.

At school, I felt as if something inside me had snapped into place, my longing perfectly matched by the neatness of the room, the white letters on green chalkboard, the children silent except for their pressing pencils. I loved this regimen which would make my mind grow a little every day, which would teach me to read and write.

I loved my wooden pencil, the coolness of the lead against my teeth, the smell of the pink eraser. At school, I could use a real pencil sharpener to keep my pencil as sharp as I liked. At the Slow Farm, when I wanted my pencil sharpened, I had to find Jack and have him whittle it with his pocketknife. He did expertly flick the wood chips, but he wouldn't sharpen my pencil again until I'd worn the tip all the way down.

As I wrote, the room disappeared, and then my hands, until nothing was left but the dragging lead. The universe was only the movement of these lines straight up and over and out and stop and a new letter growing. Theboyhitthe . . .

Looking at my "the," I realized I'd forgotten to put spaces between my words. Slowly, the page around my words, the desks, the strip of alphabet letters and numbers around the top of the room all reappeared. "I forgot to put spaces between my words," I whispered to Judy, sitting next to me.

Judy looked down at her paper. She'd forgotten her spaces too.

My idea came quickly, perfect and fully formed, "We can draw circles around them."

Judy agreed and we carefully drew a circle around each word, dividing them from each other.

Ingrid walked behind the children, looking over their shoulders.

She paused behind us. Usually, Judy talked, but this time I spoke first because I wanted Ingrid to know I was the one with the good idea. "We forgot to put spaces between our words, so I said we should put circles around them."

Ingrid's words were sharp, cutting through the warmth created by gray lines on gray paper.

"What do you think erasers are for?"

She moved to the next child, "Good, good. Nice letters."

And then the part of me that lived all the way to the edge of my skin, to the hairs on my arms, sucked in, leaving a fleshy layer between itself and the air.

The molded, conditioned, disciplined, repressed child—the unfree child, whose name is Legion, lives in every corner of the world . . . He sits at a dull desk in a dull school; and later, he sits at a duller desk in an office or on a factory bench. He is docile, prone to obey authority, fearful of criticism, and almost fanatical in his desire to be normal, conventional, and correct. He accepts what he has been taught almost without question; and he hands down all his complexes and fears and frustrations to his children.

Summerhill: A Radical Approach to Child Rearing
A.S. Neill, 1960

WHAT I FEARED: BEING A DIRTY GIRL

During recess, the children huddled in clusters and told dirty stories. Two people would lock fingers in a particular way, crack open their hands and peek in, then scream or turn away. "Yuck!" When it was my turn to look, I knew I was supposed to see something sexual. "See it? See it?" I nodded, but I only saw darkness and fingers.

The bum story, however, rattled in my mind and stayed there for days, making me feel hot-sticky. Finally, on a weekend morning, late September, I decided to tell Rima, hoping the story would leave my head, float in the air, and then evaporate.

We lay on our stomachs, hidden in the meadow grass. Jack and Janet had taught us there should be no secrets between people, between adults and children, no topic is "bad," but I didn't believe them:

"A little girl's parents told her to buy some ham for dinner. They gave her some money to go to the store."

Rima breathed more deeply and nestled into the yellow grass. She loved stories.

"But the girl bought candy. She knew she was going to get in trouble, so she cut off one side of her bum and gave it to her parents."

I imagined the bum-ham, pink and raw, and felt a little sick.

"Her parents said the ham was the best they'd ever tasted!"

Rima giggled. Her legs, layered in dirt, stretched out behind her.

"So her parents told her to go to the store and buy some more. She bought more candy. So she cut off the other side of her bum and gave it to her parents. They said the ham was even more delicious."

Rima's face was open.

"So her parents told her to go to the store and buy some more. She bought candy again. When she came home without any ham, her parents were mad. They told her they were going to spank her," I paused dramatically, "but when she pulled down her pants, she had no bum!"

Rima laughed and laughed. "Again," she said, "again." And again and again and on other days again.

I shouldn't be telling this story to Rima, especially not over and over, this story found at the secret edges of the playground, away from the ears of grown-ups. I'd wanted to be innocent again, but instead, my light-headedness, my warm-faced naughtiness, settled over us both and grew with each telling.

It would be of some advantage to live a primitive and frontier life, though in the midst of an outward civilization, if only to learn what are the gross necessaries of life . . .

Walden
Henry David Thoreau, 1854

WHAT I LEARNED
ABOUT FIRE

Jack was having trouble lighting the wet wood in the stove.
Even his newspaper balls and fine kindling couldn't ignite it.
Finally, he poured on kerosene.

"That's too much," Janet said. "You don't need that much."

"I know what I'm doing."

I came a little closer. I wanted to watch the pattern of fire,
to see the green and blue flames that sometimes rose when
Jack burned old magazines.

"Stand back."

He struck the match on the bottom of his boot rather
than on the box. "Real men strike matches on their boots—or
teeth." He threw the match, slammed the door, and the stove
erupted like a storm or a roaring lion clawing up the stovepipe. I stepped back.

"I told you that was too much." Janet said. The stovepipe
rattled and shimmied and leaned dangerously to the left.
"The sparks could start the roof on fire."

"I know what I'm doing."

Rima held up a piece of kindling. She wanted Jack to open
the door so she could throw it in. "Not yet." Rima wasn't afraid

of flames, even after she'd started her hair on fire, even after she'd leaned her bum against the wood boiler in the bathhouse in Pocahontas Bay and her skin had stuck, then peeled. Jack still had to warn her and over and over not to shake the box of wooden matches.

I, on the other hand, heeded warnings. When Janet was a teenager, she'd tried to light the pilot light in the oven: the gas exploded, hurled her backward, singed her eyelashes, and burned her eyebrows right off. The week before, she'd over-bleached her hair to almost-white and now that she was eye-browless, Wuh-Wa refused to be seen with her in public. Jack told me stories about middle class children whose polyester nightgowns, in fires, had melted to their skin. I knew this was a lesson, not only about fire, but about plastics and the hubris of the middle class.

The fire sank back to a safe roar, and Jack and Janet disappeared into their books. I lay on the floor and drew. Rima played with Kanga, our stuffed kangaroo, bouncing her on the floor, then, when she got bored, on Jack and Janet's feet and the backs of my legs. We'd named Kanga after the character from *Winnie-the-Pooh*, and she too had a baby Roo who fit in her pocket. (In the books, I liked Tigger best because his name started with a "T" and he wanted to climb trees. Rima liked Roo because Roo was the youngest and because "Roo" was Jack's special nickname just for her. Janet liked Eyore, depressed Eyore, which concerned me a little.)

Our stuffed Kanga was normal looking, but Roo was ugly—a red-orange, stringy-furred finger puppet, shapeless as a ghost. We adored her.

Rima looked under the chair where Jack was reading. She looked up Janet's pant leg. "Where's Roo?"

"I don't know," the three of us mumbled, not ready to emerge from the stories we were creating for ourselves.

Then Jack stirred from his book to add another log to the fire.

Jack used his quick, emergency voice to speak to Janet. "Roo's in the fire."

She jumped up behind him. "She must have gotten stuck on the end of that log."

Jack reached his arm into the flames.

"Don't burn yourself, Jack."

He snapped his hand back. A smell of burning fingernails, burning plastic. Through the net of Jack and Janet's arms, I could see the tips of Roo's fur, curling in the flames. Jack tried to hook her with a piece of kindling, but it was too late. She'd melted into a black ball. There was nothing Jack could do but close the door.

"I didn't see her." Jack looked close to tears.

I waited to feel as sorry as Jack and Janet looked, but I never felt a wash of grief.

For that moment, I understood Roo was only a bit of fabric, brought to life by my family's shared imagination. Jack and Janet weren't trying to save Roo's life; they were trying to protect Rima and me from sorrow. So, instead, I was grateful. Even though we'd lost Roo, even though fires could burn out of their control, Jack and Janet, in moments, could move with one desire to save what they loved.

1973

January 22	Supreme Court Case Roe vs. Wade protects right to an abortion in the first three months of pregnancy.
January 11	Senate Democratic Caucus votes to investigate Watergate allegations.
January 27	Cease fire in Vietnam; Nixon does not call it defeat but "peace with honor."
February 28	AIM (American Indian Movement) members begin 2-month stand off with federal agents at Wounded Knee, South Dakota on Pine Ridge Reservation.
March 29	Last of troops withdrawn from Vietnam.
April 30	Because of Watergate allegations, four of Nixon's top aides resign.
July 24	Supreme Court rules Nixon must turn over White House tapes.
October 10	Vice President Spiro Agnew resigns after allegations of income tax evasion and accepting bribes.
December 6	Gerald Ford sworn in as the 40th Vice President.

WHERE WE WERE FROM

When Jack was a little boy, he listened every week to radio shows: the Hornet, the Shadow, The Lone Ranger (he hummed the theme song for us), and his favorite, Sergeant Preston of the Yukon, which, Jack confessed, might be his secret reason for moving us to Canada.

Our radio was a silver rectangle with silver knobs and two round, olive-green speakers. The stations we could receive occasionally broadcast a children's show, but usually ran news from the CBC. The news meant nothing to me, except Jack and Janet leaned forward in their purple chairs and shushed us when we tried to talk.

One evening as Jack and Janet listened to the radio, I marched around them, reciting a chant I'd learned that day at recess:

"Hey! Hey! Get out of my way! I just got back from the U.S. of A!" I liked the sound of it, the rhyme and stomping rhythm: hey, way, U. S. of A. Ay, ay, stomp stomp ay. Stomp, stomp, stompity stomp, stomp, stomp, ay. Rima marched behind me, but her steps were off rhythm.

"You shouldn't sing that song," Janet looked over at me. Her voice was heavy.

"Everyone at school sings it." I continued stomping.

"But you're from the U.S. and they're not."

"I am not." Jack and Janet looked at me. "I'm from Colorado." When they didn't respond, I added, doubtfully, "I'm American."

Then Jack tried to explain to me about states and provinces and countries and places inside other places, but I was too busy considering, for the first time, the meaning of my chant: I was from the U. S. of A. and people from the U. S. of A. are bossy, self-important bullies. Like the Canadians, I felt the U.S. as an immense, sharp-edged presence. This new knowledge of my origins made me feel both more powerful and ashamed. At school, I'd keep my birthplace a secret; I wouldn't tell anyone to get out of my way.

When Jack and Janet listened to the news, I noticed, for the first time, the strange, strong words and how they were almost always associated with the United States: Agent Orange, My Lai, Nixon, Vietnam, Viet Cong, Watergate. Sometimes, as Jack and Janet listened, they were quiet and somber; other times they spoke angrily back to the radio. They were glad to be in Canada, they said, where they could get the real story, glad to be building another sort of life in a gentler place   But sometimes Janet, after hearing of too many deaths, would say, "I'm not sure we're doing enough," and then wave her hand around the room. "How can this be enough?"

A Country So Large and So Small

Size of Canada	9,984,670 sq. miles/3,855,103 sq. km By area, after Russia, the largest country in the world
Size of British Columbia	11,185 sq. miles/18,000 sq. km Larger than California, Oregon, and Washington combined; 2.5 times the size of Japan; 4 times the size of Great Britain
Population of Canada 1971	21,568,311
Population of California 1971	20,346,000
Population of British Columbia 1971	2,240,472
Population of Los Angeles 1970	2, 811,801

WHAT I LEARNED ABOUT TEETH AND DECAY

I didn't think much about my teeth before the teeth people came. We brushed if we remembered and if we felt like it.

I did like Jack's toothbrush, though, which had an orange rubber point for cleaning between his teeth, sticking out of the base of the handle. I never saw him use it though: at restaurants, Jack always picked his teeth with a toothpick; at home, with the end of a match. When Jack wasn't watching, I pushed the rubber between my teeth. It was satisfyingly itchy. I asked Jack if I could chew it off and he said no.

The teeth people were a man and woman, sent by the province to rural classrooms, to educate children on proper oral hygiene. The man had loose curls and the woman had light brown, shoulder-length hair. They both looked freshly scrubbed, and their clothes seemed brand-new clean, so even the town girls' dresses looked gray in comparison. I knew they didn't have children because they had a childlikeness in them, an eagerness that hadn't been wearied. I admired their shininess and how much they knew about teeth.

They brought an oversized model of white, even teeth set in pink plastic gums. The model reminded me of Janet's teeth, straight and well proportioned, although hers were slightly yellowed from smoking. She said her teeth were soft and that was why she had so much silver in her molars. I worried about her soft teeth. She said Jack's side of the family had hard teeth and she hoped I did too. Jack's top teeth were hidden by his mustache. His bottom teeth were slightly crooked and grayed near the gums. Rima's teeth were like little pearls with spaces between them.

The teeth people used the model and an oversized toothbrush to show us how to hold our toothbrushes at a forty-five degree angle and stroke upward, at least five times on each tooth. We had to brush away plaque, which could eat holes in our teeth. They recommended brushing our tongues too, to keep our breath fresh. Then they showed us how to use a string to scrape between our teeth.

As they left, they gave us each a gift packet—a child-sized toothbrush, a miniature container of dental floss, and red plaque-exposing pills—and reminded us to brush our teeth at least twice a day. Then they said we must go home and teach our families what we'd learned. I couldn't wait to give teeth lessons.

At home, I couldn't get Jack to stop working. He mumbled something about the bourgeoisie and schools telling him how to raise his children. Janet listened and nodded, not because she was interested, but because I cared so much. Still, I hoped my information could strengthen her soft teeth. Rima was only interested in the red pills that came two by two in foil wrappers.

So I explained the pills to Rima: we would brush our teeth as best as we could and the red pills would tell us where we'd missed. I knew I'd brush better than Rima because of my special training, but I did give her advice. I brushed my teeth twice, paying attention to each tooth. I brushed my tongue, all the way to the back so I almost gagged. I even brushed the inside of my cheeks. Then I showed Rima how to floss. I wrapped the string around her finger, but it kept unwinding. I wrapped my string too tightly and my fingertip turned bright red, then deep red, then purple.

"If I don't take it off," I said to Rima in my best teacher voice, "my finger will die and fall off."

We dissolved the pills in our mouths.

"That can't be very good for you," Janet said, followed by a lecture on the dangers of red dye number two.

"Your teeth are red," I laughed at Rima. Her tongue and the insides of her lips were also cherry-bright.

"Yours are, too."

"No, they aren't."

"Yes, they are."

I looked in Janet's hand mirror. Although paler than Rima's, each of my teeth was red at the gum line. I stuck out my tongue. It was vibrant and furry with a broken crack down the center. I brushed my teeth again and again, but still the red, although fading, persisted.

For the next several weeks, I tried to brush my teeth before school, but Jack told me not to: only adults have to brush their teeth in the morning. I asked Janet what he meant. She said grown-ups drink coffee and smoke cigarettes and it makes their breath bad, but she thought it was something else too: when people became teenagers, their mouths started to get coated and bad tasting.

I brushed and flossed every day until my dental floss ran out.

"It doesn't matter," Jack said. "They're just your baby teeth. They'll all fall out."

Even though I'd tried my best, I knew with my red teeth and unconcerned parents, I'd let down the teeth people. Most of all, I was afraid of the new knowledge that although I believed I was clean, something invisible could eat away at me, a fault line of decay I could neither see nor fix.

Texada's Rise and Fall

Minerals:	Iron ore, limestone, marble, gold, copper, silver, lead, quartz
The year iron ore was discovered:	1876
The year gold was discovered:	1880
The year copper was discovered:	1890
Names of the top producing mines of the Texada Mining Company in 1889:	The Golden Slipper, Caledonia, Silver Tip, Blue Bell, Viwar Eagle, Grand Devon Canada
Culture in 1900:	Texada boasted the only opera house north of San Francisco; favorite bar was *Bucket of Blood*.
Approximate population in 1897:	300
Approximate population in 1900:	600
Population in 1971:	1443

Population in 1991: 1089

Most famous rock: The Texada Rock, its exact form found nowhere else in the world: black basalt specked with white feldspar starbursts.

Claim to fame: The primary source of limestone for the cement, chemical, and pulp industries for the entire west coast of North America, from Alaska to Southern California.

HOW I FELT ABOUT KISSING

After lunch, Rima and I followed the two Hagman children. The autumn sunlight stretched in lazy rectangles on the hard-wood floor, over the blue throw rug and the scattered trucks. I felt shy, because even though the boy was in my class, I'd never spoken to him. He was stockier than me, with perfect freckles and clean, blonde hair. The girl, just Rima's age, was already holding Rima's hand and pulling toys from the toy box.

Young Mr. Hagman and Roxy had invited our family over for a Saturday afternoon. I'd never been in a town person's house before, so at first I was a little nervous. I assured myself we were superior to the Hagmans: Jack had been to college; Janet didn't approve of Roxy's red high heels; and although we didn't have as much money as the Hagmans, Jack had cho-sen his life on the island while the Hagmans, island natives, had been born, unquestioning, into theirs.

But, secretly—I knew better than to say so—I was in awe of their wealth. Roxy had fed us peanut butter and grape jelly sandwiches on store-bought white bread with crinkly potato chips. She cut our bread diagonally—which I assumed must be the fancy, middle class way, because Janet, rebelling against Wuh-Wa, always cut her sandwiches into rectangles. The Hagman's also had running water, an indoor toilet, electric lights, and, in the living room, wall to wall carpeting and, diagonal in the corner, a TV.

As Roxy made the tuna fish sandwiches for the grown-ups, Young Mr. Hagman, put a hand on Roxy's hip. He was a stocky man with dark hair. Roxy looked at him, their eyes locked, and he moved closer. A charged warmth encompassed them. Although Jack and Janet were often naked in front of us—believed, as did other hippies, in the naturalness of sex—I rarely saw them touch. Janet turned her face away from Jack as he tried to kiss her goodbye; in bed Jack yelped as Janet put her cold feet on his shins.

We watched a show on TV. A man and woman rolled down a hill in a passionate embrace. Jack and Janet had been frank with us about sex, but, it seems, not clear enough. Rima thought when a man lay on top of a woman, they were having intercourse. So as she watched the couple, she said to herself, "Now they're having sex, now they're not. Now they're having sex, now they're not."

Too shy to talk to the Hagman children in their room, I pulled a Viewmaster, red with a white handle, out of their toy box. I inserted the circle of slides. At first the African animals looked flat, but when I turned the Viewmaster toward the window, the animals burst into three-dimensional form. The tiger's dark stripes were opaque, but its orange-muscled fur and marble-green eyes seem carved of light.

Then the four of us played a game which loosened us up and made us laugh: as fast as we could, we rolled over the top of the Hagman boy's bed, into the crack between the bed and the wall, onto the floor, out, and up again. We screamed, trying to catch the person in front of us. Again, I rolled over the top, down the crack, onto the floor, but the boy-in-my-class had stopped under the bed, blocking me from rolling out. I was out of breath and dizzy.

"K-I-S-S me," he whispered. My brain and body and vision all seemed to tilt to the right. It took me a moment to figure out what he was spelling. "K-I-S-S me," he whispered again. The air seemed wet. The mattress above us bulged through criss crossing wires. The boy-in-my-class was heavy with money and good looks; next to him, I felt long and spindly, like some fallen twig.

"Do you know what that spells?" he asked.

"Yes," I whispered back. I couldn't let him think I didn't know how to spell just because I missed kindergarten. But I didn't understand why he wanted me to kiss him. With my flaky eyes and crooked teeth and jagged hair, I wasn't pretty. I wasn't a town girl. He wouldn't whisper those letters to a pretty town girl.

I worried about Rima. I knew she couldn't spell, but what would she think when I didn't roll out from under the bed? I stayed silent—motionless and alert.

"What are you doing?" Rima asked. She tipped her head to peek under the bed. Her face was in shadow and the light behind her made the edges of her hair glow.

The boy-in-my-class scooted out. I lay for a moment, by myself, feeling dirty, a little hazy, trembly in my chest.

Driving home with Jack and Janet, I didn't tell them about the whispers under the bed. I talked about Viewmasters. I said I wanted a Viewmaster, but that was not what I really meant. I wanted to be a tiger, muscled and glowing and always just out of reach.

Van Anda / Vanada?

In the late 1800's, Tacoma businessman Ed Blewett, hoping to make a fortune, moved to Texada and opened the Van Anda Copper and Gold Company, named after his son, Van Anda Blewett, who, in turn, was named after well-known New York newspaperman Carr Van Anda. In 1897, Blewett founded Van Anda City, adjacent to Texada City. In 1943, the two towns merged into one: Van Anda. Eventually, the two words melded into one, Vananda, only to be separated again in the late 1990's upon the insistence of zealous local historians.

WHAT I LOVED:
BALLET

When I heard most of the girls in my class were going to take ballet lessons, I wanted to take them too. Jack thought ballet was too middle class and might encourage fragility. But he did like the fairies in the books he read us, so I talked him into my lessons by telling him that being a ballerina was kind of like being a fairy.

Janet agreed because she loved dancing. When she was six years old, she'd worn a red sequined costume and sang and tap-danced a whole routine to "Santa Claus is Coming to Town" in Bossier City's Christmas show. She re-enacted the parts she remembered for us. In Pocahontas Bay, she danced when she washed the dishes, or she danced with us in her arms, twirling and shaking us until we laughed; sometimes she danced even when there wasn't any music. But she didn't dance at the Slow Farm.

I thought ballet was a strange word; it should have been pronounced bal - ett. Janet said ballet was a French word so "et" makes the "ay" sound. She said if she were French her name would be Jan - ay, with the accent on the "ay." When she said her French name, she tossed her head as if she were a fancy lady.

The ballet lessons were held in a converted porch in a home in Vananda. Faded roses leaned against the house. The town girls wore white tights and pale pink shoes with bows; I had baggy pants and bare feet. But none of us had taken dance before. My feet naturally turned to the proper angles, and I quickly memorized the first three positions. I loved my straight spine, my tall head, my breath coming from a deep place, my muscles stretching and tightening on my legs, my arms, my stomach.

"Good, Tarn, good," the teacher said, and then she reached down to adjust the feet of the other girls.

I loved the special names and rules for the way I held my feet, elbows, and hands, even the angle of my head. I knew I couldn't explain this love to Jack, who wanted to create for us a world without rules. I couldn't explain to Jack, who wanted to remove us from the painful flow of history, that, most of all, I loved my sudden sense of belonging to a history.

When I moved my foot, it seemed to have an echo, an echo of all the other feet that had ever moved that way.

I was living in a very interesting time, sort of on a cusp between two eras. Half of me wanted to do something different, but half of me felt loyal to this vision of wife and mother.

Cindy Wilson, former president,
Ms. Foundation for women

THE LADY WHO FLOATED ABOVE MY BED

I awoke to the sound of Jack and Janet's voices in the living room. Jack's voice—normally even, quiet, and authoritative—was high, tight, pleading. Janet's, lower than usual, faded so I couldn't hear it, then flashed back loud and sharp.

A shaft of yellow light fell through a doorway onto the old plywood. Neither the light, nor the warmth from the wood stove, could turn the corner and settle over us in our beds in the shadow of the log walls.

"Be quiet, you'll wake the girls," Janet angry-whispered.

I wanted to pull my wool blanket, the one with the red stripe and moth holes, around my neck, but my body was still heavy-asleep.

"Tarn, are you awake?" Rima asked.

"Yes, are you?"

"Yes."

I couldn't follow the words of their fight, but I could hear the longing under the words, the meaning hidden from each other.

Under her words, Janet said, "I'm lonely, I'm lonely, I'm lonely. My father is dead and I'm desperate for love, and always I'm not good enough for love."

Under his words, Jack said, "I built a world for you. I work hard for you, and all I do, I do for you."

Jack and Janet's emotions rose and fell in me, from my navel to my collarbone, sloshing and bruising. I tensed my muscles as if my tightness could stop Jack and Janet from spinning out of themselves.

They hadn't fought before we moved to the Slow Farm. We wouldn't have moved if I hadn't asked to go to school. The fighting was my fault, for being so hungry for school and for disagreeing with Jack.

Part of me lay in my bed, still and listening, numbed by too many waves of feeling. The other part seemed to be floating above the bed, by the ceiling, looking down. She had no age but seemed older than me, a grown-up even. She was calm. She told me I was a character in a story.

"This is the sad and interesting part of the story," she said. "Look. Don't you feel sad for those two sisters? Look at them."

I saw Tarn and Rima curled in their beds. I felt compassion for the sisters, compassion in gentle, manageable proportions. Because they were in a story, I wasn't afraid for them.

"Tarn, are you awake?" Rima asked again.

I was back inside myself.

"Yes, are you?

"Yes."

In the morning, I felt damp and tired. But no one spoke of the fight. Rima wrapped herself in a blanket and dragged it around the house, her cheeks still puffy with sleep. Janet smoked and stirred granola in a big frying pan. Jack put on his gumboots and jeans and stepped into the cool morning, into the water droplets that hung on all the blades of grass. I let the conflict fade from my mind, sink into that same place where I stored the strangeness of the night, the anxiety of dreams which disappears in the light of day.

One learns to act like a warrior by acting, not by talking. A warrior has only his will and his patience and with them he builds anything he wants.

Carlos Castaneda
A Separate Reality, 1971

WHAT I FEARED: DEATH

Janet coughed often, a sound like sorrow settled in her chest. She told me she was sick because of Texada's damp climate. She hadn't coughed that way in Colorado where the air was so dry, it turned bread to toast and marshmallows to rocks. I couldn't imagine such a place; in Pocahontas Bay, a slice of bread could mold in a day. Suddenly, our air, which I'd never noticed before, seemed soupy. It carried invisible creatures that stuck in Janet's lungs and clogged her tubes. Janet added that even though her face would probably stay young looking in British Columbia—puffed up with all that moisture—she'd rather live in Colorado and be dry and wrinkly. But Jack didn't want to go back, and he didn't believe in being sick: sickness was a character weakness that could be overcome by will.

I don't remember how Janet got to the hospital in Vancouver or how long she was gone. But I remember the word whispered at the edge of my hearing: pneumonia. I pretended I hadn't heard what Jack's friends had tried to keep secret, but Rima didn't believe in whispers. So she announced loudly to anyone who walked in the front door, "Janet has ammonia."

"Not ammonia, pneumonia," Jack answered her. "It starts with an 'n' sound." And then he turned to me, "but pneumonia is actually spelled with a 'p.' Pneumonia comes from the root 'pneuma' which means air."

"Janet has ammonia," Rima said to the next visitor.

I didn't ask Jack if Janet would die like the pioneers in the books he read to us. I let that fear float, black and formless—next to the knowledge that when Lynn went to the hospital, she didn't come back. I thought instead about this new word, which broke the phonics rules I'd learned in school. I'd thought all words followed my school rules.

When Janet finally returned, she moved slowly and her lips were almost white. Her hug felt bony. She was kind, nodded at my stories, stroked my back, but it seemed more a kindness of long habit. Something in her was far away and unsettled.

"I could've died you know," she said to Jack, like an accusation.

She took doses of pink penicillin—another long and important word that started with a p, but a p that made a proper sound. She seemed set on proving to Jack she wasn't weak or exaggerating like her Southern sisters.

"The doctors said my green phlegm was a dangerous sign," she said, continuing her one-sided argument. "I would have died, the doctor said, if I'd gone any later."

vananda, n. A place where loose-ends naturally collect, and where lost objects are likely to be found. A port in a storm; a bolt-hole, an asylum.

Passage to Juneau:
A Sea and Its Meanings
Jonathan Raban, 1999

WHAT I LEARNED ABOUT POWER STRUGGLES

Rima and I invented the "direction game" to play in the car. When Jack stopped at an intersection, we guessed if he were going to go left, right, or straight. Whoever guessed correctly earned a point, and we kept score on our fingers. If we guessed "straight," Jack announced, like a slogan, "I'll never go straight!" If we guessed "right" he said, "If I turn right four times, we'll end up where we started." I tried to visualize the pattern, but just as I could almost see it, my mind jumbled. Janet neither played nor commented, but looked silently out the side window.

One day, playing the direction game on the drive to Vananda, I noticed a clicka-clicka-clicka noise and a flashing green arrow on the dashboard.

"What's that?" I asked Jack.

"What?"

"That flashing thing."

"A blinker."

He didn't say more, but after several turns, I'd figured out its function. At intersections, I began to make loud, confident guesses. Rima knew something had changed.

"How do you always know?"

Jack was silent, waiting to see what I would do.

At first I liked my power over Rima and the secret I had with Jack and wanted to keep it. But the exhilaration of winning soon gave way to boredom and, even worse, a sense of my own meanness. After several more turns, I confessed. Rima was annoyed I'd tricked her, but even more sorry we'd lost our game forever.

The errands in town began in the usual way, with Rima and me arguing in the back seat. I was hot and irritable and didn't want Rima to touch me, so she repeatedly kicked me "by accident."

"Girls, do I have to stop the car?" Jack warned.

The car smelled like decaying fabric. Bits of rust flaked from the ceiling onto the back seat.

After I yelled at Rima, Jack added a new threat: "If you don't stop, Tarn, you're going to have to get out and walk."

Part of me didn't believe him, because he had never actually stopped the car, and part of me hoped to be punished—hoped he could rein in the meanness growing in me.

"Stop touching me!" I yelled at Rima.

Jack jerked the car to the side of the road and pulled up the emergency brake.

"Get out."

Everyone was silent. Rima froze, except for her right foot, in a white sandal, which rocked back and forth.

"Jack, don't," Janet said, reaching her hand towards his knee.

"I said she'd have to walk." He opened his door and leaned his seat forward. "Now get out."

"I can't take this . . ." Janet said.

I crawled out from behind his seat. I was shocked, but I didn't blame him. I didn't want to be with myself either.

I expected to cry or be angry or frightened, but it was a relief to be outside under the curve of gray sky. Next to the road, ferns curled their yellow edges. Blackberry bushes tumbled over themselves. Behind them, roses clambered over tilting picket fences and climbed the walls of the wooden houses. The salty breeze cleared out the muttering between my ears. I knew Jack and Janet would drive back for me, but for this brief space, I was freed from myself.

I kicked bits of gravel.

One rock flashed at me. I picked it up. One side was quartz crystal, white and translucent; the other was layered in plates of gold pyrite. I didn't know how such beauty could end up in my hand when I was so bad. Texada, the island itself, did that for me—scattered jewels at my undeserving feet.

NICKNAMES FOR TEXADA

Canada's Most Precious Rock
Golden Isle
Isle of the Blest
Jewel of the Straits
Surprise Island

WHAT I HOPED: WE COULD BE MENDED

By mid-October, I regularly complained of stomachaches. I sat on the front stoop, curled over with my forearm pressed into my waist. My stomach felt as if it were curdled, twisted on a stick. Jack suspected I might be faking, and after the first complaints, ignored me. I was used to Jack being right—wanted him to be right—but bent over the alternating dull and stabbing pain, I didn't think I was faking.

In the beginning, Janet quizzed me on what I'd eaten and brought me mugs of chamomile tea. When I continued to have attacks, Janet sat next to me on the step. I cried in frustration. She was quiet for a moment, watching me.

"I think you're having tension stomachaches," she said. Her voice was serious, private. I lifted my head from my lap and looked at her. "That means your stomach hurts because you're upset."

She'd given my illness a name, proving she believed me, but she seemed to be implying that I was making myself sick.

"What does she have to be upset about?" Jack said, when Janet told him. "She's just a kid."

I'd been proud of my coordination and balance, but recently, I'd lost both. I fell off the pine stump and hit my face on the ground. My brain felt as if it had been jostled. My mouth pulsed. Janet opened my mouth to see if I'd lost any teeth and pulled out her fingers covered in blood.

"I think we should take her to the doctor."

"She's just bitten her tongue. Tongues bleed a lot, but they heal quickly," Jack said.

Janet rinsed my mouth out with water, touched my tongue. "No. Look. Her front tooth went through her bottom lip." Blood filled the gully between my lip and gum.

"There's nothing a doctor could do," Jack said.

My lip swelled large and tender, so it was difficult to speak.

A few weeks later when the hole in my lip had already closed into a half-moon scar, Jack took Rima and me with him to town to run errands. He parked the Volvo in a gravel parking lot, which happened to be near the doctor's office, and told us to wait.

We were soon restless. We rolled the windows up and down. Then we stood on the side windows and waved at each other over the curve of the roof. Chalky blue paint rubbed off on our hands. I crawled onto the roof. Rima couldn't reach, so she stepped on the hood, and I pulled her up. From the roof we could see in the distance a line of pine trees and the strip of beach where people with buckets dug for clams. We jumped. The metal under us dented and popped. So we stomped harder. I spun and stared at the sky. The treetops were a whirly blur.

I heard screams from the gravel below me. When my eyes stopped spinning, I could make out Rima's face—her forehead and cheek streaked in blood. I jump down beside her. Blood and tears filled her eyes. I patted her back. Rima pressed her hand against her face. When she saw the blood on her fingers, she shrieked. Jack raced across the parking lot, his legs grow-ing longer with each step toward us.

He grabbed the oil rag from the back seat and used a clean corner to wipe around her eye, but the blood wouldn't stop flowing. He scooped her under his arm and ran her to the doctor's office. I stayed behind with the dented car and watched the blood soak into gravel.

I shouldn't have let Rima on top of the car. I was supposed to take care of her. I sat on the log at the edge of the parking lot and curled over my stomach, which had tightened into a throbbing knot.

When they returned and had loaded back into the car, Jack was cheerful. Rima hadn't damaged her eye. Rima was happy too. She had a purple lollipop in her mouth. The doctor had given her lots of attention, and she now she had her own, exciting story to tell, with a visual aid: three stitches above her right eyebrow. I was impressed by those black threads poking out of Rima's forehead, by Rima's courage—I couldn't imagine letting someone sew me—and by the new knowledge that a person could be mended like a piece of fabric.

I was also strangely relieved by Jack's urgency and by the seriousness of the event, as if our free-floating emotional chaos had finally organized itself into visual damage about which we could speak and act—and about which even Jack had consulted an expert.

We hold these truths to be self-evident:

- *That all species are created different but equal;*
- *That they are endowed, each one, with certain inalienable rights;*
- *That among them are Freedom to Live, Freedom to Grow, and Freedom to pursue Happiness in their own style;*
- *That to protect these God-given rights, social structures naturally emerge, basing their authority on the principles of love of God and respect for all forms of life;*
- *That whenever any form of government becomes destructive of life, liberty, and harmony, it is the organic duty of the young members of that species to mutate, drop out, to initiate new social structure, laying its foundations on such principles and organizing its power in such form as seems likely to produce the safety, happiness, and harmony of all sentient beings.*

The Declaration of Evolution
Timothy Leary, 1968

WHAT I LEARNED
ABOUT LOVE:
THE SNAKE

I couldn't stop thinking about the offer in my latest *Ranger Rick* magazine: fill out the postcard and receive information on how to keep a garter snake as a pet. I'd catch a snake and make its strangeness familiar. It would be mine, and not Rima's, and it would wait for me and lift its head when I opened its cage. I'd care for it and it would need me.

I couldn't ask Janet to help me because she didn't want a snake in the house. Jack agreed, but wouldn't stop work on his truck long enough to fill out the form. I felt as if I were in a dream: I had an urgent message, but as soon as my words touched the air, they lost their shape—and Jack smiled and nodded at my gibberish. Finally my repetition edged into Jack's awareness and he scribbled our address.

The day after he'd mailed it, I asked him to drive back to the post office to pick up my packet. Jack explained it would take a long time to arrive, especially since it was coming from the States. During the weeks I waited, my hopes got bigger, until I visualized a large box, with my name on it and an aquarium inside with rocks and plants and a little pool I could fill with water. When the business-sized envelope finally arrived, it was addressed to "Tom Wilson" and contained only two pieces of paper. Still, I was hopeful.

I pestered Jack until he emptied his shoebox filled with nails, screws, nuts, bolts, and washers and gave it to me. I followed the diagrams. I layered ripped grass on the bottom of the box, then nestled in a plastic lid with water. In the meadow I caught a snake, long and black with three yellow stripes, and put it in my box. It tried to escape by climbing up the walls, making a brushing sound against the cardboard. When it couldn't slip over the side, it pressed itself into a corner. Its eyes were glass beads.

In the morning, the snake was in the same position. Its eyes were cloudy. Some of its skin was peeling. The grass was limp, the snake was limp, and the box smelled like the snake's fear juice.

After all my begging, I was ashamed to ask Jack if I should let the snake go.

Janet was in the dark-even-in-the-day kitchen chopping carrots. I held the box in my arms.

"Should I let it go?"

"It's up to you." She seemed sad and distracted.

My box was heavier on the snake side. The snake lunged for the opposite edge, and the weight of the box tipped again. So much muscle in such a small space. I carried the box back across the road and turned it on its side at the edge of the meadow. The snake eased into the tall grass and didn't even turn back to say goodbye.

"I'm glad," Janet said when returned with my empty, stained box. She was wiping down the plywood counters. "I don't think it's right to keep animals who would be happier free."

*I can think of a number of reasons why Janet
left Jack but neither she nor Jack ever told me
even one.*

Letter to me from Granny,
January 29, 1997

THE MOMENT I CAN'T
REMEMBER

This is what I remember: Jack walks in front of us. His flashlight battery is low and makes only a feeble, yellow circle. My eyes are fuzzy, half-closed with sleep, but I have the path memorized and follow the dark shape of Jack and Janet's backs toward the front door.

That morning, Janet had awakened early to feed the animals. She spent the morning at the Laundromat; made all our beds with freshly washed sheets; harvested the last of the season's vegetables; swept and scrubbed the house; and then left for work, evening shift, at the Texada Arms. That night after midnight, Jack, Rima, and I picked up Janet from work and drove back to the Slow Farm.

It's late October, just a few days before Janet's twenty-sixth birthday and less than a month before my sixth. The sky is a crisp black. Jack stops, speaks.

"I didn't leave the door unlocked."

I'm instantly awake.

His flashlight illuminates the latch on the front door, a chunk of wood that spins on a nail. It's turned to the side and the door is open a crack. We hear noises, like footsteps, like a woman walking in high heels. Jack pushes the door open. I think he's incredibly brave.

This is what I don't remember, the story I only know from listening to Janet tell it years later, laughing, to women friends:

The billy goat is standing in the middle of the kitchen table. The nanny goat is just swallowing the last of the vegetables, a carrot top hanging out of the side of her mouth. In the middle of each freshly made bed is a steaming pile of goat droppings. She yells, grabs the billy goat by his horns and wrestles him out the front door. The next day, she packs her bags.

Even now, I can taste the blackberries on the hill behind the pub, the sweet cherries from the twisted Slow Farm tree—can still see the single peach, pointed at the bottom, which hung in front of the outhouse—but I can't remember the moment Janet left Jack, the center around which all the other Texada memories build or recede.

I want the story to belong to me, the order of events, the reasons, a clear moment at which the marriage ended, the story I'll never have. But maybe I can't remember because she didn't leave on a day, but in a series of moments, which, distracted by childhood's bright fruits, I couldn't see.

Is it not possible—I often wonder—that the things we have felt with great intensity have an existence independent of our minds; are in fact still in existence?

Virginia Woolf
A Sketch of the Past, 1939

WHAT I FEARED: WE WERE PERMANENTLY BROKEN

In the months after Janet left, the Slow Farm felt still—a small and listless stillness. Our dirty clothes piled on the floor. In the morning, our blankets were covered in rat droppings, which we shook off. When it rained, the roof leaked and dripped into dented cooking pots. Janet had always crawled out of bed in the night to empty them, but Jack forgot: the water overflowed, and, afterward, the floor and carpet never fully dried.

Jack, whose skin and hair was usually tinted with gold, seemed grayed. Cloud shadows crossed his face. Even walking seemed an effort. He didn't sing to us or read us stories in his many voices. Various friends, or friends of friends, came to stay for days or weeks—mostly men with long hair who were kind and poor housekeepers. Jack let them cook and feed us, and sometimes there wasn't enough food.

Rima and I longed to be held by Jack, but he didn't touch us. He didn't throw us into the air, or spin us around by the arms, or let us pretend to be rabbits and squeeze through the space his knee made when he crossed one leg over the other.

We didn't crawl into his bed to wake him or climb the mountain of his back.

Before Janet left, Rima had been comfortable with anger, which shot through her arms and legs like electric shocks. But she must have required all three of us, a wall around her, to feel safe enough to lose herself, because she no longer had temper tantrums. Instead, she cried—not stubborn, willful screams—but continuous dripping, as if the slightest touch could cause her to overflow. My tension stomachaches, which had been periodic, were now almost continuous. They radiated from my center into my heart and lungs and shoulders.

To soothe myself, I played on the corner of the Persian carpet with the little animals I'd unearthed in the sandpit or gathered from tea boxes. When I made stories for the animals, they became large and alive and I disappeared. For a moment, my own dark feelings, lapping at me like too much water, retreated. My favorite animal was a lead bulldog, one of the sandpit's last treasures. He was heavy with a wide chest and serious face and had crawled out of the sandpit to protect me and keep me company.

One morning, Jack, wearing work boots, tromped by me on his way from the back bedroom to the kitchen. Crunch-snap. My bulldog lay on his side on the carpet, almost camouflaged in the dark patterns. But when I looked closely, I could see his leg, broken at the shoulder, next to him.

I cradled the dog and leg in my palm and marched it to Jack. "You stepped on my dog and broke it."

"You shouldn't have left it on the floor." He reached for his lukewarm cup of coffee on the counter.

He could have looked more carefully. He could have walked more lightly. But I didn't have the courage to say so.

"Can you glue him?"

"He could be welded, but I don't have an iron." Jack sipped his coffee. "And it wouldn't look the same." He set his half empty mug on the counter, wiped his mouth with the back of his hand, and walked out the front door.

I curled over on the floor and put my forehead on the carpet and cried. I cried for the bulldog. I cried because we had been four and now we were three, because Jack's blind stumbling had caused it. I cried because I'd thought Wilsons had flexible bones, but really we were ugly and broken.

A warrior doesn't know remorse for anything he has done . . .

A warrior acts as if he knows what he is doing, when in effect he knows nothing.

Carlos Castaneda
Journey to Ixtlan, 1972

WHAT SURPRISED ME: I COULD TRICK JACK

Janet completed her separation paperwork with the court in Vancouver, and Jack agreed to send us to her—although he kept summer visitation rights.

Several weeks before we were to leave, I drove with Jack to Vananda to run errands. A man, a friend of Jack's, sat in the passenger seat with Rima on his lap. I sat between them. No one talked. When Jack shifted, the gearshift rammed into my leg, and he didn't notice me trying to squeeze away from it. The air in the cab felt sticky and smelled of engine grease and men's sweat. Rima played with the man's long beard.

To entertain myself, I started to make a noise, a quiet, high-pitched whine in the back of my nose and throat.

"Eeeeeeeeeeeeeeeeeeeeeeeeeeeeee."

Then I experimented, taking big breaths first so I could squeal as long as possible, while keeping the noise an even volume and pitch.

"Eeeeeeeeeeeeeeeeeeeeeeeeeeeeeeeeeeeeeeeee."

I sounded like a whirring machine. Maybe Jack would think there was something wrong with the truck engine. I kept my mouth closed and my face relaxed.

"Eeeeeeeeeeeeeeeeeeeeeeeeeeeeeeeeeeeeeeeeeeeee."

"Did you hear that?" Jack asked the man.

"What?"

"That high-pitched whine." He shifted his body forward and cocked his head to listen to the engine.

I was surprised the story I'd just told myself was unreeling. I hadn't truly believed that Jack could be fooled.

"No."

"Listen."

"Eeeeeeeeeeeeeeeeeeeeeeeeeeeeee." I told myself I was playing, but my play was tainted with a sense of superiority for having tricked him, even for a moment.

"I can hear it now," the man said.

"Shit."

"Eeeeeeeeeeeeeeeeeeeeeeeeeeeeeeeeeeeeeeeee."

Jack drove faster to see if speed affected the pitch of the squeal. The pitch stayed the same. He drove slower, poised and listening.

"Tarn?" he finally said, looking at me. "Is that you? Are you making that noise?"

"Yes."

"*Why* didn't you tell me?"

I'd wanted his ear, carefully attending to the whir of the engine, to attend to me, to see my sorrow, to adjust me. I wanted to lose just enough respect for him that when Janet called for us, I'd be able to leave him.

"I don't know."

I looked out the passenger side window so I couldn't see his face.

VANCOUVER

FALL 1973 – SPRING 1974

WHAT I LEARNED ABOUT COMMUNISM

My first night in Vancouver, I lay awake on a foam mattress on the hardwood floor of a second story corner apartment. Never had I tried to sleep in a night so bright and noisy. Light from the street lamps glittered on the glass of the double-hung windows and illuminated the shapes in the room: a low couch, a coffee table, a bookshelf, a plant. The forced air heater clicked; the room was warm and nose-tingling dry. Near me, Janet and Rima sighed and turned in their sleep. On the street below, cars stopped, started, sputtered. Men and women walked in groups, murmuring. A siren wailed; red and white lights flashed across the high ceiling.

The apartment belonged to Jim Green, a union organizer and the ex-husband of Janet's friend Nancy. Jim wasn't like Jack: he was chunky and dark-haired and had a booming voice. The next day, sitting on the couch under a picture of Chairman Mao, Jim explained about the coming Revolution. He told Janet she'd have a lot to contribute. "The women in China," he said, "are the backbone of the movement." When I asked Janet about Chairman Mao, she said he helped the poor people in China get food and land. He sounded nice, but his face was stern. While Rima and I crawled over Jim's wide lap, Jim quoted to Janet from Mao's *Little Red Book*.

I thought that was an odd name for a book.

"Is the *Red Book* always red?" I pulled at Jim's black hairs poking out of the top of his shirt.

"Yes." Jim didn't explain as thoroughly as Jack did.

"If they put a blue cover on it, would it still be called the *Red Book*?"

"It's always red."

"Is there a *Blue Book*?"

"No." He pushed my hands away from his chest.

He was more interested in talking to Janet. "Freedom comes at the end of a barrel of a gun," he boomed.

Janet and Jack hadn't believed in guns, but now Janet wasn't sure. Later, when we were alone, she told me, "I don't know what I think about guns . . . they may be necessary. At least Jim is *doing* something."

A Communist should have largeness of mind and he should be staunch and active, looking upon the interests of the revolution as his very life and subordinating his personal interests to those of the revolution; always and everywhere he should adhere to principle and wage a tireless struggle against all incorrect ideas and actions, so as to consolidate the collective life of the Party and strengthen the ties between the Party and the masses; he should be more concerned about the Party and the masses than about any private person, and more concerned about others than about himself. Only thus can he be considered a Communist.

Mao Tse Tung
The Little Red Book, 1965

WHAT ZOË TAUGHT

As much as Janet ached for the suffering of all oppressed people, she was too busy figuring out how to make a living to think much more about the Revolution. First, Nancy helped us find a communal house. It was Victorian, several stories, with a concrete basement. More women than men lived there, and all seemed in a general state of agitation. So many bodies together: unfamiliar smells and footsteps and voices. Everyone cooked and ate together, usually some flavorless, pale stir-fry with gummy brown rice. The house was always dirty. Rima rode around and around the backyard on a tricycle. When I tried to sleep, I could hear water roaring through the pipes.

There was another child my age in the house, Zoë. I loved her name, so short and zippy, with two dots, but she was too absorbed by her conflict with her mother to notice me. Zoë wouldn't eat anything but bread with butter and jam. She and her mother argued about this every day, and Zoë always won. Everyone in the house had an opinion: some believed in freedom of choice for children, an idea I liked, while the more health-conscious voted for making her eat some vegetables. While they were preoccupied with this discussion, I secretly sucked on my own heaping spoonfuls of butter, which tickled the back of my throat. Zoë's mother finally decided Zoë's body must know what it needed.

About a year after we left, we heard Zoë had rickets—a disease caused by vitamin deficiencies, which had curved the bones in her legs like a cowboy's. This sounded like a horrible lesson about eating your vegetables from one of those Victorian children's book of manners, the kind Rima and I mocked.

In five years, from 1971 to 1975, I directly experienced est, gestalt therapy, bioenergetics, Rolfing, massage, jogging, health foods, tai chi, Esalen, hypnotism, modern dance, meditation, Silva Mind Control, Arica, acupuncture, sex therapy, Reichian therapy, and More House—a smorgasbord course in the New Consciousness.

Jerry Rubin, activist

WHAT I LEARNED ABOUT
THE NEW JANET

Even though we lived in the communal house, we spent most of our time at Nancy's. Janet knew Nancy in high school in Boulder, but they had become friends when they were both married, with new babies, living on Sugarloaf Mountain. Sometimes I pretended Nancy was my mother because I liked her soft curly blonde hair, her small bones, and the way, when she talked, she whistled a little on her *s*'s. Mostly, I liked her gentleness; she never wanted to hurt anyone's feelings.

At Nancy's house, I met a Janet I hadn't known before. She traded her gumboots for platform sandals, her old jeans for fashionable, flared ones with seams down the front. She brushed on a little mascara, and she and Nancy went out at night to bars, to the Ike and Tina Turner concert, to see the Reggae movie *The Harder They Come*. Sometimes they stumbled home, drunk and laughing. The next day she'd tell me Nancy was carded again.

"Because of my complexion," Nancy would complain.

"No, you're beautiful. You just look so young!" And they'd laugh at some secret, shared memory. Janet's stories now happened where I couldn't see them.

Nancy

Nancy had a stereo, so Janet rediscovered the rhythm and blues musicians she'd loved in high school—Etta James, Aretha Franklin, Otis Redding, Marvin Gaye, and James Brown—and she turned up the music full blast. It pulsed in my head, rattled the house, and tired me out. Janet and Nancy danced around the living room in their tight, bell-bottomed pants and tight, scoop-necked T-shirts. Janet grabbed me and twirled.

"Dance," she ordered. "Dance." She twisted her hips, lower, then higher. I didn't want to; I still felt too stiff. Rima jumped up and down and reached for Janet's hands. "Come on, dance." Janet looked over her shoulder at me, shot her hip out, and snapped her fingers. I tried a little bum wiggle. "Thatta girl."

"Listen, now listen to this . . . " She crooned along to Otis Redding: "Sitting' on the Dock of the Bay." Then she screamed James Brown's "I Feel Good!" Rima put up her arms, hoping to be held, but Janet didn't notice.

"So much *soul*. Now. Listen to *Aretha*." She pretended to hold a microphone as she sang in my face: "R-E-S-P-E-C-T, find out what it means to me, R-E-S-P-E-C-T!" I could see the fillings in her back teeth. The new Janet was so loud and energetic, but I didn't know how to get inside her enthusiasm with her: it was too sudden and new. She and Nancy played the same albums over and over until I had all songs memorized—whether I'd wanted to or not.

Nancy had a friend, a hip black man who owned a record store, and she and Janet started visiting him about once a week. He introduced them to soul greats: Al Green, Bobby Bland, and Donny Hathaway. At home with her invisible microphone, Janet sang along with Bill Withers, "Keep on using' me, till you use me up." Then they moved on to more cutting-edge, funk-fused soul: the Meters, Herbie Hancock, Rufus with Chaka Khan, and the Average White Band.

I crawled into the images on Janet's album covers as I used to crawl into the pages of my picture books: the great yellow pincher bug robot who played the keyboards on Hancock's *Headhunters* Album. Steve Wonder sitting on the sand in long braids and an African tunic. The cursive initials AWB, for Average White Band, the W rounded so it became a woman's bum. My last name started with a W, so I had a bum in my name too.

Of all Janet's music, Rima and I liked Steve Wonder best, and we memorized the lyrics from the *Inner Vision* and *Talking Book* albums. He told me the truth: cities are hard if you're black and poor, the innocent suffer. He encouraged me, "Keep on movin' until you reached the higher ground." He soothed me, "Don't you worry 'bout a thing." And he had the voice of the perfect father, the one who understood you, the one who forgave you, the one who promised, "You are the sunshine of my life; that's why I'll always be around."

Sometimes Nancy and Janet turned down the music, sat on Nancy's couch with their feet curled under them, drank coffee, and talked. They complained about their mothers and ex-husbands. I stayed near and tried to listen—and not to listen. More words than I had ever heard from Janet, about a Jack I hadn't known.

"He *thinks* he's so smart, but remember when we moved from the apartment in Boulder? He filled a *refrigerator* box with books—and then tried to carry it down the stairs." Janet laughed, a bitter cough.

I dumped out a barrel of plastic monkeys and then hung them in a chain by their arms. Alternating yellow and red.

"All those cars he couldn't fix. And his *clothes.*"

Yellow monkey. Red monkey. Nancy had monkeys on her wall, too: monkey-shaped clay beads on a macramé wall hanging.

"He has *no* social skills. I was embarrassed to be married to him."

I stood in front of Nancy's *Yellow Submarine* print and memorized the details.

"I never loved him . . . I only married him to get away from my family." She sucked on her cigarette and blew the smoke out of the side of her mouth.

I whispered the Beatles' song to myself: "We all live in a yellow submarine, a yellow submarine, a yellow submarine."

"The abortion was worth it. I wouldn't have been able to leave him." Nancy, her daughter Geneva, Janet, Rima, and I should all live in a yellow submarine. I didn't know where Jack should live. To miss him would be to betray Janet, so I tucked his memory away and tried not to think of him.

Radio Music

My favorite Song
Bad, Bad, Leroy Brown

Song I memorized
Delta Dawn

Songs I Liked and Memorized Most of
Ain't Too Proud to Beg
Band on the Run
Cat's in the Cradle
I Shot the Sheriff
It's Only Rock and Roll (and I Like It)
Jesus is just Alright
Midnight Train to Georgia
The Night That the Lights Went Out in Georgia
Ramblin' Man
Rocky Mountain High
Some Kind of Wonderful
Sweet Home Alabama
We're an American Band
Your Mama Don't Dance

Songs I Didn't Like, but which Stuck in My Head
Ain't No Woman Like the One I've Got
Could It Be I'm Falling in Love
I'll Have to Say I Love You in a Song
Killing Me Softly with His Song
When Will I See You Again

WHAT I WANTED: SOLITUDE

Nancy helped Janet get government assistance and job training. After her divorce, Nancy had trained as a welder; Janet chose secretarial school. First, Janet brought home a set of our own silverware, paid for by the government. Then her program gave her professional clothes for interviews. She was placed in a job, and soon we rented our own clean, pretty house: two stories, a front porch, and hardwood floors.

By ourselves, Rima and I would walk several blocks to the Chinese grocer's. We passed houses with slanted green lawns, concrete steps, and overgrown flowers. Most of the exteriors were sprayed in a gravel stucco mixed with quartz crystal or bits of shells. The gutter next to the sidewalk disgusted me, but I looked anyway: twigs, cigarette butts, envelope corners, a faded candy wrapper.

The grocer's was small with crowded, musty shelves and high ceilings—and in a perpetual twilight. Cigarettes. Ice cream sandwiches. Stacks of cans and boxes with red labels. For twenty-five cents apiece, we each bought a Wagon Wheel: a layer of marshmallow squeezed between two graham cracker circles and coated with chocolate. We ate them on the way home, shedding a trail of chocolate flakes. Always, the next day, unaccustomed to walking on sidewalks, the bottoms of our feet, even our bones, felt bruised.

In our new house, we each had our own bedroom. Rima wasn't sure she liked the idea, but I wanted my room with the slanted ceiling all to myself. I needed a retreat from the noise, not just the sirens and car horns, but the distant sounds that blended into an ever-present, pulsing background hum. Car engines. Car doors closing. Front doors. Closet doors. Light switches. A hammer. A drill. A telephone. Water piped through walls, under houses, in lines under the streets. Radios. Stereos. TVs. Lawn mowers. Pruning shears. Laughing. Yelling. Singing. Stomping. Yawning. Electric wires. Chopping, boiling, frying. Timer dings. Flushing toilets. Creaky mattress springs. So many heartbeats.

Maybe I also needed a retreat from Rima and Janet. Early evening, Janet would call me into her room. I sat on her bed. She had new books on her shelf: *The Bell Jar, The Golden Notebook, Fear of Flying, Rubyfruit Jungle, Gestalt Therapy.* Stories by Alice Munro and Margaret Atwood. Sometimes she told me a funny story about someone at work. Other times she cried and told me how frightened she was to be alone—proud, too, but scared. And she was worried about money. And so angry at Jack.

Rima wanted me to play with her more, the games we used to play, but, for reasons neither of us understood, they no longer interested me. Instead, I lay on my bed—stomach, back, side, stomach—and read books. My favorite was *Sunflowers for Tina*, about a young black girl who wanted a garden and couldn't have one because she lived in the city. She tried to plant the carrots from the fridge in the dirt behind her house and got in trouble.

"You're always *reading.*" Rima stomped out of the house. I couldn't seem to muster the energy, or generosity, to do anything else. Later, I sat with her on the couch with her favorite picture book, *The Snowy Day*, and made up the dialogue between the characters for her.

I opened my window. Often it rained and the air smelled different than the air on Texada, the same wet-green but mixed with car exhaust and the dusty scent of wet concrete. I closed the window to muffle the city noise. My room was simple and bare: white walls, a single bed, a dresser from a second hand store, and a bookshelf. I arranged all my books in descending size order; those that were the same height I organized by numerical publishing code.

Books were full of conflict, but all neatly contained in words, in paragraphs, in pages, in stories that had a beginning, a middle, and an end—and all on my shelf confined within covers so their chaos couldn't spill out and disturb the books next to them. Anytime I wanted, I could open to a wild world; then, when I was ready, stuff all its tendrils of feeling back inside, slam it closed, and tuck it on the shelf. When Rima borrowed a book without asking and put it back in the wrong place, I yelled at her. She screamed back:

"I put it where I thought you wanted it! . . . And why are you so *mean* now?"

I decided I'd make my bed every day, as other children were supposed to. "Why bother?" Janet asked. "You'll just mess it up again."

I tried to pull my sheets perfectly smooth, but as soon as I'd erased one wrinkle, my elbow or knee creased another. Exasperated, I threw myself on my bed, punched it, pounded it.

The house also had a family room Janet gave to us as a playroom. She bought an old couch that could be pulled into sections. I suggested Rima and I each take an end and turn it into a corner, making nests. I cut out pictures of Inuit art from a calendar and pasted them in my corner. Then I told Rima she couldn't come in my nest unless she asked. "Why do you have to have your own nest? You have your own room!" But, at night in bed, I dreamed of even more solitude: a house split in two, with Janet and Rima on one side and me on the other, Janet helping me only with what I couldn't do myself.

Janet got a call from Rima's cooperative preschool. During playground time, Rima had been caught in the cement pipe play structure, kissing a boy. Janet didn't know whether to laugh or be concerned, so she asked my advice. I didn't know how to answer. Listening to Janet and Nancy talk, men were frightening. I couldn't imagine being close enough to kiss one. But a silent, uneasy instinct told me Rima was healthier than I: she erred on the side of open arms.

Tina took the carrots and a dirty spoon from the sink and went outside. She knelt down on the cracked concrete in front of the little square of earth by the fence, not even noticing that she scraped her knee. The ground was dry and hard. Tina dug at it with the spoon, but she couldn't make much of a hole. The handle of the spoon bent, and she hurt her hand trying to straighten it out ... At last Tina had planted four carrots in a neat row in front of the fence. The green feathery tops stuck up cheerfully in the sun. She watered them with great and affectionate care ...

Tina's mother stood squarely in the doorway, her hands on her hips. She stared at Tina.

"What on earth ...?"

"I planted it myself," said Tina proudly.

"You didn't—!"

"Carrots," explained Tina. "They should grow." But her voice sounded uncertain by the end of the sentence.

"Oh no," said Tina's mother with a look of dismay. "Not our supper. You just dig those right up again."

Anne Norris Baldwin
Sunflowers for Tina, 1970

WHAT I NEEDED: THICKER SKIN

Several times, Janet showed me how I would walk home from school. The streets in Vancouver confused me. I couldn't make a map in my mind of the overlapping curves and squares. Cars, without warning, sped up, stopped, turned. Walk signs flashed. Stoplights blinked their yellow-red-green, yellow-red-green. Buses with long antennae on the back attached to overhead wires careened around corners, the wires sparked, the antennae fell down. The bus drivers opened their doors and ran to the back to reattach them.

I would be home before Janet, so she threaded a house key on a string and tied it around my neck. She dropped it inside my shirt; for a moment, it was ice against my chest. Did any other children at my school live only with their mothers? Would any of them have a key-on-a-string? If we all hid our keys under our shirts, they wouldn't be secrets—like all those people on our streets who left keys under their front mats for Rima and me to find.

Lord Nelson Elementary filled an entire city block—bigger than any building on Texada—and was surrounded by asphalt. Janet walked me into the front office. My hands and feet were numb, my tongue tingled. Even my thoughts were sluggish. Janet leaned over a tall counter to fill out paperwork. I stood next to her, focusing on the scratch of her pen. She pushed the papers toward the woman behind the counter and handed me a paper bag. "Your lunch, honey . . . I'm going to be late for work." She squeezed my shoulder.

The office lady walked me to my classroom. The clip of her shoes echoed through a maze of hallways.

"Your grade one teacher is Miss Pinrose," the lady told me, as she opened the door to a room thick with the smell of laundry detergent, pencil shavings, and damp breath.

Miss Pinrose was like her name, an old rose pinned to a hat, formal and faded. She assigned me a friend for the day, Margo, who was shorter than me, with black curls. She strode toward the door, happy to have been chosen—until she saw me. She looked me up and down, then sucked back into herself.

The students were almost all Italian, with dark hair and dark eyes and pretty skin. They attended one of two Catholic churches, and they could recite the morning prayers read over the loudspeaker. "You say prayers in public school?" Janet asked. Jack wouldn't want me to say prayers, so I tried not to learn them.

The Italian boys moved smoothly. Under their button-down shirts, they wore white T-shirts. I didn't know how they kept their shirts so white, so neat and soft looking. I asked Janet why they wore them. She said to keep their top shirts clean, which she said was a silly idea. A tall boy named Joseph sat in the back of the room drawing perfect people and houses and cars. I admired him, but I was disappointed too. In Vananda, I'd been the best artist in grade one.

Generally, the girls were shorter than me and more compact. The smallest girl in the class, Gina, wore her hair in a whale spout, spraying up on top of her head and filled with plastic barrettes and bobbles. "Why does she do that?" I later asked someone.

"I don't know. I guess her mother likes it."

I tried to decide if I wanted brightly colored plastic objects floating on the top of my head. Janet would never force me to wear my hair a certain way, but she didn't have time to fix my hair anyway.

All the girls had pierced ears. Later, when the girls told me they'd had their ears pierced since they were babies, I wanted mine pierced too. When I asked Janet, she told me when she was a teenager, Wuh-Wa wouldn't let her pierce her ears because "only *common* girls pierce their ears." I didn't know what *common* meant, but it seemed to have something to do with being poor and sexy. Wuh-Wa, Janet said, wore elaborate, jeweled, and painful clip-on earrings, which was hypocritical—as well as dumb. Janet wore long, dangly earrings from India.

Janet finally took Rima and me to a doctor of Eastern medicine, and he pierced our ears with strange, long studs we were supposed to wear for months and which flopped about and made the other children ask questions. He pierced my holes too close to the edge of my ears, and one earring ripped out. Rima's got painfully infected. Janet removed our studs and let our ears heal over.

That first day, when I went to get my lunch in the coat room, that cave out of the view of the teacher, I opened my paper bag and unwrapped my sandwich: tuna fish with apples and walnuts on whole wheat.

"Eewwooooo, what's that smell?" complained several students with metal lunch boxes.

I stuffed my sandwich back in my bag. The other children chewed on white bread sandwiches with baloney and mayonnaise or peanut butter and purple jelly. They unwrapped yellow Twinkies from their cellophane. I stuck my hand in my bag to get my oatmeal cookies. Someone had stolen them.

As the children ran out to recess, Miss Pinrose called after them, "Margo, don't forget our new student." I followed her to the playground, where the boys and girls were segregated to different areas. The gray-white light filtered through high clouds. Scraggly trees lined the sidewalk on the other side of a chain link fence. The asphalt was painted with yellow lines for hopscotch and four square, games I'd never played.

Two girls turned two jump ropes "double dutch." I lined up behind Margo and four other girls.

Cinderella dressed in yellow,
Went upstairs to kiss a fellow,
Made a mistake,
Kissed a snake,
How many doctors did it take?
One, two, three . . .

I didn't want to play, but I didn't know how to get out of it. When it was my turn, the bottom rope tangled my ankle while the top whapped my head.

"We're going to play hide-and-seek. You *do* know how to play hide-and-seek?" Margo asked. I thought I did, but once we began, I realized we were playing a more complicated version with counting and running and home and safe and out and it. By the end of the first game I was it.

"You're it, you're it," Margo screamed at me.

"What do I do?"

"Close your eyes and count to a hundred. No, put your head down like this and cover your face."

"One, two, three, four . . . "

"Count faster . . ."

"Five, six, seven, eight . . ."

The school bell rang—like a tugboat horn, only louder—vibrating the insides of my head. I opened my eyes just in time to see all the children streaming through double doors. I followed into the hall, but all the children had been sucked into their rooms with the doors closed behind them. I walked, trying to find a familiar landmark, worried Miss Pinrose would be angry, worried all the children would stare when I opened the door. Finally, I walked by the same office where Janet had filled out paper work, and the lady came out, irritated.

"Why aren't you in your class?"

I started to cry. She patted my back and led me to my room. She opened the door. All the students, who had been cutting with scissors, looked up from their desks. So many children. Rows and rows of them, bits of white paper scattered all around their desks. Miss Pinrose looked surprised—she hadn't noticed I was gone. I wiped my tears. I wanted those children to stop looking at me.

"Margo," Miss Pinrose said as soon as the door closed, "I thought I told you to stay with her."

"I *thought* she was following me." Margo glared.

The grade one girls were too complicated for me. Later, I heard Margo and her friends making fun of another girl, Cindy, who had a round, simple face and a wide bum. "Cindy doesn't wear underwear," they whispered to each other. When they included me, they used a grown-up tone of confidence and condemnation: "Cindy doesn't wear underwear." I found Cindy sitting on the steps outside the girls' bathroom, her head in her hands, crying. I sat down next to her.

"Sometimes I don't wear underwear," I said.

She looked at me, incredulous: "Why?"

I didn't answer and we sat, silent and confused together.

The afternoon of that first day, I began my walk home, following what I had thought were Janet's directions. I was relieved to be alone, outside, looking at the bright moss in the sidewalk cracks, the hydrangea bushes covered in great snowballs of icy blues and stained pink. I passed the tree I loved, the one with branches like long, swinging monkey tails. I was almost home.

But then I didn't recognize any houses—or parked cars, or toppled children's bikes, or the shape of any bushes. I couldn't move without making myself more lost. I was a deer on Texada, frozen in the headlights: thoughts squeezed flat, my heart racing. I sat on a lawn.

After about half an hour, the woman of the house saw me through her window. Although I didn't know my address, Janet's phone number, or even my street name—only that my porch had wavy yellow plastic siding—she found my house, several blocks away and stood with me as I unlocked the door. "Are you sure you don't want me to stay until your mother gets home?" I was grateful, but wanted to be alone.

I sat on the floor next to Janet's stereo speakers and cried as I listened, over and over, to Dolly Parton's "Coat of Many Colors."

When Janet got home, she set her bag of groceries on the counter. Rima—dirt smudges around her mouth and a couple of crumpled drawings in her hand—trailed behind her.

"Finally, something to eat besides rice and beans . . ." Janet kicked off her heels and leaned over to massage her feet. "We need a car. The bus is okay. But groceries and laundry are hard . . ."

She grabbed the milk and opened the fridge door. "How was your day?" Her voice echoed inside.

When I didn't answer, she closed the door and looked at me. Her eyes were puffy, her beige skirt wrinkled.

"Fine."

She opened the kitchen cabinets, which she had painted yellow, and started stacking cans inside.

"You like your class?"

How could I burden her, who had so many worries of her own? I put my hand around the key on the string. It was the same temperature as my body.

"Mmm-Hmmm."

I had to get tougher where my skin touched the world.

My coat of many colors
That my momma made for me
Made only from rags
But I wore it so proudly
Although we had no money
I was rich as I could be
In my coat of many colors
My Momma made for me.

So with patches on my britches
Holes in both my shoes
In my coat of many colors I hurried off to school
Just to find the others laughing
And making fun of me
In my coat of many colors
My Momma made for me.

    Coat of Many Colors
    Dolly Parton, 1969

WHAT I WANTED: god

Supposedly, I'd met Nancy's daughter shortly after she was born—when we all lived on Sugarloaf Mountain—so even though we didn't remember each other, because we had "known each other since we were babies," we were automatic-without-question best friends.

Everything about Geneva fascinated me: her pale olive skin, wide nose, almond colored eyes and blonde afro. Her father was a black intellectual, who moved in and out of university jobs, wrote difficult poetry and occasionally landed in jail. When Geneva was three, they had traveled to France so her father could meet the black expatriates. At that time, Geneva wanted to be a dog. She put her tights on her head, as ears, and demanded Nancy tie a leash around her neck and let her walk on all fours. They strolled the streets of Paris as the French stared at them, in contempt both for their child abuse and lack of style.

Even though I was taller and two months older than Geneva, she was bossy and confident and knew the complicated ways of the city. She had endured a separation from two fathers—her own and then Jim Green—and only seemed the more worldly for it. She took dance lessons and Chinese lessons and rode the public bus by herself. Her long, narrow bedroom smelled like nail polish: bottles lined her white vanity; spilled polish dried in pools on the hardwood floor. The paint on her nails chipped off, leaving only red cuticles. She had a teenage foster sister who lived upstairs who had a boyfriend—Geneva caught them with their hands inside each other's jeans—and posters of Bruce Lee all over her room. Once, Geneva had seen Jim Green sucking on his girl-friend's nipples: I asked her why, but she wasn't sure about that part.

We both wanted long hair, so we draped beach towels over our heads and pretended we were princesses. Sometimes we let Rima play. Geneva always chose her hair color first, pink, and was head princess. I wore the faded, navy blue towel, and Rima was left with the short green one with frayed ends. When Nancy told Geneva to clean her room, Geneva, in turn, ordered me to do it—which I did.

"You don't have to clean Geneva's room for her," Janet said on the way home. I knew she was worried about the strength of my character.

"I don't mind." I wanted to be near her. Besides, Geneva bit people when she was mad.

Once, when Geneva wouldn't stop jumping on the couch and throwing puzzle pieces, Nancy grabbed her. Geneva chomped her forearm. Several times Nancy had received a call from Geneva's daycare that she had again bitten a student or teacher. Nancy and Janet worried over it in hushed tones.

But I wasn't afraid; I just wanted to be in the presence of this force of nature who knew how to use her teeth to get what she wanted, who knew how to make all the adults just a little bit afraid.

Rima, who wanted to impress Geneva, told her she could speak Chinese.

"No you can't."

"Yes I can."

"Talk then."

"Gubbity, gubbity, gubbity."

Geneva laughed and I laughed and Rima ran crying to Janet who laughed, even as she tried to comfort her.

Mostly, Rima felt left out, but when Geneva tried to teach us how to be sexy—shimmy our shoulders, swing our hips, toss our towel hair, and throw a pouty glance over our shoulder—Rima got it right away. I flirted like a robot. Geneva and Rima showed me again, united, this time, against me. "Just shake your shoulders ... like this. Put one foot right in front of the other and swing your hips." They both cat walked across the floor and, at the end, added a fancy turn.

Nancy took Geneva and me to see my first movie, *The Life and Times of Grizzly Adams*. I sat in the squishy red seat next to Geneva, my fingers greasy with popcorn butter, and watched Grizzly Adams with his friendly beard. The theater disappeared and I was in the woods, in the trees. At the end of the movie, a pretty young woman returned from the wilderness to the city. The credits rolled; the trees receded. Outside the theater, sirens moaned.

"Tarn? Are you crying?" Nancy turned me around to look at my face. "What's wrong?"

"That lady." I had an aching ball of sadness in my throat.

"What lady?"

"She went to the city."

"In the movie? The daughter? . . But Tarn, she wanted to go back. She's happy."

"But I don't want her to go," I sobbed.

Geneva grabbed the fringe on the bottom of Nancy's leather coat and they both watched me. I had no words to share . . . only private images: fox gloves, stinging nettles, fuzzy cedar bark, bare-skinned arbutus, the fiddlehead tips of new sword ferns, my own twisted cherry tree covered in lichen, cool air which slipped into my house at night. And Jack, all alone now, with no one to read his stories to.

But when I spent the night at Geneva's, together in her single bed, I did tell her some of my secrets. The forced air heating in her room still felt new to me, so dry and warm. Only one blanket covered us. How could I sleep with so little weight pressing me? Outside, cars rolled past, louder, softer, a rhythm like the breaking of ocean waves. The streetlights through the curtains illumined, in shades of blue-gray, the smooth outline of Geneva's cheek. She smelled like a mix of fruit candy and a warm, clean dog.

"I don't like the words penis and vagina," I whispered.

"Me either," she whispered back.

I knew Jack and Janet believed they should teach us the proper, scientific words for genitals, not the absurd-baby-words of their childhoods. But "penis and vagina" were not short and friendly ordinary words such as "arm" and "leg" and "nose." They were not funny words such as "elbow," "knuckle," or "belly button." They were formal and foreign. Even grown-ups said them strangely—monotone and with a straight face, while underneath, a dozen other, unreadable faces flashed and disappeared.

"I don't like the words shit and pee," I added. The words were harsh and smelly, like unattended outhouses. They made my mouth sticky. "Don't give me any of that shit," Janet said sometimes when she was mad. "I'm not going to take any of his shit," she said about Jack. The word intensified her anger.

"Me either."

But we didn't know the words other children, other families, used instead.

"We could call pee 'apple juice,'" I suggested. Geneva agreed. We couldn't think of a word for shit and finally settled, tentatively, on "hamburger."

The next day, I practiced our words with Geneva: "I have to go apple juice. But I don't have to go hamburger."

"Me too."

I wouldn't say the words in front of Janet though, first, because she might think I was criticizing her and, second, because she might laugh. She and Nancy laughed all the time. Also, in the clarity of the day, it seemed unsavory to mix the names of food and excrement. Within a day and a half, "apple juice" and "hamburger" evaporated. I returned to saying pee, but never again did I use the "s" word—too much anger in it.

Another night, as Geneva was almost asleep, I whispered, "Let's believe in God."

Jack didn't want me to believe in God. God was just a thinner version of Santa Claus, wearing white robes and sitting on a cloud. God had to be just a story, for how could He hear everyone's thoughts at once? The telephone lines of his brain would get crossed. My reasoning made me feel superior to the Italian Catholic children in my class, but I was jealous of them, too. I wanted a God who could see into my inner parts and sit gently with my secrets—a Love who couldn't forget me, even for a second.

"Okay," Geneva said.

Then, in the few moments before sleep, the room was filled with what seemed both a structure and a presence: a form thicker than the walls. Heavy, peaceful, alive. It filled every space, rested on us, a just-the-right-weight blanket.

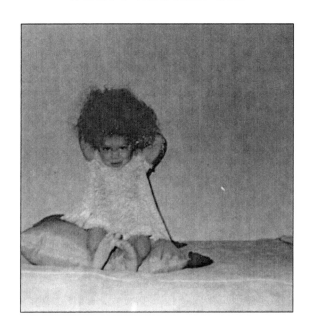

Geneva and Tarn, Boulder, Colorado, 1968

RETURNING TO TEXADA

SUMMER 1974

WHAT I LONGED
FOR AND FEARED:
SEEING JACK AGAIN

By the time Jack pulled up in front of the house, I was so nervous I thought I might throw up. So strange to have him on our doorstep, his body out of place in a house full of women. Tall and angular. His hair was longer, flipping just above his shoulders.

He and Janet stood back from each other: low voices, formal greetings, averted eyes. Janet hugged us and then Jack threw our military duffle bags—jammed mostly with stuffed animals—over his shoulder and into the back of his car. From the front porch, Janet waved goodbye-for-the-summer. Rima wanted the front seat; I let her have it. I would get used to Jack again from a distance. On the drive to the Horseshoe Bay Ferry, Rima and I alternated between self-conscious silences and talking too fast, trying to tell Jack everything that had happened in the last six months. My mind raced and froze, raced and froze.

But standing at the rail on the deck of the ferry, a little space and wind and silence between us, my nervousness stilled. I breathed deeply. The jangled buzz of the mainland receded. I warmed my hands on the hot chocolate Jack had bought us. The wind blew patterns on the chocolate foam. I stirred it with my finger, then put my finger in my mouth and tasted the ferry soot. Islands drifted by like pods of familiar whales. Lord Nelson Elementary School was last night's dream. Even Nancy and Geneva, although more alive, seemed like characters in a book. Janet, I couldn't think about Janet. I didn't so much miss her as feel as if one of my essential organs were missing.

Jack folded his newspaper over and started the crossword puzzle. I thought I was happy to see him again, to smell him, but the newness had already begun to crack, to give way to a familiar emptiness I'd thought was his absence. The wind flapped the bottom of my jeans, puffed out the sleeves of my jacket. I felt a sudden urge to jump from the ferry: to be suspended for a moment, midair, and then drop—disappear into impersonal blackness. So I talked to myself in an extra firm, logical voice: The water will be cold. Someone will notice. The captain will turn the boat around and throw you a life ring. Everyone will be worried. Late. Angry.

"Can we buy comics?" Rima asked. Jack handed her the coins from his pocket. I chased after her.

"Don't buy *Archie*," Jack called. "Get *Uncle Scrooge*."

He liked to read our comics and didn't approve of our city-girl attraction to teenage fashion and romance. So we secretly skimmed a few stories about Archie, Betty, and Veronica and then bought the comics about Donald Duck's rich uncle. Back on deck, I stayed away from the ferry rail and dived, instead, into the comic book frames.

We, therefore, God-loving, peace-loving, life-loving, fun-loving men and women, appealing to the Supreme Judge of the Universe for the rectitude of our intentions, do, in the name and by the Authority of all sentient beings who seek gently to evolve on this planet, solemnly publish and declare that we are free and independent, and that we are absolved from all Allegiance to the United States Government and all governments controlled by the menopausal, and that grouping ourselves into tribes of like-minded fellows, we claim full power to live and move on the land, obtain sustenance with our own hand and mind in the style which seems sacred and holy to us, and to do all Acts and Things which independent Freemen and Freewomen may of right do without infringing on the same rights of other species and groups to do their own thing.

The Declaration of Evolution
Timothy Leary, 1968

WHAT I FEARED: THE POLICE

I thought the Slow Farm might ease what was unsettled in me. But the Slow Farm, when we arrived, was different. All the animals were gone, except the tortoise-calico descendants of Lynn and Len's cat, who streaked past us into the bush. The chickens had been rounded up and caged in the chicken house, although some still escaped to make secret nests in the grass. The plywood stove and steam shovel, which Jack had made for us for Christmas, had been left outside and disintegrated in the weather.

The Slow Farm didn't belong to just us anymore, but to the many people who wandered through to spend an afternoon or week or month. Skinny men with beards and long hair. One carved spoons out of the burls of cedar trees. Another made tables by slicing interesting shapes from cedar stumps, polishing, shellacking, and attaching branches for legs. One man hunted. He hung a doe from the side of the house and sliced her stomach open. He left her warm heart in the kitchen sink.

The women, who stayed for shorter periods of time, were beautiful. Long thick straight blond hair. Thick, black, curly hair. Milky complexions. Indian skirts. Filmy shirts that showed their shapes. Black hair growing on their legs. Three were from

San Francisco. One played the banjo. One played the guitar and sang folk and old jazz tunes. One sewed little bags made out of satin and velvet and ribbons. One made beaded earrings. Younger than Janet, they had no children. They were like older sisters. Sexy. Kind. Sometimes they lavished us with attention, making us macramé necklaces, inviting to us sew with them, giving us postcards with fairies on them; sometimes they forgot us, interested, as they were, in the shifting attractions between grown-ups. They disappeared, in changing pairs, through the door—which had been cut out of the wall in the room where Rima and I slept—into the windowless, tarpaper room, large enough only for one bed. Through the Indian fabric, hung in the doorframe, floated damp smells and animal sounds.

Rima and I loved best a man named Richard, who was shy with other grown-ups, perhaps even a little neglected by them. We climbed on his lap and up on his shoulders. He was patient with us in the way Jack used to be. He didn't talk often, but laughed when we gathered his hair into a ponytail above his forehead and hung little toys on it, which dangled in front of his eyes. When he didn't have money to buy us a gift, he made us a box out of cedar shakes, with two compartments, one for each of us. In each side was a rubber ball he'd made himself out of old rubber cement.

When I needed to be alone, I sat in my twisted-trunk cherry tree, eating cherries, tossing the pits on the roof, and writing in a small spiral notebook cherry recipes which I'd invented but not tested: cherries pressed between two crackers, cherries brewed like tea, cherries roasted on a stick like a marshmallow. There was relief in the scratch of my pencil across the page, ideas ordered in a small book with clean borders.

When I looked down, I could see the marijuana plants growing behind the house, thick as bushes. The grown-ups dried the leaves on hand-built racks in the attic. It was an accomplishment to dry anything in British Columbia, where fruit and clothing and bread slices decayed into black soil.

Around the house, packs of papers for rolling joints were scattered everywhere, on windowsills and small tables. Rima and I asked to eat marijuana brownies because they were baked with real sugar and chocolate. Desserts on the Slow Farm usually consisted of halva and sesame snaps and the occasional bite of carob, which the women exclaimed tasted just as good as chocolate, but didn't. Jack said we could. They were overcooked, crusty at the edges, and we felt no effects other than the strange aftertaste of flavor like potent parsley.

The RCMP rolled up to the house in a clean car—long, flat, and humming.

Jack worked in front of the barn, removing a car engine with a pulley. Near him, Rima and I had been playing school. I was the teacher. I'd asked for Jack's old distributor cap, washed it, turned it upside down, and stuck pencils into the holes. Then I dictated spelling words and addition problems. Rima squatted on the gravel and wrote the answers on Jack's yellow legal pad. I corrected her mistakes and drew stars on the top of her paper.

"The cops!" somebody yelled.

The grown-ups tried too hard to act normal, to keep working, polishing a table, hammering on the side of the house.

When the cop car door opened, it released a heavy silence. Two officers and a dog stepped out. The officers' hair, the color of mice, was cropped even as a mowed lawn—not like the Slow Farm men whose long hair soaked up smells of sweat, wood smoke, and stir fry.

I saw the Slow Farm through police eyes: the tall weeds on the side of the road, several cars without engines in front of the barn, two children with dirty feet and scabbed legs. They could probably tell we'd eaten marijuana brownies.

I liked the officers' tidiness, the clean lines of their uniforms. At school, I'd learned the police help kittens and children and old people. But then I remembered the ranger in the brown uniform who shot Blue.

The police dog was a German Shepherd with black around his mouth and eyes. I wanted to pet him, but he put his nose to the ground and started running back and forth on the length of his lead, as thoroughly and systematically as Janet with her carpet sweeper.

Jack walked toward them, wiping the grease from his hands on his jeans. "Can I help you?"

"We got a report of drugs on this property. We have to follow up. You understand."

"Sure, go ahead," Jack's voice was natural, but I felt a stiffness travel up his spine.

"We need to search the house."

"Go ahead," Jack said.

As the police strode toward the door, Rima and I tried to grab Jack's hands. He pulled them away.

"Why are they here? Why do they have the dog? What's the dog doing?"

"He's sniffing for drugs." Jack looked straight ahead. "If they ask you any questions, just say you don't know."

I felt as if black ants were biting the backs of my legs. If those officers asked me any questions, the truth might burst right out of me without my permission. The grown-ups would all go to jail and it would be my fault. My throat jammed below my Adam's apple.

"What if they ask my name?" I whispered.

"You know what I mean."

Inside the Slow Farm, the attic door was partially open, but the officers didn't look up and the dog kept his nose to the ground. The officers came out holding one small baggy of marijuana—the one sitting in the handmade pottery bowl next to the chair in the living room—not even enough for a full joint. They didn't find the plants that grew like bushes behind the house.

Afterward, the grown-ups laughed, called the officers "pigs" in loud voices. "It wasn't about the dope," they said. "They just wanted to hassle us."

I learned the incredible fact that there is no police force in the community. The RCMP apparently come over about every second weekend. It was hard for me to conceive of a North American community in the 1970s without a force for law and order to prevent it from falling into a state of anarchy.

A tourist reporting in the *Powell River News* about his recent visit to Texada Island, 1971.

THE PROMISE I MADE

Jack leaned over my sleeping bag and touched my shoulder. "I'm going to town to get the truck, Tarn. No one else is here today, but I'll be back this afternoon."

Jack, who prided himself on his mechanical ability, had only reluctantly surrendered his truck to Cecil May's Garage. Now he had to walk the six miles to Vananda to pick it up.

"Wait," I said, suddenly awake. "I'll go with you." I was afraid to be left alone. Rima and I often played by ourselves, but we always knew where to find a grown-up if we wanted one.

"It's too far," he whispered. His breath was warm and smelled of coffee tinged with sadness.

I opened my sleeping bag, shimmied down the bunk bed, and grabbed my shorts and shirt from the damp pile next to my bed.

"I need you to stay with Rima."

Rima opened her eyes. "I'm coming."

"It's too far. I can't carry you."

Rima crawled naked out of her sleeping bag. Her white hair tangled on the back of her head.

"I'm strong. I'll carry Rima."

I wasn't afraid of accidents or strangers or wild animals, but without the sound of Jack's tools banging, the silence that would settle over the Slow Farm might crush us.

We followed Jack out the front door, followed his olive-green velour shirt and dark yellow smell of cigarettes and sweat. He walked toward the gravel road. I knew he was trying a trick—acting as if we were obeying him in hopes we would. When I stepped on his heels, he turned around.

"I said," and he paused, gathering his anger, "stay here." Then he lowered his voice an octave, "I mean it, girls. I'm not going to say it again."

Rima and I squatted under the Slow Farm sign and watched him walk away. From the back, his blond hair looked greasy and curled in odd ways. He seemed unusually thin as I watched him cross the Three Billy Goats Gruff Bridge, hands in the pockets of his jeans.

First a silence and then a humming filled the place where Jack had been—buzzing insects and the burbling creek and the almost audible sound of plants growing and sap surging through the pines. The edges around the Slow Farm seemed suddenly to spread high and wide, with no clear boundary.

We sat down in the dirt and threw bits of gravel across the road to the old horse pasture. I thought of the fathers in the books at school and the fathers of the town children. Those fathers would never leave a six and four-year-old alone. Janet had never left us alone.

Then I had an idea, an idea which made me feel brave and which lifted, for a moment, the constant, soupy uncertainty I'd been feeling all summer. I looked at Rima: her eyes were shiny-mischievous. She'd had the same idea.

Rima didn't want my help dressing but did let me buckle her sandals. We skipped past the bridge, past the pastel-tree rock, farther than we had ever been on foot, past the marsh of cattails filled with squeaky-gate red-winged blackbirds, past clumps of dusty bracken ferns and blackberry bushes and fox-gloves and thistles, past little hidden springs surrounded by rubbery skunk cabbage.

When we began to tire, we sang lines from songs Jack had taught us. "I've been working on the railroad, all the live-long day." "Oh Susanna, oh don't you cry for me." "Froggy went a courtin' and he did ride, uh-huh." "Grasshopper sitting on the railroad track, pickin' his teeth with a carpet tack."

We slowed. With Jack out of sight for so long, I forgot my indignation. We were hungry. When Rima felt she couldn't walk any longer, I hoisted her on my hip as Janet did. She slid down. I carried her on my back, as Jack did, but the walking was slow and she couldn't clasp her arms and legs tightly enough.

We recognized a particular roll of blackberry bushes, whitened from lime dust, and knew we were close to town. But there was a turn we needed to make, and I wasn't sure I'd recognize it. I didn't know exactly how to get to Cecil May's Garage, and what if Jack had already left and we'd missed him? How would he find us?

We crawled into the ditch on the side of the road to avoid cars, keep out of the wind, and watch for him. Lime-covered grasses curved over our heads. I picked some blackberries for Rima, but they were hard. We told each other Jack would be proud of us for walking so far. A chill descended. For hours, we wrapped our arms around our knees and pressed together to share heat.

When we'd waited beyond what we felt capable of waiting, we heard a car, but it wasn't Jack. Another car passed, and another. We began to cry. We were half-afraid, half-impressed that we were like girls in one of our storybooks, two sisters huddled in the ditch, hungry and shivering. Jack would be sorry he'd left us and would hug and feed us. Maybe he'd take us to Mary's Cafe for a hamburger and chips and a chocolate milkshake to apologize.

Just as I was imagining we'd spend the night, we saw the familiar grill of Jack's truck, the front windows separated like two big eyes. We crawled to the side of the road, stumbling over our stiff feet. We jumped and screamed and flailed our arms. Just as we were sure the truck was passing us, it shuddered to a stop.

When Jack got out of the truck, he didn't look at us or speak. He opened the squeaky passenger door, and when we had crawled in, he slammed it behind us. Twice, for good measure. Jack had never before been angry-beyond-words at me.

"We walked almost to town," I said.

Jack didn't answer. Jack faced forward, his face rigid. I picked at the dried foam in the rip of the vinyl seat. In the past, his anger hadn't really been anger, but sharp barks for our own good.

Then I was ashamed of my hopes Jack would be proud of me; ashamed I hadn't kept Rima home and distracted her; most of all, ashamed that my anger, which had been slowly growing all summer, was hardening into something permanent.

Jack accidentally ground the gears, and the gearshift ball came off in his hand. He jammed it back on. I looked everywhere but at him—at the cracked dashboard; the gas gauge stuck on empty; the tree-branch fractures in the windshield; the half-squished paper coffee cup skidding around his feet. Through the vents, I smelled burning oil. I thought the engine might start on fire, but I wouldn't warn Jack and be the first to break the silence: we'd just have to burn to death together.

And slowly, I felt a dark promise taking shape in my chest, a promise too big and too stubborn: I wouldn't love Jack again, not, at least, in the openhearted way of children. Even then, I knew it wasn't a promise I should make, but I made it anyway.

How to Cook Stinging Nettles

Because of the nettles' irritating proclivities, the hands should be protected when nettles are gathered, preferably when they first appear in the spring. Leather gloves and a knife make the task easy. You can get along alright, too, by using two sticks as tongs. It would be reasonable to expect that nettles would require lengthy cooking. As a matter of fact, you only have to drop the young shoots into a container of boiling water that may be then set away from the heat. As soon as the dark emerald greens have cooled enough to be eaten, they may be forked out and served.

How to Stay Alive in the Woods
Bradford Angier, 1956

RESENTMENTS I
COLLECTED

I began to collect resentments against Jack.

Every day Rima and I had to retrieve the half dozen eggs from the chicken house. We loved reaching our hands into the upper nest boxes and feeling an egg, like a treasure: still warm, a little straw stuck to it. And brown. Middle class people had white eggs. We had healthy brown eggs with little speckles.

But the path to the chicken house, which dipped into a marshy gully, was lined with nettles that stung our legs—a little electric shock, then red bumps and itching. One of the women at the Slow Farm told us we could soothe the stings by rubbing them with foxglove leaves. I imagined foxes wearing purple flowers over their paws when attending parties—but as medicine their leaves were useless.

"We don't want to get the eggs," I told Jack one morning. "There're too many stinging nettles." He stood beside the open hood of his truck, a large, greasy part in his hand.

Rima nodded. Her face looked firmer, older than it had. I hadn't really looked at her in Vancouver, hadn't noticed her growing.

"Put some pants on then," Jack said. He twisted a bolt with a wrench. He looked different too, the skin on his face rougher.

"Our pants are too small and you won't buy us any more."

He grimaced. Then focused all his strength on another frozen bolt. I'd touched a sensitive nerve: Janet's complaints he was tight with his money and didn't care for us properly.

I tried another tack. "Robyn says she'll get the eggs for us." The women at the Slow Farm didn't like to see us upset.

"We all have jobs to do. That's the only thing I've asked of you. You'll do it. Now." His head disappeared into the engine well.

A few days later on the chicken house path, the paper wasps attacked.

Some years wasps skimmed our ankles and we had to avoid stepping on them. But that summer, as Jack described it, the wasps were "flying high." They seemed military-like: streamlined, tails curling under, waists disappearing into little strings. They attacked Rima's face and my upper arms.

"Wasps don't sting unless they're provoked," Jack said. "Don't bump or swat them."

Jack wouldn't believe us when we told him we were doing neither. He pinched a stinger still hanging from my biceps. "Make sure you pull these out—they can still pump poison after the wasp is gone."

I asked him to coat our stings in baking soda—as Janet had. He seemed burdened by our complaints—as if his mind were mulling over some mathematical problem from which he didn't want to be distracted, but he mixed the soda and water. We stood outside the front door of the Slow Farm as he pressed the paste on my upper arm and on Rima's forehead. To have him so close, warm and smelling of sweat, reminded me, for a moment, of Pocahontas Bay.

Jack refused to relieve us of egg duty, but he'd thought of a solution. He disappeared—a red can of kerosene swinging in his right hand—down the path toward the tree with the wasp nest. From the gravel in front of the barn, we saw only the spiral of dark smoke. But afterward the wasps neither died, nor disappeared. Instead, they were out for revenge and stung us every day. Jack didn't believe us when we told him the wasps were angry and had a plan.

"Insects have simple brains. They don't have emotions."

We still had to collect eggs. I feared their poison was filling up my veins.

Jack also failed as a Tooth Fairy.

First, my tooth moved, just a little. I pressed it with my tongue, rocked it with my finger until I worked the first sharp edge from the gum. I ran my tongue over and over the sharpness, the opening to a cave. When it loosened more, I pressed it up and popped it back into place, like a puzzle piece.

A couple times a day, I'd inform Jack of its progress: "Look how loose it is now!" And now. And now. When it was looser, I twisted it, until it hung by just one root. I didn't have the courage for the last pull, but neither could I leave it alone. So I massaged the tooth with my tongue until my gums were numb and the tooth was so loose it wouldn't stay in place and let go with one gentle tug. And then the raw hole: tender, too soft, tasting of metal.

When I'd lost my first tooth in Vancouver, I placed it under my pillow and the Tooth Fairy traded it for a quarter, which I spent on a Wagon Wheel at the Chinese grocers.

I knew I'd have to remind Jack about the Tooth Fairy.

"I'm really looking forward to the Tooth Fairy coming tonight," I repeated " . . . or the Tooth Weasel." The Birthday and Easter Weasels had visited us in Pocahontas Bay.

The next morning, I slipped my hand into the cool under my pillow. I touched something polished and sharp edged, like a chip of oyster shell—and pulled out my own tooth. Rima was disappointed. Even though the quarter wasn't coming to her, she loved traditions.

"The Tooth Fairy didn't come last night," I told Jack as he pulled on his gumboots.

The following morning, I couldn't find anything, and finally touched that same tooth at a far corner.

"She didn't come, again," I informed Jack, businesslike, as if it were the fairy who'd failed, and I trusted him to deliver the message.

The next day, I felt a single large coin. I lay on my back and held it to my face. A British pence, a giant copper coin that said "Penny" on one side—the same one I'd dug from the sandpit weeks ago, played with almost every day since, and left on the living room rug in my glass animal city.

"The Tooth Fairy made a mistake," I said to Jack, who had stopped back into the house that morning to get something. I held up the pence. "This is my penny. I found it. It was here with my animals. Tell the Tooth Fairy I'll put it back under my pillow. She can bring me a quarter." He nodded absently and clumped out the front door.

The Tooth Fairy never returned.

The history of the white, menopausal, menda-cious men now ruling the planet earth is a his-tory of repeated violation of the harmonious laws of nature . . .

- *They are bores.*
- *They hate beauty.*
- *They hate sex.*
- *They hate life.*

The Declaration of Evolution
Timothy Leary, 1968

THE FIRST TIME
I WAS DRUNK

Texada Days, the weekend festival with cotton candy and gunny sack races, had its parallel in the hippy community: Texada Daze. In the booths that lined the perimeter of the meadow at Shelter Point, the Slow Farm people offered their cedar spoons, tree stump tables, beaded earrings, macramé necklaces, and reversible velvet bags. New faces from the mainland and local islands displayed crystals, finger puppets, handmade pottery, tie-dyed scarves and T-shirts, carved wooden bowls and walking sticks, embroidered shirts from Central America. Those who didn't have money traded. The visitors scattered their tents and tarps throughout the camping sites and woods. Behind the booths, the locals set up blankets, and the half-dressed children with tangled hair and smudged faces wandered between them, looking for snacks and fun.

With his pickup, a man hauled in a mobile sauna shaped like a little shingle-sided house. Naked men and women entered and exited. The man blocked the door with his arm when Rima and I tried to go in. "No children." On his T-shirt were the words *Buzzed Bunny* and a drawing of Bugs Bunny with bloodshot eyes. I didn't know what *buzzed* meant, but I didn't like the way Bugs looked or the scowl on the man's face.

A man in a jester's hat with bells on his wrists marched through the crowd, waving his hands, calling himself the Pied Piper, and announcing the children's show. We joined the parade behind him and followed him to a plywood stage, painted in swirly colors. Paper mache puppets in velvet clothes with pretty buttons argued and hit each other, then kissed and hugged. Two men with faces painted on their stomachs made their bellybuttons talk. The Pied Piper juggled. A man played guitar and sang *Puff the Magic Dragon*. The performers passed a black top hat and the grown-ups put in money or marijuana or bags of walnuts. Some children threw in handfuls of grass or rocks. Afterward, there was a belly dancing class.

Just before dark, The Band began to play. I was proud because I knew some members: Rol and Nancy on violin, Kathy on banjo, Vic on the guitar, and Vic's sister Louise on vocals. Louise—small, with fine features and dark hair in long, loose curls—was a regular at the Slow Farm. Many men loved her, not just because of her pretty face and curves, but because she listened, laughed easily, took care of people. She seemed to enjoy talking to Rima and me, so I was especially proud my friend Louise was singing: bluegrass, a little jazz, folk, rock.

Women gathered in the meadow in front of the stage: bare feet, ankle bracelets, long skirts, long and tangled hair. They didn't dance to the rhythm of the music. Instead, they pulled off their shirts and moved as if they were performing underwater ballet. When they spun, their breasts flew out. The men, wearing wooden beads and cotton pants rolled up at the bottom, joined them; a few flow danced like the women, but most jumped up and down or rocked stiffly from side to side.

When Louise sang my favorite song of hers, "Damn this traffic jam, hurts my motor to go so slow," Rima and I wanted to dance too. We'd show off a few partner spins we'd invented. But the grown-ups didn't see us. They bumped us with big elbows and hips, stumbled. They smelled of herbs and dirt and sweat. A woman with a few flowers stuck in her tangles stepped on my foot. The sun was setting, the crowd was getting larger and more oblivious, so we edged our way to the perimeter.

A large, red-haired man lay on his back in the dirt. His hairy stomach hung out of his half-buttoned shirt. His eyes were closed, his mouth hung open. A deep, pink indent sliced across his forehead. We were certain he was almost dead. New dancers on the way to the stage stepped over him. We ran to tell Jack, who was pulling a bottle of whisky from behind the seat in his truck.

"That's Gary. He got hit in the head with an ax and now whenever he has even one drink, he passes out. He's fine."

"Hit with an ax?"

I could tell from Jack's face that wasn't a story he wanted to tell, so he was relieved when three men sauntered up. Jack handed them the bottle.

Rima and I wandered away to explore the lengthening shadows on the edge of the meadow. In one small, secret clearing, we stumbled upon a group of about eight people sitting in a circle, passing a jug of Baby Duck.

"I think those are Jack Wilson's kids," someone said. "You Jack's kids?" We nodded. It was almost dark, and I was cold in my shorts and bare feet. "Wanna join us?"

A man and a woman scooted over and made room for us. The women tucked their feet under their long skirts. When the jug reached me, the man showed me how to hook my index finger around the handle, rest the jug on the top of the V of my bent arm, and tip my elbow toward my mouth. The bottle was too heavy for Rima to lift, so the woman and I held it for her. Every time the jug passed, Rima and I took another swig. The wine tasted like bitter syrup, but I'd learned a new trick and the grown-ups roared and clapped every time we took a swallow. I wasn't cold any more.

"Whoa, slow down there," they said to Rima when she gulped.

I awoke in the back of Jack's truck. My mouth tasted sour; my shirt smelled of throw up and wine; my temples pulsed as if my heart had migrated to my head. Louise murmured while she tucked blankets around us.

She interrupted her mother-dove cooing to yell at Jack, who'd just appeared. "What were you thinking? They're children!"

Jack didn't answer.

"They need to go home!"

"They just need to sleep it off. They're fine there."

Their voices were disembodied. Stars were tossed like chicken feed, thick across the sky.

"Damn it, Jack. Give me the keys."

Every bump in the road felt like a punch to my head. But the night air was cool across my face. I turned my head into the sweater Louise had folded as a pillow and closed my eyes. I wasn't mad at Jack. Not like the eggs and Tooth Fairy when I had asked him for something and he hadn't given it. In this case, I knew I'd made my own decision. But I did bask in Louise's sweet belief in my innocence.

None can be an impartial or wise observer of human life but from the vantage ground of what we should call voluntary poverty.

Walden
Henry David Thoreau, 1854

JACKS' FAILURE: THE BATHTUB

In Vancouver, Rima and I had become accustomed to being clean. We took regular baths with floating toys and Mr. Clean bubble bath poured from a pink box and argued over who sat in the front of the tub and controlled the temperature. I usually won and ran the water too hot for Rima, whose legs turned splotchy.

At the Slow Farm, I was tired of hair so greasy it felt like snakes, tired of the grime I could scrape from my forearms, tired of the black wrinkles on the back of my ankles I couldn't scrub clean, even with soaking. One night, as Jack waited for me to crawl up to my bunk, I finally blurted I didn't want to put my dirty feet in my sleeping bag. And my scalp was itchy.

"You girls have been living with Janet for too long."

Several days later, Jack emptied the cast iron bathtub. It had been forgotten next to the house, filled with firewood, old leaves, a few moldy walnuts, and stagnant water. He grabbed a couple of Slow Farm guys and they dragged it to the middle of the field, between the house, the outhouse, and the strip of pine trees. Rima and I ran out to see. A bathtub in a field! The spots where the enamel had chipped looked like black muscle under white skin. Jack stuffed an old rag into the drain, then ran a hose across the road from the creek. He sucked on the end of the hose to prime the water.

When Rima and I finally stepped in, the water was so cold, our ankles ached. "It's too cold!"

"Cold water is good for you. Builds character. Makes you strong."

We couldn't force ourselves to sit down.

"You used to swim in ocean water colder than this," he said, almost to himself.

I felt sorry for Jack's disappointment, but my body wouldn't move. He lifted us out and stood us on the dust next to the tub. We shivered as Jack scrubbed us, quick and rough, with a bar of soap and a cloth. His whole body was stiff. "Lean your head over. Farther." He spoke in simple, flat commands. I leaned, and he poured water over my hair with an empty tobacco tin, water so cold my temples throbbed.

Several days later, at dusk, Jack called us out of the house. "Girls, come here! I want to show you something neat." His voice was joyful, as it used to be. He'd dug a pit under the bathtub and filled it with cedar logs, which were burning tiger orange against a landscape already darkening toward night. We ran to the tub and waggled our fingers in the lukewarm water. We shook our hands at the fire. *Sizzle.* Jack smiled. His body was loose again. We dipped and shook again. *Sizzle.*

"Not too much water, girls, you'll put out the fire," Jack said, but his voice was full of pleasure.

Attending school in Vancouver, I'd realized my life with Jack was unusual, and at that moment I felt a pride in that difference—the beauty of a fire glowing under a lion-footed tub, stars just beginning to blink in the sky. I'd slide down the slanted back into deep, hot water.

Little bubbles clung to the bottom. "Can we get in now? I don't want to boil!" We leaned over the rim and swirled our arms in the water. The side of the tub felt chalky, almost too hot, but the water was still disappointingly tepid.

"Go ahead!"

We stripped off our shorts and T-shirts and stepped in. We squealed and scrambled out.

"It's not *that* hot, girls."

I knew how hard Jack had worked. I wanted to play in water under a sky turning purple-black at the edges, but the bottoms of my feet still stung. To prove us wrong, Jack pressed his hand on the bottom of the tub. Then snapped it back.

He picked up the shovel and threw dirt on the fire. His upper arms flexed. He held his breath. Little leftover flames mixed with rising dust.

"You believe everything Janet says about me," he breathed out.

I didn't know what I believed. If I told Janet about the bathtub—which I later did—she'd make a story out of it. She rolled her eyes, "What did he expect? The tub is made of iron."

My feelings for Jack, which before had been solidly formed into worship, had broken into fragments, cracked by pity and Janet's disdain—and my fear I'd driven Jack away: I'd complained about wasps and nettles; I couldn't hold my alcohol; I'd asked him, when he was too busy and sad, for clean ankles and tooth fairy quarters.

The proper home is one in which children and adults have equal rights.

Summerhill: A Radical Approach to Child Rearing
A.S. Neill, 1960

JACK'S ADVICE

I curled up in the decaying 1940s armchair, whatever color and pattern it had been long faded to gray, reading *Tintin*. Rima lay on her stomach on the filthy Persian carpet, rotating the knobs on her Etch-a-Sketch. The room smelled of dust and old fabric with a hint of marijuana. Scattered around us were comic books Slow Farm guests had left behind: *Felix the Cat* about a sex-crazed feline; *Mr. Natural* who wore nothing but big boots and a long beard; the *Fabulous Furry Freak Brothers* starring three wild-haired men who smoked dope and tried to escape the police and the threat of a regular job. I loved comics, but those were for grown-ups, full of jokes I didn't understand and which made me feel squirmy. So I fell into Jack's copies of *Tintin*, the hardback comics starring the little red-haired Belgian reporter who solves mysteries and has wild adventures with his dog Snowy. At that moment, I was rereading my favorite, *Tintin in Tibet*.

Jack strode through the living room and called out over his shoulder, "Clean up this mess, girls."

I looked up and watched him step over crayon bits, a tangled slinky, Go Fish cards, Parcheesi pieces, abandoned Snakes and Ladders game, and chips of colored wax Rima and

I had dislodged from the windowsills where candles, jammed in wine bottles, had melted.

He'd never asked us to clean before. Usually, he was too busy thinking to notice dirt. Once a woman visitor had ranted, "How can you live like this?" His answer: "I don't look down."

So although I'd heard his order, I didn't believe him. I thought, for a moment, about the possibility of cleaning and then nestled back into the snowy fields of the Himalayas where Tintin was about to meet a yeti. Rima didn't move from her position on the floor where she had just figured out how to draw a cityscape.

"Girls, I told you to clean up," Jack said as he walked by again, several dirty coffee mugs in his hands. "I'm not going to ask you again."

I felt an unexpected surge of anger pulse down my center. Actually, I didn't like our house so chaotic. But even more, I didn't like Jack telling me what to do: he was changing the rules of our house. I didn't want him to clean for other people when he'd never cleaned for Janet. As far as I was concerned, it was too late for him to change for the better.

I turned my page and tried to disappear again into Tintin's white land. But Jack was at the door again. I pretended not to see him, but his silence filled the room, melting my Tibetan snows.

"The trick, Tarn . . ."

I reflexively lifted my head. The silver cobwebbed windows on the other side of the room came into focus.

"The trick . . ." He leaned against the doorframe. " . . . is to *look* like you are working. Even when you aren't."

Then he was gone.

My mind tumbled. He'd surprised me. I liked it when he tossed my thinking upside down. But he was disappointed in me again, not for my disobedience as a normal dad would be, but for my lack of cleverness. I was working hard to stay angry at him, and he wasn't helping. He was confusing me instead.

Still looking at my *Tintin*, I stepped one foot on the ground and accidently ripped the cover of a *Felix the Cat*. I stood. Rima looked up at me, her face round and bright like the moon. I picked up Parcheesi pieces with my toes and tossed them vaguely toward their crushed box.

Tarn's Drawing

WHAT I'D TRY TO BELIEVE

I tried to keep myself at a distance from Jack, but he tempted me with stories. He read to us again before bed. Old favorites. "The Bull Beneath the Walnut Tree." "Peter Pitkin and Witch Wookie." He hadn't let us take our books when we'd left with Janet; maybe he believed stories would bring us back to him. He read us new, longer books, too: *Charlotte's Web; Charlie and the Chocolate Factory; The Lion, the Witch and the Wardrobe; The Wizard of Oz.*

We met before bed on Rima's bottom bunk, on her ragged wool blankets that smelled like dusty dogs. Jack settled between us, at the head of the bed. Voices in the living room rose and fell, then shattered into laughter. He adjusted my pillow behind his back, the one with stains from my sometimes-nighttime bloody noses, and opened *The Wizard of Oz.*

My spot was between Jack and the log wall, and I pulled as far from him as I could, without touching the moss or chalky brown circles growing on the logs. The light from the kerosene lantern barely reached me, abandoning me in deep twilight. The light played on the side of Rima's face. She pressed into Jack's ribs and pulled her stuffed monkey under her arm.

Usually, Jack only brought us stuffed animals he found at the dump, but several weeks before, he'd returned from the mainland with new stuffed monkeys, a white one for Rima, a brown one for me.

Rima loved monkeys because, like her, they were mischievous. She especially loved her white monkey and didn't want Jack or me to smudge or mat it with our oily fingers. At first, she hid it in the far corner of her bunk, but she couldn't resist sleeping with it, and soon its fur was clumped and gray and she carried it with her everywhere. In general, I didn't like monkeys. The ugly ways in which they looked human, with flat faces, curlicue ears, and bare wrinkled hands, made me sad. (I did love Curious George, however, even though Jack and Janet had told me the Man in the Yellow Hat, who seemed so nice, was actually a poacher.) I was secretly attracted to Rima's impractical, glamorous white-furred monkey—but also proud Jack had given me the brown, the more sensible and understated, one, the one I guessed he liked better. A signal, I hoped, of approval.

Still, I kept my body tight, resisting Jack, this moment. But as soon as he started to read, the log wall disappeared, the bunk bed above me opened to sky, the voices in the living room turned to birds, and I was lifted into the air with Dorothy and her friends by winged monkeys.

In one of my early memories, I'm on Jack and Janet's foam mattress on the floor in the back of the school bus. Jack leans against the wall, and I rest my head on his chest, firm and soft in his flannel shirt, and suck my thumb. He reads from *Alice in Wonderland*.

Soon, I no longer hear his voice. I hear the rhythms of Lewis Carroll. Then I hear a new blend of voices: the voice of Jack and Carroll and the voice in my head and the voice, which is no voice at all, but only the story. Jack laughs and tries to explain the math and logic jokes, which I still don't understand.

In the story, the mouse tells Alice a tale about a court case between a cat and a dog. As the mouse speaks, Alice watches his tail. The text is written in the shape of a mouse's tail, waving back and forth, getting smaller and narrower until it almost disappears at the tip. My mind plays in the white space around the tail. All else disappears: the bedspread beneath us, the metal wall behind us, my own body. Then I understand, without Jack telling me, the tale is a tail. I laugh. I laugh in a too self-conscious way to show Jack I understand, but also because I don't know how to speak my delight at the way my mind can hold two meanings at once.

I march with Dorothy and the Lion and Tin Woodsman and Scarecrow into the Emerald City and the palace of Oz to claim our rewards for killing the Wicked Witch—our courage and heart and brains and our way home. But the sniveling Wizard is not the wonder we'd believed.

"I thought Oz was a great Head," said Dorothy.

"And I thought Oz was a lovely Lady," said the Scarecrow.

"And I thought Oz was a terrible Beast," said the Tin Woodsman.

"And I thought Oz was a Ball of Fire," exclaimed the Lion.

"No, you are all wrong," said the little man meekly. "I have been making believe."

"Making believe!" cried Dorothy. "Are you not a Great Wizard?"

"Hush, my dear," he said. "Don't speak so loud, or you will be overheard—and I should be ruined. I'm supposed to be a Great Wizard."

"And aren't you?" she asked.

"Not a bit of it, my dear; I'm just a common man."

The next morning, Rima called from the bottom bunk. "Are you awake?"

I opened my sticky eyes and hung by my waist over the edge of my bed. The blood pooled in my head. She held up her monkey. Silver wings sprouted from its back. They flashed in the gray morning light.

"Look at yours," she said, suddenly worried the magic had only happened for her.

I pulled myself out and found my monkey next to my head. The tinfoil wings crinkled and fell a little to the left.

Rima crawled out of bed. She wore Jack's green flannel shirt, which hung past her knees. Her stomach still had a little of its firm roundness, but her legs were thin—longer than I'd remembered—sticking out under the shirt. "I'm going to show Jack," she said, pushing her monkey toward me. It seemed to be smiling, an angelic sort of smile.

She waited for me to answer, to follow her. But I lay on my back and held my monkey above me. His face, slept on for too many nights, was lopsided, his fur crusted with spots of sap, car oil, and honey. His wings slumped. I squeezed his stomach and his mouth seemed to twist, as if he were disturbed to have been wakened, decorated for some game he didn't understand. When I didn't move, Rima skipped away.

I split again, as I had the night Jack and Janet fought. The me still in bed remained cynical, solid, and closed. Angry Jack's magic couldn't return us to the way we were. Ashamed at my closed-ness, which felt like meanness, which felt like holding my breath.

But my other, bigger self, a woman, floated above the bed, just under the ceiling, as if she too had wings. She loved Rima, who was tingly with this new monkey magic. She loved even the me still in my bed with the closed-heartedness I had chosen.

And then the floating woman showed me an image: Jack, late in the night, sitting by the kerosene lamp, cutting cardboard wings, over and over, until they had just the right graceful curve, just the right proportions, and then wrapping the cardboard in tinfoil, bending it so it wouldn't rip, so it would catch the light. This man, who had wanted to learn everything, who didn't know how to keep his wife or make me happy, had made us magic monkeys. He had returned the monkeys to our beds, softly, so as not to wake us.

I wanted to be this floating woman—who loved Jack and Rima and me as a tender mother would, who forgave us all— but she was still above my body and I couldn't reach her.

I grabbed my magic monkey and moved toward the living room to see Jack and Rima. I'd make them think I believed in winged monkeys, but instead, I'd try to believe in something else: in love which is lumpy and lopsided and mistimed—yet is love none-the-less, as wide and generous as it knows how to be.

RETURNING TO TEXADA

SUMMER 1996

Climbing Along the River

Willows never forget how it feels
to be young.

Do you remember where you came from?
Gravel remembers.

Even the upper end of the river
believes in the ocean.

Exactly at midnight
yesterday sighs away.

What I believe is,
all animals have one soul.

Over the land they love
they crisscross forever.

William Stafford

WHAT TO KEEP

Traveling through Vancouver Island, I overhear a stranger say *Texada*, and my stomach flips—the sort of flip you feel when, at an unexpected time and place, you hear news of a long-lost love. No other place-name causes the same reaction, not the places we lived before: Sugarloaf Mountain, Alexandria. Nor the places after: our summer haunts with Jack all over Vancouver Island and the Gulf Islands, the cities we bounced between with Janet after we moved back to Colorado—Golden, Boulder, Denver, Loveland, Colorado Springs—over twenty houses as Janet tried to settle that voice inside her crying "House for Sale!"

The twenty-minute ferry ride from Powell River to Texada is familiar: the steep-hilled islands, thick with trees, bow to the water; the ferry churns white wash behind the boat; the sky and the water reflect that same mercury-gray-silver. Looking at my map of British Columbia, I'm surprised that Texada, which I'd almost come to believe exists only in my imagination, is so large and clearly marked.

On the drive to Van Anda on Blubber Bay Road, the island looks more worn than I'd remembered, like a mother of too many children. Trees, cut many times over, have grown tall again in dense forests, interrupted by patches of clear cutting.

Down dirt roads, I glimpse craters from over a hundred years of mining. How is it possible Texada has any guts left?

In Van Anda, the road rolls, curves, and splits past the same little wooden houses hugged by roses, sweet peas, and blackberries. But the town has changed too. The Laundromat is boarded over. M. and M's Variety store is a post office. Mary's Cafe, smaller than I'd remembered, is a Credit Union. I'm surprised by my twinge of sorrow. I hadn't realized how much I'd wanted purple and red soda pop in glass bottles, a chocolate milkshake with an ice cream lump, French fries called chips and served with vinegar, and sugar cubes I can stack, put in my pocket, and feed to horses in a field. I talk to some shop owners: the new, massive log cabin on the crest of a hill overlooking the town belongs to Young Mr. Hagman and Roxie. Old Mr. Hagman has died.

On the way to Texada, I visited Jack, and he armed me with directions to the Slow Farm, a rough map of the property, an old photograph Richard had recently given him, and a warning the land might look very different since it had been bulldozed for a pipeline.

The photo was faded and strange: a sun-like flash of light under the walnut tree blurs the left side, but the house itself is clear—Scandinavian-style, interlocking logs. A cement pad stretches under the open front door where Rima and I stand. I wear white shorts and a halter-top. Rima, a head shorter than me, wears overall shorts. On the outside wall, next to us, hangs a handsaw and, underneath, a yellow road sign:

MILES
PER HOUR
SPEED LIMIT

I drive the gravel High Road, wider, better graded than it used to be. I pass a familiar-looking marshy field on the right.

The road crosses a creek, but over a drainage culvert instead of the wooden Three Billy Goat's Gruff bridge. The pasture to the left could be the one with the horses and the creek, but it seems too narrow. Suddenly, the thought of finding the Slow Farm makes me nauseous and I almost turn back.

The smell of mildew and rotten eggs. The old sleeping bag where Tristan kisses me on the leg. Peter cooks a snake, snakes squirm in a pit, a snake swims through the water. Peter, naked, chases me. Rima falls through the tarpaper roof. Mr. Hagman tells me to put on clothes. I tell Rima a girl cuts off her bum. I can't get the sap off my skin. I sit on the front step and curl over my stomachache.

I park in a field that should be the Slow Farm. But the property seems too small. And too flat. I don't remember the butter and egg flowers, nor the dragonflies, hovering at the height of my knees. I begin to hunt for artifacts. Tractors have bulldozed everything into gullies: a rusty frying pan, a refrigerator door, an overturned car. From the tangled grass, I pull a white, enameled chamber pot, a teapot lid. I turn over charred wood beams; roly poly bugs skitter underneath.

Janet beats the rug. In the dark, an unlocked door swings open. A wasp stings. Again. Couples disappear into the dark, tarpaper room, into hot, dank smells. The police come, with their vacuum cleaner dog. Rats poop on my bed. Too many women try to heal Jack of his grief.

I find a collapsed outhouse, just a few shakes over a gooey pit. Like ours, a fruit tree grows next to it. But I'm not sure. I can't fathom that the walnut trees with their soft-large hands, the taffy-twisted cherry tree, the Twelve-Acre wood are gone. I have no absolute proof the Slow Farm isn't my own murky dream.

Then, through the trees I see an old cabin, the back collapsed into a hill—perhaps the through-the-wasps-and-stinging-nettles chicken house. I scramble through the salal and sit in the doorway. But I'm still not sure. I'm tired and disappointed and inexplicably angry. I kick at more objects I don't remember. Old nails. A carburetor. A blue, plastic turtle.

I am about to leave when I feel, under the grass, concrete. Maybe the entry way in the photograph. I step to the side and the grass beneath me bends, like metal. I scrape away the dirt, find a sharp edge, and peel the sign from the ground. The yellow lacquer has melted, bubbled, turned bruise-green in the heat of a fire, but the black words are clear:

MILES

PER HOUR

SPEED LIMIT

I want to cry with relief.

From the fallen sign, I map the whole property. Yes, the chicken house. The barn. The bathtub first here, under the tree, then in the field, and then in the house. The Twelve Acre Wood, with a stump to jump off. Garter snake pit. A horse's hot breath. Ashes in the outhouse. I stand on the side of the road under an imaginary Slow Farm sign.

Back at the car, I look again at the butter and egg flowers, those chubby bubble candy flowers, and the dragonflies. The present superimposed over the past: a field of grass over a log cabin, a mound of dirt and open sky over a pair of walnut trees. I'm at the Slow Farm. The curve of the land I loved. All that long-buried sadness. It's more than just a story. It exists.

From our complicated pasts, how do we know what to keep and what to let go? I don't know. But I put the sign—and the blue turtle—in my trunk.

The Slow Farm was owned by Texada Log when I arrived. The building had been destroyed by fire but, as you noted, the chicken house was still standing. Ernie Jago, the caretaker for Texada Log at the time, told me he burnt it down after having trouble trying to evict some hippies.

Letter from Bob Blackmore,
local historian, July 31, 1997

THE ORB IN THE CENTER
OF MY CHEST

Driving to Pocahontas Bay, I focus only on the overgrown road through lumpy ferns and stream beds and alder groves. But when the firs finally open to the water, my heart double-skips.

The bay is half the size I remember and the buildings are gone, but the shapes are the same: the steep arc of the bay; the vertical logs on the hillside where the logging trucks dumped their cuts into the water, the stack of logs—settled and shifted—where Rima and I had waited for Ishkin and Bishkin to arrive in their silver airplane.

I sit on the beach, sheltered from the wind by the two long arms of land, and pick up little pink-edged clamshells, cedar wood chips. I breathe the breath of arrival. Here was the Eden Jack wanted to give us—although he did not so much create it as stumble upon it. For how can any of us create an Eden when we have to carry ourselves with us, dragging our history, wherever we go?

But for Rima and me, Pocahontas Bay was as close to an Eden as we would ever find. Even though she was two years younger, Rima remembers too—the snap of ocean air against our cheeks; the dappled light that filtered through the trees; the feel on our tongues of huckleberries, dry fiddleheads, furry thimble berries; a big leaf upside down on our heads and a fern around our waists. The slippery skin of Seaweed Mamas. Light from the kerosene lantern belly-dancing on the ceiling. Before bed, Jack scratching out Witch Wookie's voice, "Is that you Peter Pitkin? Then you'll catch it!"

For both of us, the Pocahontas Bay of our childhood has become an inner landscape that does not exist in time but floats, a self-contained orb, in the center of our chests—a secret, hidden world which we have carried with us, like a talisman, into our more conventional lives in more suburban neighborhoods than we care to admit.

Rima and I share memories of the contour of the land and the games we played, but Rima, not even three when we arrived, has almost no memory of Jack and Janet there—and no memory of them together. In Rima's memory, the weather on Texada was always sunny.

For me, Texada was gently overcast, always the temperature of my own skin.

For Janet, it was always raining. She remembers our life on Texada only vaguely—a year and a half in her mid-twenties—and doesn't care to remember more. She was too isolated, too lonely, too young for such a place. She's ashamed of who she was then, the drugs she used (always hidden from me), her numbed silence in her marriage, how ignorant she was about herself. Her time on Texada seems the life of another woman, so different from the make-up wearing paralegal she'd eventually become. She never let go of her fierce belief in social justice, but her own life became defined by the practical—a single mother with limited education trying to pay the bills—and by her restlessness that kept her forever on the move and starting over.

Only Jack remembers the weather as it was—the toss of storms, the long gray winter with its misty rains, the blessed summers—the weather that followed him to nearby Vancouver Island where he finally settled. He carried with him two equally weighted, contradictory expectations for himself: he should be self-sufficient, independent, spontaneous, artistic, and adventure-loving, a man who needed nothing more than his hands and some land. And he should earn a fortune, invent something, make a lasting intellectual contribution, be a man he imagined his father would admire. He could never reconcile these visions, which led to a roller-coaster career—his name on British Columbia's most promising businessmen lists, invitations to join important boards, followed by spectacular tumbles. He founded a computerized marine mapping business and a company that made robotic arms for remotely operated submarines (and, once, robotic spiders for a Hollywood movie). Between, he was a log salvager, a community college professor, a rescue boat operator, and a bookstore owner.

He married a woman from the Slow Farm and kept in touch with his Slow Farm friends. They all grew into middle age together.

Rima and I still escape to the trees as often as we can. In our careers, we've married our father's idealism with our mother's practicality. Rima, after earning a graduate degree in planning and working for a city, devoted herself to building beautiful, environmentally responsible low-income housing for seniors. I'm a public high school teacher. We've committed ourselves to the slow, laborious, often frustrating effort to improve the world from within the system, which might, after all, be the most ambitious—certainly the most humble—form of idealism. But, still, we are filled with our parents' doubt; we are never sure we've made the right choices and are doing enough.

I'm still the child I was, seeking truth and finding, always, that whatever I conclude needs revision. In the end, I'm usually forced to hold two realities at once. The tale is a tail. Utopia is a good place. Utopia is no place. My childhood was challenging. My childhood was a blessing.

I walk through the marsh grasses at the end of Whisky Still creek, then tromp through the woods behind what used to be the Big House. Back on the dirt where our house had been, I find a fresh piece of broccoli left by a camper, evidence

I've not opened a secret door to the past. I have to share the island. In Texada time, my two years were a blink. Over the decades, thousands of people have made their homes on the island. They've never heard of me. Or even of the Slow Farm. The historical record *Texada* by the Powell River Historical Society mentions no hippies who came for a while and then drifted away, stealing a few Texada natives. I'm not in Texada's stories of itself.

But lining the road, just below the hill to Janet's old garden, I find evidence Pocahontas Bay had once belonged to us: a new generation of Janet's daffodils—not in bloom, but green and vigorous.

One Pocahontas Bay morning, Rima and I found a large basket waiting for us on the kitchen table, overflowing with ruffly-necked daffodils. Little morning suns. They dazzled us, all that yellow blazing against a gray morning. Nestled underneath, in nests of fresh grass, we pulled out dyed, pastel eggs.

"I'm sorry, girls." Janet's face was sad. "I forgot it was Easter. I couldn't get to the store for candy or toys. That's all I had."

I didn't know how to assure her that bright beauty, arranged especially for us, was enough.

Years before, someone had bulldozed the three little houses—and the chopping block and pile of oyster shells—into a mound. I clamber up the incline. The earth begins to sag, so I excavate, yanking dead grass and roots and old boards, a little afraid of the strange caverns and the smell of rot. Then I find it. A chunk of wood. Soft on one side, purple paint on the other. The royal purple of the trim of our house, unfaded.

I want to send Janet a purple paint chip. I want to send her a photograph of the daffodil leaves. I want to send her the picture of where her garden had been, where sunflowers, three times our size, bowed over us.

Janet remembers her own early childhood, Diane's hundred crayons; Billy in the teacup; parts of her tap-dance routine to *Santa Claus is Coming to Town*; her father, home from work, swinging her in his arms, calling her his darling Teddy. I can't stand fully in those memories with her; and, even though she was with me, she can't stand in mine.

I want to tell her, but she won't hear, that I found, at the center of Pocahontas Bay, not decay, but the gifts she gave me without thinking, the ones she can't remember: a house in purple trim, an Easter basket full of daffodils, bread rising under a cloth on the stove. She pushes the bread down, kneads it, rolls it, pats it. With flour on her hands she laughs, "This feels just like a baby's bum."

On my way to Texada, I saw Jack for the first time in years. My parents' long bitterness; the years he didn't see us; his habit, an echo of his own father, of meeting each of his children's accomplishments with criticism, filled me with grief. I wanted to heal our relationship, but didn't know how. I tried to interview him about our time on Texada, but he was resistant. I asked a few questions before he closed the conversation.

Did he think the ranger had shot Blue because Jack and Janet were hippies? He didn't remember his rage and insisted there had been no tensions between hippies and the loggers, miners, and rangers on the island, and all his conversations with the ranger had been friendly. "The man was just doing his job." He didn't remember the story of the raven and the French toast either, although he smiled when I told him and didn't doubt it was true.

This disturbed me, that stories I'd memorized through his retelling, and retold myself dozens of times, had escaped him, that I might hold what he had lost, that we all might hold forgotten bits of other people's lives. That other people could hold parts of me I've chosen not to know.

Finally, in their fifties, Jack and Janet, after years of court disputes over custody issues and back child support, made a tentative peace. Before I left for this trip, Jack and Janet talked on the phone. Janet complained she couldn't understand why Texada was so important to Rima and me. Jack, she reported, agreed.

Maybe it's because our days in Pocahontas Bay were designed for children, our rhythms governed only by our needs for play, food, rest, and slow exploration. At just the right moments, Jack and Janet lavished us with attention or abandoned us to our private worlds.

Most likely, it was our age. Rima and I tumbled out of the school bus into Pocahontas Bay at just the stage when children are in love with the ordinary world, when they first explore, independently, the boundaries of their own backyards. Ours happened to be a lush, almost primeval forest. And I confess, even now, I can't fully let go of the feeling that Texada, with its salty silences and black soil and heavy silver light, has some special magic, that the island—in the unworried, affectionate way of a distant but benevolent grandmother—loved us.

Maybe I'm obsessed because our family began its slow decay long before I recognized the signs; I'm compelled to sift through memories, looking for hints I missed. Maybe I tell myself this lie: if I can recognize the patterns, I'll never be so surprised again.

I'm sure only of this: for years, I could write about nothing else but this sweet, gouged, cut, abundant island. That it rose in my consciousness, over and over. Texada is, for me, that great shining, rising and disappearing back of a whale.

Remembrances of the joyful day of your birth and following days have been drifting through my brain. The first snow of the season was falling lightly, with promise of more. You came close to being a home birth. When the doctor handed you to me, just arrived, I had an overpowering experience—you looked at me and "connected." The doctors at the time said "impossible"—newborns cannot focus, eyes or attention—but more recent data says yes sometimes they do. In any case, you were the most aware new baby I've ever seen and the moment was burned into my brain forever.

E-mail from Jack
November 19th, 1998

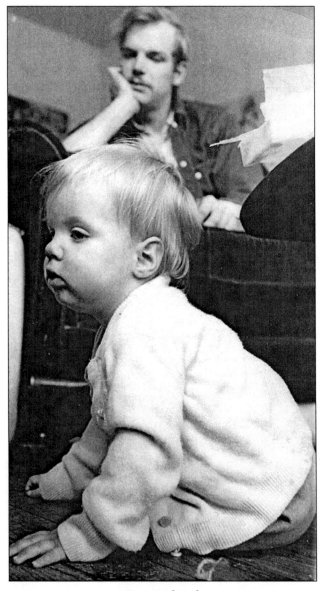

Tarn and Jack

COWICHAN BAY, VANCOUVER ISLAND

SUMMER 2005

I went to the woods because I wished to live deliberately, to front only the essential facts of life, and see if I could not learn what it had to teach, and not, when I came to die, discover that I had not lived.

Walden
Henry David Thoreau, 1854

DEAR JACK

When I arrived, you hadn't been out of the house for weeks. But you came out for me. Every morning, I met you on the deck of Starfish Studio, your last business—a marine charts/used book/local art/coffee and muffin shop. Around us, old men gossiped and smoked and flipped through the newspaper. For an hour, you drank coffee; we made small talk. Seagulls with hungry eyes scanned for crumbs. Then you went home to rest.

On our last morning, you said, "You haven't had much fun since you've been here," as if I'd come to be entertained.

You piled me and your dog Hobbes into your old Volvo, so covered in dog hair, it looked as if the whole interior had been woven in German Shepherd.

In my childhood, when we visited you in the summer, you'd seen it as your duty to provide us with adventures: a summer in a teepee, a tree house, a houseboat, a 1900 fishing boat. But I'd been heartbroken by what you hadn't given me: the money you didn't send; a year, two years gone by without a phone call; how I felt you couldn't love me unless I made myself you—and not even then, because you didn't love yourself.

"I'm sorry this isn't more exciting," you said, "I wish I could take you to camp on the beach in Tofino."

The Volvo bounced up a steep, potholed road. You'd left your oxygen tank behind. Your arthritic dog remembered the route and ran back and forth in the back seat. His dog hair floated, sunlit, in the air.

When we reached the top of Maple Mountain, we got out of the car. The air was cool with the scent of ocean and cedar. You couldn't climb the last moss-covered rock to see the view of Maple Bay below, the little shimmery sailboats. I took a picture with my digital camera so I could show you.

And then I turned to take a picture of you. You didn't see me.

On the next shot, you noticed.

"Why are you taking pictures?" You were a little angry.

I didn't answer. We both knew you were dying, though you would never tell me. I wanted to keep a part of you with me.

I'm glad I stole that photo. I caught you in a private moment, and you are so fully yourself: Your profile, looking up into the trees. Your lean frame, hands in your pockets, shoulders slightly shrugged. A posture I've known since my birth, a posture I suddenly recognize as my own.

Hobbes stands next to you, his back to the camera, but looking the opposite direction, your favorite way of being with someone you love: silent, a balance of solitude and companionship.

Snapping this photo shows my hunger for more of you, but over the years, I've let go of much. My need for you to approve of my choices. My desire to close the gulf between us. Even my chatty e-mails asked too much of you. So I moved more quietly and slowly. I tried not to hope for anything. Most difficult of all, I had to give up even my longing for your stories. My questions made you silent. So I didn't ask and you didn't speak. But, sometimes, when I had sat long enough, you talked:

Your sister tossed Kerouac's *On the Road* on your bed when you were seventeen and your life was never the same. In Boulder, Neal Cassady (famous muse of the Beats) camped on your front lawn. One night in our cabin on Sugarloaf Mountain above Boulder, your friend the Black Panther accidentally shot a hole above my crib while cleaning his gun, and you threw him out. That same year, your cat, who hiked and rock climbed with you, was eaten by a mountain lion and you had to listen to his cries.

And the reward of all this letting go is that the bruised-heart, hollow-ache that has companioned me since that day in the ditch was finally, and miraculously, gone.

We looked at the Douglas firs, in silence, together. I was flooded by tender gratitude. Even though you couldn't give me everything I wanted, you gave me what has become most dear to me: reading and nature and stretches of solitude.

Several months later, when I saw you last, you could no longer walk outside with me. Through the window of your small industrial loft, we watched the docks below: the gulls and kingfishers, and great blue herons. The dog eyed seals.

I handed you a copy of the photograph, hoping it would carry all I couldn't say. But who among us can see the beauty in our own frame, or in the shape of our lives?

You glanced at it and tossed it on the table.

"Look at that old man."

There are no events but thoughts and the heart's hard turning, the heart's slow learning where to love and whom. The rest is merely gossip, and tales for other times.

Annie Dillard
Holy the Firm

IN MEMORY
JACK 1942—2006
JANET 1947—2007

ACKNOWLEDGMENTS

Special thanks to the Texada Heritage Society, the Powell River Historical Society, and Bill Thompson for his book and labor of love *Texada Island*. Thanks to Bob Wishlaw for use of his photographs and to Beverly Blackmore for permission to quote from her late husband's letters. Fayette Hauser, counterculture artist and former member of the Cockettes, was so generous in our phone interview.

I'm indebted to the Rainier Writing Workshop, founded by Stan Rubin and Judith Kitchen, for all the ways the program supported and stretched me and for the remarkable community they have created. I was so fortunate to have as my mentors the wise, skillful, and compassionate Brenda Miller and Peggy Schumaker.

Most of all, gratitude to Judith Kitchen, who believed when I had lost faith and challenged me in all the right ways. I am in awe of her sharp literary mind and her vision, energy, enthusiasm, and generosity.

I owe my writing group, who, for over a decade, has endured endless drafts: Michael Karpa, Madelon Phillips, Wendy Schultz, and Jan Stites. Thanks for your expertise, loyalty, encouragement, and your own inspiring work.

A residency at Hedgebrook gave me the space and time to make major revisions. Thanks, not only for the Snow White cottage and lunch delivered in a basket, but for commitment to women's voices.

Most recently, I thank Angela Dellaporta, Karen Myers, Ginny Moyer, and Lynne Navarro who read the full manuscript and shared their insightful responses on a perfect summer day in Angela's backyard. Thank you, Ginny, for our enduring writer's friendship.

The book was designed by artist Marc Gleason. See more of his work at marcgleason.net.

Jenny Munro is adopted family and my Grammar Queen. Thank you for all the copyediting (and dog cuddling, cozy teas, and movie watching)! Gratitude to the writer Lita Kurth for her feedback on the manuscript and for our motivating writing dates.

Thanks to Marc Vincenti for his belief in the book, valuable suggestions, and all he has taught me about writing and teaching. Deep gratitude to the poet Kasey Jueds, who offered much needed advice on early drafts and whose friendship and example inspires and sustains me. Thanks to Sarah Tiederman for our years of committing to weekly goals together. Pamela Kaye's writing friendship continues to be a foundation and an inspiration.

Lynda Matthias is not only my greatest cheerleader, but an example of how to live an artful life. Barbara Van Slyke, June Riley, and Ron Ballard kept my sanity and sense of possibility alive. Dear friends Debbie Gotchef and Tom Haak read early drafts and gave me courage to continue. Martha Elderon cheered me on and gave me helpful suggestions.

Thanks to professor Dr. William Fox Conner—writer, gentleman, farmer—who introduced me to the personal essay and in whose freshman class I wrote the feeble beginnings of what would become this book.

I'm grateful that this book brought me a new friendship with Texada's Angie Hagman, pretty town girl, who had her own hard story and who, like me, found her solace in Pocahontas Bay with her beloved grandpa, Old Mr. Hagman.

Big appreciation to the whole Kato family. I couldn't have been adopted by a nicer bunch. I will never stop being grateful.

Christopher Louis Bell nudges me to my office when I should write, pulls me back out when I need to eat, tucks me in when I need to sleep, and most of all, makes me laugh. Thanks for the encouragement and technical support.

The book is dedicated to Jack's daughters: to Tammy in whose kind and animal-loving footsteps I'm privileged to follow, to Tori who is the daughter of Jack's heart, and to Rima, who gives her two boys the best of our childhood: books, independence, time outside, and a sense of wonder.

Tarn Wilson's essays appear in *Brevity, Defunct, Gulf Stream, Harvard Divinity Bulletin, Inertia, Ruminate, South Loop Review,* and *The Sun,* among others. She is a graduate of the Rainier Writing Workshop and lives and teaches in the San Francisco Bay Area. Visit her at tarnwilson.com.

OVENBIRD

Judith Kitchen's Ovenbird Books promotes innovative, imaginative, experimental works of creative nonfiction.

Ovenbird Books
The Circus Train by Judith Kitchen

Judith Kitchen Select:
The Slow Farm by Tarn Wilson
The Last Good Obsession by Sandra Swinburne
Dear Boy: An Epistolary Memoir by Heather Weber

www: ovenbirdbooks.org

CPSIA information can be obtained
at www.ICGtesting.com
Printed in the USA
LVOW11s2309081116

512210LV00001B/129/P